Emerging Cognitive Abilities
in Early Infancy

Emerging Cognitive Abilities in Early Infancy

Edited by

Francisco Lacerda
Stockholm University

Claes von Hofsten
Uppsala University

Mikael Heimann
Göteborg University

2001

LAWRENCE ERLBAUM ASSOCIATES, PUBLISHERS
Mahwah, New Jersey   London

44683588

Lawrence Erlbaum Associates, Inc., Publishers
10 Industrial Avenue
Mahwah, New Jersey 07430

Cover design by Kathryn Houghtaling Lacey

Library of Congress Cataloging-in-Publication Data

Emerging cognitive abilities in early infancy / edited by Francisco Lacerda, Claes von
Hofsten, Mikael Heimann.
    p. cm,
    Based on a symposium held in Grangärde, Sweden.
    Includes bibliographical references and indexes.
    ISBN 0-8058-2669-6 (cloth : alk. paper) -- ISBN 0-8058-2670-X (pbk. : alk. paper)
    1, Cognition in newborn infants--Congresses. 2. Cognition in infants--Congresses. I.
Lacerda, Francisco. II. Hofsten, Claes von. III. Heimann, Mikael.
    BF720.C63 E44 2000
    155.42'23--dc21
                                                                    00-060984

Books published by Lawrence Erlbaum Associates are printed on acid-free paper,
and their bindings are chosen for strength and durability.

Printed in the United States of America
10   9   8   7   6   5   4   3   2   1

Participants

Christin Andersson
Department of Linguistics
Stockholm University
Stockholm, Sweden

Elliott Blass
Department of Psychology
University of Massachusetts
Amherst, MA

Barbara Davis
University of Texas at Austin,
Austin, TX

Qi Feng
Department of Psychology
Umeå University
Umeå, Sweden

Mikael Heimann
Departments of Psychology and
    Education
Göteborg University
Göteborg, Sweden

Bert Johnson
Department of Psychology
Umeå University
Umeå, Sweden

Mark Johnson
MRC Cognitive Development Unit
London, UK

Peter Jusczyk
Department of Psychology
Johns Hopkins University
Baltimore, MD

Annette Karmiloff-Smith
MRC Cognitive Development Unit
London, UK

Patricia K. Kuhl
Speech and Hearing Sciences
University of Washington
Seattle, WA

Catarina Kylander
Department of Linguistics
Stockholm University
Stockholm, Sweden

Francisco Lacerda
Department of Linguistics
Stockholm University
Stockholm, Sweden

Maria Legerstee
York University
Toronto, Ontario, Canada

Björn Lindblom
Department of Linguistics
Stockholm University
Stockholm, Sweden

Susanne Ljungberger
Department of Psychology
Stockholm University
Stockholm, Sweden

Andrew N. Meltzoff
Department of Psychology
University of Washington
Seattle, WA

Katarina Mühlenbock
Department of Swedish
Göteborg University
Göteborg, Sweden

Yuko Munakata
Department of Psychology
University of Denver
Denver, CO

Linda Polka
School of Communication Sciences
    and Disorders
McGill University
Montreal, Canada

Kerstin Rosander
Department of Psychology
Umeå University
Umeå, Sweden

Elizabeth S. Spelke
Department of Brain and Cognitive
  Sciences
Massachusetts Institute of
  Technology
Cambridge, MA

Ulla Sundberg
Department of Linguistics
Stockholm University
Stockholm, Sweden

Tomas Tjus
Department of Swedish
Göteborg University
Göteborg, Sweden

Eva Ullstadius
Department of Psychology
Göteborg University

Claes von Hofsten
Department of Psychology
University of Virginia
Charlottesville, VA

Contents

Preface

Enjoying the wonderful weather and the long daylight periods of the Scandinavian summer, a group of scientists spent a full week discussing the issues that had brought them together: *Emerging Cognitive Abilities in Early Infancy*. The initial intention of this meeting was simply to provide an opportunity to discuss broad implications of experimental data on different aspects of infant development that was being collected at the universities of Stockholm, Umeå, and Göteborg. We gathered at the small village of Grangärde, in the middle of Sweden, at a respectable distance from the mundane temptations of the big cities. With the inspiring view of a wonderful lake and peaceful surroundings, and all the attention of our excellent hosts, we engaged in our brainstorming discussions on nearly a round-the-clock schedule. It had been agreed that the three of us, project leaders at each one of the universities, would invite just a few international guests and several doctoral students to the meeting, but we soon realized that what we had started was far too important to be kept to ourselves. The group dynamics, the atmosphere of the symposium, and its geographical location all generated spin-off effects that were far beyond what we initially expected. Our free time was used to carry out informal spontaneous discussions of matters addressed during the joint sessions and the idea to produce this volume was born.

Our driving force was to consolidate knowledge from different areas of infant development research in an attempt to achieve an integrated view of the cognitive abilities emerging in early infancy. The discussions on which the chapters are based and the brainstorms generated by the live presentations are extremely difficult to recreate in a scientific book. Therefore, we have arranged the chapters in a sequence that we believe best conveys to the reader the line of reasoning that emerged during the meeting. We begin with chapters dealing with fundamental and general aspects of cognitive development and then sweep through the specific theme of language acquisition; we close with a return to general questions concerning different representation modalities.

The first chapter, by Condry, Smith, and Spelke addresses fundamental aspects of the infants cognitive development: Do infants sense the world in essentially the same way as adults do or do infants initially have an intrinsically different perceptual organization that is rearranged in an adult-like way as a consequence of their experience with the outside world? This central issue sets the stage for the discussion presented in the subsequent three chapters by Munakata, Johnson, and von Hofsten. Munakata, for instance, draws our attention to the fact that results from experimental research with young infants are extremely task dependent and rather often lead to paradoxical results, like when capabilities demonstrated at an earlier age seem to be unavailable some months later. Munakata raises pertinent questions concerning the interpretation of experimental results from different domains, including language development, and concludes that it is necessary to focus on the processes involved in the infant's responses to different tasks, if we are to achieve a consistent insight on infant development.

Johnson adds the neuroscientist's perspective to the issues raised by Condry et al. and by Munakata. What is "initial knowledge," how can it be interpreted in light of current data on cortical plasticity, and why do infants display that initial knowledge? Do infants really "know" or are their initial behaviors "simply" a reflection of fundamental endogenous and exogenous properties set by normal ecological frames?

In line with Johnson's suggestion, von Hofsten explores the notion that action capabilities found at birth are the result of a phylogenetic adaptation—an evolutionary mechanism that will tend to preserve action patterns that are fundamental and useful for the species—and defends the thesis that action makes a critical contribution to structure the infant's cognition.

The notions of action and plasticity are also underlying the early stages of language development. As suggested by Lacerda and Sundberg, it is possible to envisage the phonetic structure of the vowel systems observed at early developmental stages as the result of the interaction between perceptual, articulatory, and interactive components. The authors argue that the asymmetries at the perceptual and the articulatory levels underlie the dominance of high–low vocalic contrasts observed in both the young infant's choice of vowels and in the typology of natural vowel systems.

The perceptual organization of the phonetic space in early infancy is also the theme of Kuhl's chapter, where she defends her Native Language Magnet (NLM) model anchoring it on vast empirical evidence, interpreted as indicating that language development is conveyed by a complex mapping of linguistic input. Kuhl emphasizes that this stimulus input is different from the traditional Skinnerian view of learning processes and suggests that the young infant stores representations of the input signal and that these representations function like perceptual magnets, toward which similar patterns of sound are attracted, a view that is challenged by Davis and Lindblom in chapter 7. They focus on the notion of "prototype" that underlies Kuhl's NLM theory and argue that their interpretation of phonetic data describing the speech input typically available to young infants does not support the vowel prototypes. Instead, they suggest that the stability inherent to prototypes may be found at a dynamic rather than at a static level, and offer a redefinition of the notion of prototype.

This digression over the domain of language acquisition is closed by Jusczyk's chapter taking up the very pertinent question of how infants manage to recognize words under rather naturalistic conditions. Jusczyk suggests that young infants may be sensitive to the repetition frequency of the sound patterns they are exposed to and that additional visual information may help the young infant to achieve more stable representations than otherwise is possible when only acoustic information is available.

Having focused on language, we now address the question of how human infants represent different types of objects available in the outside world. Legerstee's chapter addresses the core question of domain specific representations. Infants appear to behave differently depending on whether they interact with inanimate objects or with people. How does the young infant know what to expect from his or her interaction with a live subject, and that certain of the live subject's responses cannot be expected from an inanimate object? Both Legerstee, on the one hand, and Meltzoff and Moore, on the other, address this type of issue. Legerstee builds her argument on earlier data and is inclined to favor the notion that initial knowledge may in fact be domain specific. Meltzoff and Moore explore available empirical data to build a model that attempts to account for emerging cognitive abilities in early infancy by calling on limited initial structures—an exciting model that allows us to evaluate the potential impact that different levels of initial knowledge may have on the early cognitive development.

We close our volume with Heimann's chapter addressing the issue of intermodal representations that is raised by the observations of imitation capabilities in early infancy. Heimann reviews the literature on early imitation and proposes a realistic model of the infant's imitative behavior, where specific responses are seen as carrying a stochastic component that determines their particular outcome.

In summary, we sincerely hope this volume will inspire you to ask further questions on these matters. The book is, by itself, nothing more than a very limited contribution to the integrated view of emerging cognitive abilities in early infancy. But we believe in the "butterfly effect" and sincerely expect you to join this fantastic endeavor of studying how our own species goes about organizing knowledge.

ACKNOWLEDGMENTS

The symposium of which this volume is based was supported by grants from The Swedish Council for Research in the Humanities and Social Sciences (HSFR), The Bank of Sweden Tercentenary Foundation (Riksbankens Jubileumsfond), Magnus Bervall's Foundation, and Stockholm University.

Francisco Lacerda
Claes von Hofsten
Mikael Heimann

1

Development of
Perceptual Organization

Kirsten F. Condry
Massachusetts Institute of Technology

W. Carter Smith
Hampshire College

Elizabeth S. Spelke
Massachusetts Institute of Technology

When newborn infants first look at their surroundings, do they perceive a radically different world from older children and adults, or is their perceptual world organized in ways fundamentally like our own? As infants and children grow and learn about objects, events, and scenes, do these developments change the organization that they perceive in their surroundings, or is perceptual organization constant over human life?

Theories of the development of perceptual organization can be distinguished by the answers they offer to these questions. One class of theories embraces *the continuity thesis* and proposes that the processes by which adults organize scenes into units are constant over human postnatal development. Although newborn infants sense the world with lower acuity, perceive as novel scenes that are familiar to us, and fail to appreciate the functional properties of many categories of objects, they organize their surroundings in fundamentally the same ways as adults. A second class of theories embraces *the discontinuity thesis* and proposes that processes of perceptual organization change fundamentally over development. Most proponents of the discontinuity thesis attribute these changes to learning: Children's ability to organize scenes into units develops by virtue of their encounters with scenes and objects. On this view, experiences with objects lead to qualitative changes in how objects are perceived.

The continuity and discontinuity theses cast strikingly different perspectives on the infancy period. If infants perceive the same objects and scenes as older children and adults, then infants may learn from their encounters with objects and people. An infant who views an adult eating a grapefruit with a spoon, for example, might learn about functional properties of these objects (spoons are manipulable, grapefruits are edible) and about actions that apply to them (spoons are grasped by the hand, grapefruit is chewed in the mouth). Learning during infancy might be useful later in development, because infants will be learning about the very entities—utensils, fruits, people—that older children and adults perceive and think about. If the discontinuity thesis were correct, in contrast, the things that infants learned would be of little use later in development. Imagine, for example, that infants perceived no people, food, or spoons but only momentary arrays of visible surfaces. Because adults' actions are directed to whole objects, not to the visible parts of surfaces, infants would be unable to represent actions such as eating grapefruit with a spoon in a useful way. Anything that infants learned from this event (e.g., that silvery surfaces tend to move into contact with shiny yellow surfaces) would need to be relearned later, when the child's perceptual experience shifted from a focus on visible surfaces to a focus on objects, allowing the child to realize that it is spoons (whether silver or not), not silvery surfaces (whether spoons or not) that carry food.

Ample evidence reveals that infants do learn about the world from birth: In the first days of life, they come to recognize faces (Bushnell, Sai, & Mullin, 1989), develop a distinctive preference for the sound of their own language (Mehler et al., 1988), and gain short-term familiarity with repeatedly presented visual scenes (Friedman, 1972). One might expect, therefore, that evolution would favor the emergence of perceptual mechanisms that parse faces, sounds, and scenes in the same general ways as those of the older child and the adult, in accord with the continuity thesis. Contrary to this expectation, all the evidence from studies of infants has appeared to support some version of the discontinuity thesis. Because infants' actions on objects undergo marked changes with development, Piaget (1954) and his followers proposed that there are radical changes in perception and representations of objects over infancy. Because infants' perception of a variety of simple visual displays also appears to undergo considerable changes, students of perceptual development have also proposed qualitative changes in object perception over infancy (e.g., Cohen, DeLoache, & Strauss, 1979; Spelke, Vishton, & Hofsten, 1994; but cf. Kellman, 1993). If any of these proposals are correct, then the learning capacities revealed in infants could not contribute the development of knowledge until they, or other processes, first brought structure to the infant's perceptual world.

In this chapter, we take a new look at the evidence for developmental changes in perceptual organization. Although infants' reactions to particular visual displays undergo real and compelling developmental changes, we believe these changes can be reconciled with the continuity thesis. Developmental changes in perceptual abilities, we suggest, stem from gradual, continuous increases in the precision of object representations, not from qualitative changes in its underlying processes.

To focus our review, we consider just one aspect of perceptual organization: the construction and extrapolation of object contours in 2-dimensional visual displays and in 3-dimensional scenes. We begin by discussing infants' perception of partly occluded objects—an area that has been interpreted to provide evidence both for continuity and for discontinuity in object perception. Then we discuss what may be the strongest evidence for discontinuity in infants' perceptual organization, from studies of developing perception of "illusory contours."

PERCEPTION OF PARTLY OCCLUDED OBJECTS

Amodal completion is a perceptual phenomenon in which contours are perceived or inferred despite their absence in the retinal projection (Michotte, Thines, & Crabbe, 1964). For example, adult observers perceive Fig. 1.1a as a triangle partly hidden behind a human finger. Adults appear to extrapolate the contour smoothly behind the occluding finger in accord with the Gestalt principle of "good continuation." Note that despite the visual system's principled extrapolation of the visible contours, it is possible that the contours change direction and that the removal of the finger would reveal a polygon of a different shape (Fig. 1.1b). Although the visual information in Fig. 1.1a is consistent with either a triangle or the complex polygon, the visual system favors the former. When the visible contours of a partly occluded object do not accord with the principle of good continuation, an indefinite perception results. For example, observers do not perceive a compelling, complete form behind the occluder in Fig. 1.1c. As these observations indicate, the relative alignments of the visible contours of a partly occluded object have a large effect on adults' perception of the object's unity, whether or not the contours evoke a familiar object.

The notion of good continuation has been formalized mathematically and tested in psychophysical experiments with adults. Whenever two or more spatially disjoint contours can be joined by a smooth, monotonic curve (i.e., a curve that does not inflect between convexity and concavity) observers tend to perceive the contours as connected (Kellman & Shipley, 1991), and the long edge that they form appears to pop out of a larger array of randomly oriented edges (Field, Hayes, & Hess, 1993). When these contours cannot be smoothly joined with such a curve, they are not perceived as be-

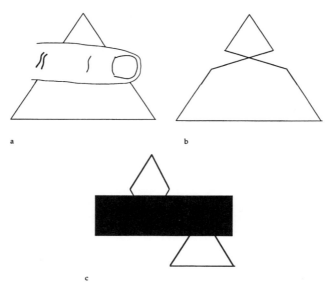

FIG. 1.1. Some partial occlusion displays (after Michotte et al., 1954).

longing to the same object and a line of such contours does not pop out of an array (Kellman & Shipley, 1991; Field et al., 1993).

Since the 1980s, the development of these organizational phenomena has been studied with infants by means of preferential looking methods. In these studies, infants are presented repeatedly with an occlusion display until their interest in the display (as reflected by their spontaneous looking time) declines. Then the occluder is removed and infants are presented with two test displays that both match the visible areas of the original display and show complete or incomplete objects. Numerous experiments, with control conditions in which the critical objects and changes in objects are directly visible, reveal that infants tend to look longer when a test display presents a new object than when it presents an object from the original display (see Johnson & Aslin, 1996; Kellman & Spelke, 1983; Needham, 1994; Slater et al., 1990).[1] This novelty preference therefore serves to assess infants' perception of the similarity between each test display and the original occlusion display.

---

[1]Bogartz and Shinskey (1998) recently introduced a different method for studying infants' perception of partly occluded objects, in which a smaller number of infants view a larger number of test displays with a single test trial of each type. Their method does not provide evidence for any novelty preferences, either in control conditions where the critical objects are fully visible or in an experimental condition in which an object first is occluded. It is not clear why infants fail to show novelty preferences in their experiments. Because of the absence of such preferences with fully visible displays, however, these experiments do not shed light on infants' perception of partly occluded objects.

Early experiments using this method presented 4-month-old infants with a stationary object whose center was hidden behind a horizontal occluder. After habituation to a partly occluded rod or triangle, infants looked equally long at a complete object and at an incomplete object composed of the two segments that were visible above and below the occluder in the habituation display (Kellman & Spelke, 1983; Fig. 1.2a). These results provide evidence that infants perceived no definite, connected object behind the occluder, despite the alignment of the visible contours of the rod and the symmetry and closure of the triangle. The findings suggested that infants fail to use configural cues such as good continuation to determine object unity.

In further experiments, infants were presented with the occluded rod undergoing lateral translatory motion behind the occluder during habituation. In contrast to the studies with stationary objects, 4-month-old infants showed a strong preference for a translating incomplete rod at test, relative to a translating complete rod (Johnson & Aslin, 1996; Jusczyk, Johnson, Spelke, Kennedy, & Smith, 1997; Kellman & Spelke, 1983; Slater et al., 1990; Fig. 1.2b). This looking preference implies that the incomplete rod was less familiar to infants than the complete rod, and thus that infants perceived the partly occluded rod as connected behind the occluder. Because the two rod displays differed only in their completeness, this preference in turn

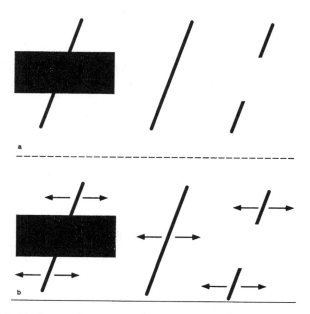

FIG. 1.2. Displays used in studies of infants' perception of partly occluded objects. Part a shows stationary rods; Part b shows translating rods (after Kellman & Spelke, 1983).

suggests that the common motion of the rod ends served as an indication of object unity. Infants' reliance on motion information to determine object unity is a good strategy given the physical laws governing object motions: Because most nonliving objects do not interact at a distance, two surfaces that move together are not likely to be separated by empty space. If two object segments visible above and below an occluder move together, therefore, those parts are likely to belong to the same object (Kellman, 1993).

Similar experiments have shown that these results generalize to 3-dimensional solids (Schmidt, 1985) and to flat, regularly textured, and/or colored surfaces (Johnson & Náñez, 1995; Termine et al., 1987; Schwartz, 1982; Slater et al., 1990). Experiments presenting different patterns of motion revealed that translation of the rod either vertically or in depth supports perception of a unified object (Kellman, Spelke, & Short, 1986), and that the object must move relative to the infant: Movements of the retinal projection due to observer motions do not yield perception of object unity (Kellman, Gleitman, & Spelke, 1987). The finding that motion specifies object unity for 4-month-old infants therefore appears quite robust, leading investigators to propose that motion provides infants' only information about objects (Kellman & Shipley, 1991; Kellman & Spelke, 1983; Spelke, 1990).

More recent studies suggest, however, that infants also are sensitive to configural cues such as the alignment of object parts and similarity of surfaces, especially when information from those cues appears within displays of moving objects. Using 2-dimensional video-displayed stimuli, Johnson and Aslin (1996) explored the role of contour alignment in 4-month-olds' perception of partly occluded objects. Infants were shown a center-occluded rod with misaligned visible ends that translated laterally behind a rectangular occluder (Fig. 1.3a). After habituation, infants looked longer at a complete rod (consisting of the two previously visible ends and a middle segment connecting them) than at two disjoint rod ends. This longer looking suggests that infants did not perceive the partly occluded rod ends as a single object despite their common motion. In a follow-up study using connected and incomplete test displays with equal numbers of corners (Fig. 1.3b), infants again preferred the complete rod over the broken rod, confirming that the differential recovery of looking time was due to the connectedness of the complete rod rather than to the presence of corners per se (Smith, Johnson, Spelke, & Aslin, 1996). These findings suggest that infants used both motion and alignment as information about object unity (see Johnson & Aslin, 1996). When two cues for determining object unity conflict (i.e., when alignment appears to specify two objects while motion specifies one) infants perceive two distinct objects rather than a unified object that continues behind the occluder.

The conflict between these recent results and earlier work may result from differences in the degree of depth information present in the displays: In 2-dimensional displays, infants may segment the surfaces differently than

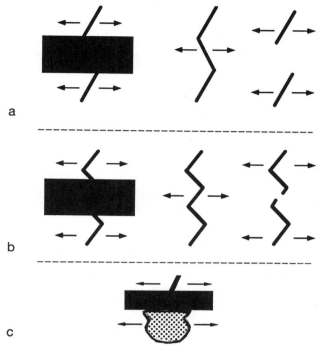

FIG. 1.3. Displays used in studies of the effects of motion and contour alignment on infants' perception of partly occluded objects (top, after Johnson & Aslin, 1996; middle, after Smith et al., 1996; bottom, after Kellman & Spelke, 1983).

they segment 3-dimensional displays. With 3-D displays, additional information about the depth of objects is available from accommodation and convergence and from motion parallax caused by the movement of the infant's head. Thus, infants' failure to perceive the misaligned, commonly moving rod ends as connected could arise from a relative poverty of depth information.

One experiment reported in Kellman and Spelke (1983) is consistent with this suggestion. Infants were presented with a moving, center-occluded compound object composed of a rod and polygon (Fig. 1.3c). After familiarization, infants looked longer at the incomplete test display, suggesting that they perceived a connected object in the occlusion display. Because the edges of the surfaces in the occlusion display were not aligned, this finding suggests that only motion influences the perceived unity of 3-dimensional displays. This possibility prompted a further study using 3-dimensional solid analogs to the zig-zag displays shown in Fig. 1.3b. Four-month-old infants again were habituated to a partly occluded zig-zag rod and then were shown a complete rod and a broken rod at test. Under these conditions, infants showed no consistent pattern of preference for either of the test displays (Smith, Johnson, & Spelke, in preparation). In contrast to results with 2-dimensional displays, infants here appeared to form no determinate perception of object unity: They did not see the occlusion display either as a single unified object or as two distinct objects.

This finding suggests that richer depth information makes the misalignment of an object's edges less salient or compelling than it is in 2-dimensional displays. Nevertheless, the misalignment must be detected by the infants, because they otherwise should have perceived a connected object in the habituation display and shown a clear test preference for the broken rod. It appears that the addition of 3-dimensional depth cues has tipped infants toward the perception of object unity, but not far enough to completely override the conflicting misalignment of the rod ends.

Why then do infants perceive the rod-polygon display (Fig. 1.3c) as a single object? In this moving, 3-dimensional display, the edges of the rod and polygon are misaligned, but infants perceive this partly occluded object as unified. The contrast between infants' perception of the rod- polygon and zig-zag displays suggest that perception of object unity depends more on the alignment of the axes of orientation of an object than on the alignment of its outer contours (see Tse, 1999). Although the outer contours of the rod-polygon would not meet if smoothly extended, the surfaces bounded by these contours would meet. Planned experiments will test this possibility.

Because the abovementioned experiments were conducted with 4-month-old infants, they raise questions about the origins of these abilities. By 4 months of age, infants may have accumulated enough experience with partly occluded objects to learn that when visible surfaces are aligned and move together, they belong to the same object. Initial results with neonates were consistent with the hypothesis that the abilities underlying the perception of object unity develop during the first 4 months. After habituation to a partly occluded rod, neonates consistently look longer at a complete rod than at a broken rod, providing evidence that the partly occluded display was not perceived as unified (Slater et al., 1990; Slater, Johnson, Brown, & Badenoch, 1996; Slater, Johnson, Kellman, & Spelke, 1994). Furthermore, Johnson and Náñez (1995) reported that 2-month-old infants showed an equal preference for the complete and broken test displays after habituation to a center-occluded rod. This finding suggests that there is an intermediate stage of object perception between birth and 4 months.

What events take place during this intermediate period? It is possible that qualitative changes occur in infants' perceptual organization. For example, mechanisms for grouping commonly moving surfaces or for extrapolating surfaces behind occluders may become functional between birth and 4 months. Alternatively, such mechanisms may be functional throughout development, but infants' perceptual systems may increase in sensitivity and precision. Older infants therefore may be better able to *detect* the common motion of surfaces that are separated in the visual array.

Research by Johnson and Aslin (1995) and Kawabata, Gyoba, Inoue, and Ohtsubo (1999) supports the latter possibility. Johnson and Aslin (1995) found that narrowing the height of the occluder at points along the path of a laterally translating rod improved 2-month-old infants' performance in a partial occlusion study. Contrary to the infants in Johnson and Náñez' (1995) study, these infants preferred the broken rod at test. Most dramatically, Kawabata et al. (1999) found that by presenting a moving high-contrast grating of repeating bars rather than a single bar, even 3-week-old infants perceived the grating to continue behind the occluder. Both grating contrast and occluder size were critical for this perception, as 3-week-old infants failed to perceive the complete grating when the occluder was widened as the grating narrowed. These findings provide evidence that these infants perceive the unity of an object or pattern over partial occlusion. The change in performance that occurs as an infant matures over the first 4 months appears to stem primarily from increases in sensitivity to motion and spatial contrast over a spatial gap. These findings support the continuity thesis.

In addition to the configural cue of contour alignment, adults also make use of the similarity of surface color, texture, and pattern in perceiving object unity. For example, adults readily perceive the dots in Fig. 1.4a as arranged in a triangular configuration despite the presence of the intermingled crosses. Similar elements tend to be grouped together. How do these surface relationships influence infants' perception of partly occluded objects?

In most of the object displays discussed thus far, the visible portions of the display have been similar in appearance and have shared such attributes as color, texture, and shape. Because the single exception—the rod and polygon display of Kellman and Spelke (1983)—was perceived as connected, some investigators concluded that young infants do not use the configural cue of surface similarity in perceiving object unity (Kellman & Shipley, 1991; Kellman & Spelke, 1983). As in the case of contour alignment, however, this conclusion was premature. There is now evidence that infants do exploit differences in surface appearance in determining object unity, especially when objects are presented in motion.

Experiments by Needham (1997) provided evidence that infants use dissimilarities in surface color, pattern, and shape to perceive object boundaries. Although most of Needham's experiments focus on infants' perception of the boundaries of fully visible, adjacent objects, one line of research focused on perception of center-occluded objects. In one experiment (Needham, 1994; Needham, Baillargeon, & Kaufman, 1998), 4-month-old infants were shown a display in which two boxes were visible to the left and

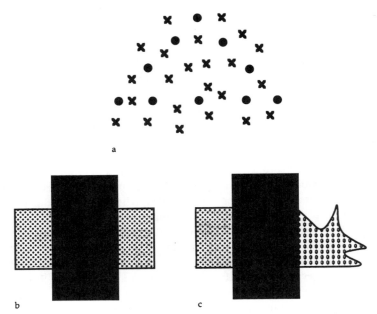

FIG. 1.4. Displays used in studies of effects of surface texture and similarity on perceptual grouping and object perception (parts b and c, similar and dissimilar boxes, adapted from Needham et al., 1998).

right of a nearer object that partly occluded them. In one condition, both boxes were red and rectangular (Fig. 1.4b); in a second condition, the left box was red and rectangular but the right box was green and irregularly shaped (Fig. 1.4c). Perception of the connectedness or separateness of the boxes was tested by comparing infants' looking time to events in which a hand moved one of the boxes and the other box either moved with it (implying a connection between the boxes) or remained at rest (implying no connection). Infants in the first condition showed an equal preference for the move-together and move-apart events, suggesting that they had no determinate perception of the unity or separateness of the boxes. In contrast, infants in the second condition looked longer at the test display in which the red and green surfaces moved together. This looking pattern provides evidence that infants had formed an expectation, based on the dissimilar appearance of the two surfaces, that these surfaces belonged to two distinct objects.

Four sets of findings nevertheless suggest strong limits to infants' use of surface color and texture similarity to perceive objects. First, infants fail to use the common colors and textures of stationary, center-occluded objects to perceive their unity (Kellman & Spelke, 1983; Slater et al., 1990). Second, infants perceive the unity of a moving, center-occluded object just as strongly when its visible surfaces differ in color and texture as when they are the same color and texture (Kellman & Spelke, 1983). Third, recent studies provide evidence that infants fail to use common *changes* in the color and texture of stationary, center-occluded objects to perceive their unity (Jusczyk et al., 1997). In these studies, infants viewed either 3-dimensional displays or 2-dimensional videotaped displays containing a moving or stationary center-occluded object. In all the displays, the object changed brightness and color throughout the study, either suddenly or gradually, at various rhythms. Infants were very interested in these changes, as judged from their long looking times to the displays. They also dishabituated to a broken object test display when the object in the occlusion display had appeared in motion. When the occluded object was stationary, however, infants looked equally at the test displays with complete and incomplete objects. Although the synchronous color and brightness changes drew infants' attention, those changes failed to specify a connected object.

Fourth, further studies by Needham (1997) showed that infants fail to use similarities and dissimilarities in the colors and textures of objects to perceive the boundaries of two adjacent objects under certain conditions. Infants were presented with two adjacent objects of contrasting colors and textures and misaligned edges. In one set of conditions, the objects were angled such that the place where they touched was hidden. Perception of the boundary between the objects again was assessed by observing infants' looking times to events in which a hand pulled one object and the other object either remained at rest or moved with it. Infants looked equally at the two test events, suggesting that they failed to perceive the boundary between the objects.

What accounts for this pattern of findings? The analyses of 2-month- old infants' failure to respond to the common motion of surfaces by Johnson and Aslin (1995), discussed earlier, suggests an answer. Infants may have the same propensity as adults to group surfaces of common colors and textures into single units. With development, however, infants may become better able to detect when two surfaces are similar and when they are not, especially when the surfaces are separated by a gap in the visual field. It is noteworthy that in all cases where infants have failed to respond to the similarity of two surfaces, the border between the surfaces has been hidden, either behind a separate occluding object (e.g., Jusczyk et al., 1997) or behind an occluding surface of one of the two objects (e.g., Needham, 1997). Following the logic of Johnson and Aslin (1995), therefore, infants should successfully use surface similarity to specify object boundaries when the area of occlusion is reduced or eliminated.

Recent research by Needham (1997) confirmed this prediction. Needham presented infants with the same displays of adjacent objects as in the earlier studies, with one change: The objects were rotated so that the point at which they touched was directly visible. In this condition, infants looked longer at the test event in which the hand pulled one object and both objects moved together, providing evidence that they perceive the two objects as separate units. Studies of infants' reactions to surface similarity therefore suggest continuity in the mechanisms of object perception over development, with an increase in sensitivity to the information on which those mechanisms operate.

We believe that these studies favor the continuity thesis for the perception of partly occluded objects. Although early results seemed to indicate that infants relied on dynamic information alone and neglected configural information in perceiving object unity, more recent studies suggest that infants are able to use all the sources of information used by adults, including motion, contour alignment, and surface similarity. Where infants' perceptions are less clear than those of adults, this difference appears to reflect infants' lower sensitivity to these sources of information. Developmental changes in perception of partly occluded objects may stem more from increases in sensitivity than from qualitative changes in processes of visual organization.

PERCEPTION OF ILLUSORY FIGURES

Illusory figures provide a second test case for examining the development of perceptual organization in infancy. Illusory contours are edges and lines that are perceived across areas where there are no luminance differences to indicate a contour. The illusion is created by the careful positioning of inducing elements, which are themselves luminance-defined figures perceived as being partly occluded by the illusory edge. Because illusory contours are experienced as real contours differing in brightness from their surroundings, the completion of the illusory figure is a case of modal completion (in contrast to amodal completion in partial occlusion displays). If the inducing elements are arranged slightly differently or rotated so that their gaps are not aligned, the display radically changes character, no longer creating an illusion. Illusory figures are useful for studying perceptual organization precisely because they exist only in the relationship between the inducing elements, and this allows for the creation of comparison figures that are highly similar in their local components but very different in global form.

The first illusory figure was introduced by Schumann (1900/1987), who made two important observations: The illusory figure appears to have sharp edges that cut across an area of homogeneous luminance, and the figure itself appears to be brighter than the background on which it appears. Schumann's discovery went unheralded for over half a century, until

Kanisza (1955/1987) developed an illusory figure that was so perceptually salient, it sparked an explosion of research that has continued to the present day (Fig. 1.5a). The Kanisza triangle consists of three circles (inducing elements), each with a trisection removed, oriented as if at the corners of a triangle. This display is perceived clearly by most adults as a central white triangle, brighter than the background, resting atop three complete black circles (Kanisza, 1955/1987).

There are several types of illusory contour displays, of which the most commonly studied are edge-induced displays and kinetic displays. In edge-induced illusory figures like the Kanisza triangle, the inducing elements are figures in themselves, perceived as objects (discs) that are partially occluded by an overlaying object (the triangle). The gaps in the inducing discs mark the corners of the occluding triangle, and illusory edges are perceived to span the open area between the discs, despite the absence of luminance changes in this part of the display. In kinetic illusory figures, the illusion is created over time by the progressive permutation of inducing elements. Kinetic illusory contours typically are created on computer displays in which the boundaries of stationary inducing elements on a solid background are altered, consistent with occlusion by a rigid object the same color as the background. This type of kinetic display leads to the perception of an illusory object that progressively covers and uncovers portions of the inducing elements (Kellman & Cohen, 1984; Fig. 1.5b).

When adults are presented with illusory figures such as the Kanisza triangle, they typically observe four characteristics. The illusory triangle appears to be occluding portions of the inducing discs, whose edges are perceived as complete circles behind the triangle. The illusory triangle appears to be closer in depth than the discs it occludes. The edges of the triangle seem to be clearly defined across the gaps between the discs, despite the absence of luminance differences. And finally, the illusory triangle appears to be brighter than the background on which it appears. Research into adult perception of illusory figures has focused on the relative importance of each of these characteristics, as well as the stimulus variables that affect the overall strength of the illusory figure.

Psychophysical research has revealed several factors that affect the strength of the illusion, and here we find similarities to the factors that influence perception of partly occluded objects as well. Early research suggested that the size of the inducing elements affected the salience of the illusory figure, and that illusions subtending smaller visual angles were less compelling (Dumais & Bradley, 1976). However, more careful psychophysical study has determined that the critical variable is the ratio of the amount of edge that is specified by the inducing element (the supported edge) to the size of the gap (the unsupported edge; Shipley & Kellman, 1992). Thus the relative amount of edge that is not specified and must be

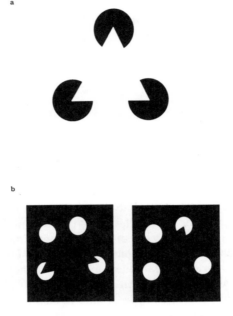

FIG. 1.5. Displays evoking perception of illusory contours in adults (after Kanizsa, 1955/1987; Kellman & Cohen, 1984).

modally interpolated by the observer has an impact on whether an illusory figure is seen and how powerful the illusion is.

Early illusory contour displays employed simple regular forms both as inducing elements and as illusory figures (e.g., Fig. 1.5a), but later studies determined that neither the figure nor the inducing elements need be simple or regular to produce the illusion (Kellman & Shipley, 1991). Regardless of their shape, however, the discontinuities in the inducing elements must be "relatable" in order for an illusory figure to appear (Kellman & Shipley, 1991). As in the case of partial occlusion displays, these discontinuities are relatable if a smooth, monotonic curve can be interpolated between them. When the elements' gaps are not relatable, no illusion is perceived, and the display appears to consist of the inducing elements alone. The common conditions on relatability for illusory contour and partial occlusion displays suggests that perceptual organization depends on similar processes in these two situations (Kellman & Shipley, 1991).

In addition to edge length ratios and edge relatability, numerous other factors have been found to influence perception of illusory contour displays, and studies attempting to specify these factors and their interrelations precisely have yielded conflicting results (see Lesher, 1995; Parks, 1986, for reviews). From the adult research, it has been impossible to find a single necessary component for the perception of illusory figures. Indeed, it appears increasingly unlikely that there is one unitary explanation for all illusory figures. This impasse provides a powerful reason for investigating the development of perception of illusory contours in infants, to examine the origins and emergence of the perception of their various characteristics. When infants first begin to see these illusions, we may ask what factors influence their perception and what other perceptual processes and capacities emerge at that time. In this way, we may shed light on the basic mechanisms giving rise to perception of illusory contours at any age.

In contrast to the wealth of research with adults, little research has focused on how infants perceive illusory figures as a means of understanding their genesis in visual processing. Nevertheless, a number of investigators have asked when infants first perceive illusory contours, and their findings suggest paths for future research to follow.

The question of when infants begin to perceive the illusion in illusory figure displays is simple to pose but difficult to resolve. Trieber and Wilcox (1980) examined how very young infants perceive a Kanisza triangle. One- to four-month-old infants were habituated to an illusory triangle and then were tested with three comparison displays: a real triangle, a nonillusory display composed of the same inducing elements rotated so that their gaps were not aligned, and an unrelated shape with the same amount of total contour (Fig. 1.6a). Results showed that infants dishabituated to the unrelated shape but transferred habituation to both the real triangle and the nonillusory display. These results suggested that infants note a similarity between the real triangle and the illusory figure, but the fact that they also perceived a similarity between the illusory triangle and the nonillusory display suggests that they may have responded to the triangular configuration of the inducing elements rather than to any perceived illusory triangle. Infants' lack of differential responding to the illusory and nonillusory triangular displays of inducing elements weakens the interpretation that young infants perceive illusory figures in the same manner as adults.

Bertenthal, Campos, and Haith (1980) advanced the study of infants' perception of illusory figures by asking whether 5- and 7-month-old infants can distinguish an illusory figure from a pair of nonillusory displays composed of the same inducing elements in the same global positions. Their central display presented an illusory square, evoked for adults by four inducing discs with a single quadrant removed, arranged as if at the corners of a square with their gaps facing centerward. Nonillusory comparison displays were created by rotating either two or four of the inducing elements outward, so that the inducing elements were symmetrically arranged into the same square configuration without creating any illusion (Fig. 1.6b). The cleverness of this comparison is that if one attends solely to the orientation of the local elements in the different displays, there is the same amount of

FIG. 1.6. Displays used in studies of infants' perception illusory contours (after Trieber & Wilcox, 1980; Bertenthal et al., 1980).

difference between the illusory display and the nonillusory display with two rotated elements as between the two nonillusory displays with two versus four rotated elements. Following habituation to one of the displays, infants were tested with the other two displays. If infants responded only to local elements, then habituation to the two-element rotated display should have generalized equally to the four-element rotated display and to the illusory contour display, and the reverse. If infants responded to the global configuration of these elements as do adults, then habituation to either nonillusory display should have been followed by greater dishabituation to the illusory display, and the reverse.

In their experiment, 7-month-old infants dishabituated to a change from the illusory figure to a nonillusory display, but not from one nonillusory display to the other. These findings provided evidence that the infants responded to the global configuration of the display rather than simply the orientation of the individual inducing elements. Five-month-old infants' attention showed a trend in the same direction, but their looking patterns were less consistent. The authors interpreted these findings cautiously to suggest that older infants attended to the global configuration of the illusory display and treated it differently from other configurations of the same elements.

Bertenthal et al. (1980) stopped short of claiming that infants perceived the illusory form in their experiments, because this stronger interpretation requires the elimination of alternative explanations in terms of lower level sensory processing. In particular, the illusory square figure used in the experiments contains a central, open area that could be distinguished from the nonillusory displays on the basis of low-spatial frequency information alone, irrespective of perception of the illusory figure. Bertenthal et al. (1980) suggested that the solution to this problem is to create a nonillusion comparison display in which the inducing elements retain the same orientation but are misaligned. This study has not yet been attempted.

A further study of young infants' perception of illusory figures used the logic of Bertenthal et al. (1980) with a paired-comparison visual preference procedure. Ghim (1990) habituated 3- and 4-month-old infants to an illusory square or 1 of 3 nonillusory shapes (produced by rotating 2 or 4 of the inducing elements) and then tested infants' discrimination of the other displays with a paired preferential looking paradigm. Infants were found to discriminate the illusory display from some of the nonillusory displays but not from other nonillusory displays. The reasons for the discrepancies among responses to the nonillusory displays were never fully explained. Because the infants did consistently treat all the nonillusory displays as indistinguishable from one another, however, Ghim's findings suggest that the successful discriminations depended on detection of some aspect of the global organization of the illusory figures.

To our knowledge, only two studies have examined whether infants perceive illusory figures in kinetic displays. The first study examined how 5- and 8-month-old infants generalize habituation between real squares, disconnected corner elements, and a variety of kinetic illusory square displays. Kaufmann-Hayoz, Kaufmann, and Walther (1988) habituated infants to either a real stationary square or a set of four disconnected right angle elements, and then tested infants with three displays in which the corners of an illusory square were specified. The test displays consisted of a standard stationary illusory square, a jiggling square in which the four inducing elements were deformed to produce the percept of an illusory square oscillating back and forth (with all four corners of the square specified at all times), and a display in which the illusory square appeared to rotate in place, such that only two corners of the illusory figure were specified at any one time. The relevant comparisons in this study were between habituation conditions. At the older age, infants dishabituated more to all the illusory figures after habituation to the four disconnected right-angle elements than after habituation to the real square. In other words, the 8-month-old infants treated the static illusory square, the jiggling illusory square, and the rotating illusory square as more similar to a real square than to a set of disconnected corner elements. At the younger age, this pattern was observed for the stationary illusory square and for the jiggling illusory square but not for the rotating square. Kaufmann-Hayoz et al. interpret these results to suggest that at 8 months, but not at 5 months, infants were able to integrate the spatiotemporal information required to perceive the rotating illusory figure.

Although 5-month-old infants did not appear to perceive illusory contours from kinetic information alone, the findings of Kauffman et al. suggest that these infants do perceive a stationary and an oscillating illusory square as more similar to a real square than to a set of right angle elements that partially match the local components of the illusory figures. Although this comparison does not necessarily provide evidence that infants see the illusory square as a real figure, it does indicate that they are not simply perceiving the local angles of the inducing elements in the illusion displays. This study is similar to Trieber and Wilcox's (1980) early work with static illusory figures, in which infants judged a real figure as similar to the illusory figure, but it is not entirely clear what basis infants are using for the judgment. The more compelling result from the older infants suggests that they are capable of the spatiotemporal integration required to perceive the rotating illusory figure, and treat that display, which is dissimilar to the real square from any static view, as more similar over time to a real square than to disconnected corners.

Using apparent motion illusory figure displays, Condry, Gentile, and Yonas (1992) examined whether 4- and 7-month-old infants could discriminate a moving illusory square from a nonillusory control pattern in a preferential looking paradigm. In the first study, 7-month-old infants were presented with a video display consisting of two rows of 10 white semicircular inducing elements on a black background. On one side of the display, four of the inducing elements were rotated so that their gaps faced inward, creating an illusory square, and on successive frames the inducing elements rotated in place, such that the illusory square appeared to move from the center to the end of the row and back to the center again. The apparent motion of the illusory figure was mirrored on the other side of the display by the same motion of a set of four inducing elements with their gaps facing outward, following the logic of Bertenthal et al. (1980). All of the inducing elements not involved in creating either the illusory or the nonillusory display on a particular frame were rotated so that their gaps did not align with any other gaps (Fig. 1.7). When adults viewed this video display, they reported clear perception of an illusory square moving on one side of the screen. They also reported that they were unable to track the movement of the nonsquare set of elements, even when instructed to do so.

To investigate infants' perception of this display, their preferential looking and tracking of the side of the display with the illusory square was compared to their looking and tracking of the other side of the display. Results

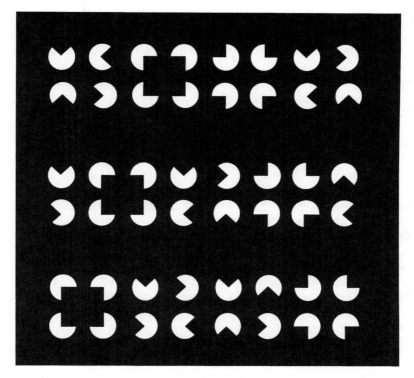

FIG. 1.7. Displays used in a study of infants' perception of illusory contours in a moving display (after Condry et al., 1992).

showed that 7-month-old infants reliably attended to the illusory square side of the display, suggesting they too perceived the illusory figure. Because this display is similar to the ones used in the Bertenthal et al. (1980) and Ghim (1990) studies, however, it is subject to the same interpretive ambiguity as those studies. In all of these experiments, infants were presented with the task of discriminating an illusory square containing low spatial frequency information (because the gaps in inducing elements all faced inward) from a nonsquare group that did not contain low spatial frequency information. In each case the infants responded consistently with the perception of the existence of the low spatial frequency information, and their response cannot clearly be attributed to the perception of illusory figures.

To address this problem, Condry et al. (1992) created a second display in which the inducing elements were alternately colored in reverse contrast (so that a white element appeared next to a black element) on a medium gray background. In this type of display, the low spatial frequency information is no longer present, indeed adults who squinted their eyes to remove high spatial frequency information were unable to discriminate the illusory figure side of the display from the nonillusory side. All other aspects of the display remained the same as in the previous experiment, and 4- and 7-month-old infants' preferential looking to this new kinetic display was measured.

Results again indicated that 7-month-old infants perceived the illusory figure in this apparent motion display, consistently attending preferentially to the illusory side of the display. To our knowledge, this finding presents the first evidence that 7-month-old infants' response to illusory contour displays does not depend on low-level contrast-detecting mechanisms but on a sensitivity to the higher level perceptual organization of the display. This finding strengthens the conclusion that 7-month-old infants perceive illusory contour displays as do adults.

Nevertheless, findings with 4-month-old infants were equivocal: These infants showed a significant side bias that was not influenced by the position of the illusory figure. Although this finding suggested that 4-month-old infants failed to detect the illusory figure, two kinds of interpretations for this failure could be offered. First, young infants specifically may fail to organize inducing elements into groups of layered surfaces so as to perceive illusory contours as do adults. Second, young infants may show lower sensitivity to real as well as illusory figures, or lower abilities to control attention so as to track figures that move. To distinguish these possibilities, a control study was conducted with the 4-month-old infants, in which a similar kinetic display that contained a real, light gray square substituted for the illusory square. Because a real square was present, Condry et al. (1992) reasoned that infants should attend to this display if their failure in the first experiment depended specifically on a failure to perceive the illusory figure. Contrary to this prediction, 4-month-old infants again showed inconsistent preferences between the two sides of the display. These findings are consistent with the possibility that spurious display factors prevented the young infants from responding to both the illusory and the real square. Condry et al. (1992) concluded, therefore, that 7-month-old infants' responses were consistent with perception of the illusory figure but that the results from the 4-month-old infants could not be clearly interpreted.

The question whether infants perceive the central illusory figure in standard illusory contour displays thus receives an affirmative answer at 7 months, but it has yet to be answered satisfactorily at younger ages. And what of the other characteristics of adults' perception of illusory contour displays? Only one study has attempted to determine whether infants perceive the amodal completion of the inducing elements in the same manner as adults. Four- and seven-month-old infants were habituated to either an illusory square with incomplete discs as inducing elements or to a nonillusory display in which all four inducing elements were rotated outward, and then they were tested with a single, semicircular inducing element or a single complete disc (Condry & Yonas, 1998; Fig. 1.8). If infants perceived the illusory square as occluding four complete discs, then they should have dishabituated to the single inducing element, whereas infants habituated to the nonillusory display should have dishabituated to the complete disc. Seven-month-old infants showed this pattern of response, suggesting they perceived the amodal completion of the inducing elements when they were habituated to the illusory square. The results from the 4-month-old infants again were equivocal, as the infants in both conditions showed no preference between the test displays with complete versus incomplete discs. If the younger infants had shown a clear preference for the complete disc after habituation to the illusory display, this would have suggested that they perceived the individual elements of the illusion display but not the illusory occlusion. The finding of no preference leaves open the possibility that infants noted some aspects of the global configuration and possibly even the occlusion, but did not clearly perceive the amodal completion of the inducing elements. Regardless of how one interprets the results at 4 months, however, the results from infants at 7 months provide strong evidence that they perceived the inducing elements in the illusory display as continuing behind a central, illusory figure.

In summary, there is consistent evidence that infants over the age of 6 months perceive the global organization in illusory figure displays, but more research is required to determine exactly what infants are perceiving. In particular, no research has examined whether infants perceive the brightness or depth effects in illusory figure displays. Moreover, more research is needed to probe the earlier development of perception of illusory contours. Although younger infants show trends in each study similar to the responses of older infants, they are less consistent in their responses.

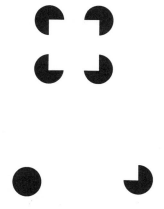

FIG. 1.8. Displays used in a study of infants' amodal completion of inducing elements in an illusory contour display (after Condry & Yonas, 1998).

Investigators also are less consistent in their findings and interpretations of young infants' responses. For example, Ghim (1990) claimed that 4-month-old infants distinguish between illusory and nonillusory figures, but Bertenthal et al. (1980) and Condry et al. (1992) were unable to find clear evidence for early perception of illusory figures using similar displays.

Careful examination of the displays used by these investigators may provide an explanation for their discrepant findings. If the amount of edge that needs to be interpolated in partly occluded figures determines whether young infants perceive completion of the occluded objects, perhaps the same factor influences perception of illusory figures as well. The illusory figure in the Ghim (1990) research subtended a considerably larger visual angle than the illusory displays in the other studies, and it had a smaller gap (unsupported edge) between the elements than did the displays of Bertenthal et al. (1980). Because the ratio of supported to unsupported edge affects whether adults see salient illusory contours, infants too may be less sensitive to edge relationships over larger gaps. Theorists agree that the alignment of the gaps in the inducing elements is critical to perceiving illusory figures. The findings by Johnson and Aslin (1995) that young infants perceive the unity of partly occluded objects and patterns when the occluder is narrowed suggests that illusory figures with smaller gaps (unsupported edges) might be perceptible to younger infants as well.

Although studies of infants' perception of illusory contours have revealed a number of changes in infants' performance between 4 and 7 months, these findings provide no clear evidence for a qualitative, developmental change in infants' perception. Instead, the evidence suggests that the organizational processes that give rise to perception of illusory contours are present in very young infants but fail to operate on standard illusory contour displays because of limits on infants' sensitivity to contour alignment. Note that the illusory contour displays presented to infants have had contour separations of 1.2° or more: far greater than the separations used in the studies of partly occluded objects. As in the case of partly occluded objects (Johnson & Aslin, 1995), therefore, apparent qualitative changes in infants' perception of illusory contours may stem from an increase in the distance over which contour alignment is detectable. If that suggestion is correct, then developmental increases in sensitivity to alignment may account for developmental changes in perception of both partly occluded objects and illusory contours. Except for these changes, the same organizational processes may operate in infants as well as adults.

IMPLICATIONS

In this chapter, we have attempted to reconcile the evidence for developmental change in object perception with the continuity thesis: the claim that perceptual organization is responsive to the same types of perceptual information, at all ages. All of the developmental changes we have considered are consistent with this thesis, if one assumes that visual sensitivity to this information increases over development. That assumption, in turn, is hardly controversial, for the thesis that visual sensitivity increases over infancy has overwhelming empirical support (see Kellman & Arterberry, 1998; Kellman & Banks, 1998). The twin theses of developmental continuity and developmentally linked increases in sensitivity nevertheless have some interesting, and problematic, consequences.

One consequence of infants' developing perceptual sensitivity is that continuous changes in underlying processes can produce discontinuous changes in perception and perceptually guided action (see Banks & Shannon, 1993). For example, as infants' sensitivity to edge alignment increases, allowing infants to detect alignment over greater and greater visual separations, infants' perception of illusory contour displays may shift from perception of a set of unrelated elements to perception of a set of surfaces, with complete edges, arranged in depth. The continuity thesis therefore is consistent with findings of certain qualitative changes in infants' perception.

A related consequence of children's developing sensitivity is that studies of perceptual development must distinguish *competence* from *performance*. For example, when one studies newborn infants' perception of center-occluded objects, one wants to know whether the mechanisms by which adults interpolate hidden surfaces and perceive unitary, partly hidden objects are present and functional at birth. When one finds, as did Slater et al. (1990), that such infants do not respond to a fully visible connected object as similar to a partly occluded one, however, one cannot conclude that this perceptual competence is absent. It is possible that mechanisms of surface interpolation are present and functional, but that their performance is blocked by limits on infants' sensitivity to the information on which they operate. This possibility, in turn, can be tested by measuring newborn infants' sensitivity to the relevant information and by designing displays that minimize the demands on their sensory systems (see Slater et al., 1996, for an example).

If visual sensitivity is extremely limited at birth, however, there may be no displays for which certain perceptual competencies will be manifest. In that case, investigators will need to change strategy to study developing perceptual competence.

One strategy is to study the competence in other animals: either animals with precocial visual sensitivity or animals whose visual experience can be strictly controlled. For example, studies by Regolin and Vallortigara (1995) and by Lea, Slater, and Ryan (1996) now provide evidence that 1-day-old chicks, who have never been exposed to any occlusion display, perceive the unity of both stationary and moving center-occluded objects. Inexperienced chicks use both contour alignment and common motion to perceive object unity, casting doubt on earlier claims that sensitivity to contour alignment depends on visual experience (Spelke, 1990).

A second strategy is to probe the mechanisms of object perception using the methods of cognitive neuroscience. For example, experiments probing the neural locus for perception of illusory contours in human adults (e.g., Paradiso, Shimojo, & Nakayama, 1989), monkeys (e.g., Peterhans & von der Heydt, 1989; von der Heydt & Peterhans, 1989), and cats (Bravo, Blake, & Morrison, 1988; Redies, Crook, & Creutzfeldt, 1986) provide evidence that illusory contour perception reflects activity in early visual cortical processing areas. As techniques for imaging neural activity in humans become increasingly available for studies of infants and children, these findings should allow investigators to probe whether similar patterns of neural activity occur in infants.

A third strategy for investigating "hidden" competencies in infants is to test for linkages, in human infants, between developmental changes in perceptual sensitivity and developmental changes in perceptual organization. For example, if infants' failure to perceive the unity of a moving, center-occluded object stems from a failure to detect the common motion of its spatially separated surfaces, then their perception should shift at the point in development when sensitivity to the relevant motion emerges. The existence of all three strategies suggests, contrary to frequently heard criticisms (e.g., Thelen & Smith, 1994), that the competence–performance distinction is not a source of untestable claims but rather a call for further research, exploring the development of perceptual capacities from multiple perspectives (see Spelke & Newport, 1998, for discussion).

Where the continuity thesis is found to be correct, and investigators succeed in tracing the perceptual competencies of adults back to the youngest infants, this endeavor has implications both for the study of vision and for the study of cognition. We end by considering each in turn.

Research on the nature and mechanisms of visual organization has focused on four problems. One is the problem of characterizing the nature of perceptual organization in human adults, a problem addressed primarily through studies of visual psychophysics. Second is the problem of characterizing the neural mechanisms that give rise to perceptual organization, a problem addressed primarily through studies of visual anatomy and physiology. Third is the problem of characterizing the computational processes that give rise to perceptual organization, a problem addressed primarily through studies of artificial vision systems. Fourth is the problem of characterizing the development of perceptual organization in relation to growth and experience, a problem addressed through studies of human infants and young children and through studies of other animals.

As already noted, these problems tend to be pursued by scientists in different disciplines, but findings that bear on one problem frequently bear on the others. In particular, we suggest that studies of infants can make a singular contribution to understanding perceptual organization at psychophysical, neural, and computational levels, if the continuity thesis is correct. In adults, basic mechanisms of perceptual organization are complemented and modulated by a wealth of acquired knowledge and learned strategies, and this knowledge may obscure aspects of their functioning. Moreover, the mature brain is highly interactive, and interactions among different subsystems complicate the task of analyzing any single subsystem. By analyzing perceptual functioning in young infants, we may see the operation of basic perceptual mechanisms in purer form.

The implications of the continuity thesis for studies of cognition and cognitive development are no less important. If the continuity thesis is correct, then infants perceive fundamentally the same world as adults. Although infants' perceptions often may be indistinct and indeterminate where those of adults are sharp and clear, infants' clearest perceptions will accord with those of their elders. Insofar as infants learn from their perceptual experiences, the things they learn should not need to be unlearned at older ages. Instead, the development of knowledge in infancy could stand at the foundation of the systems of knowledge that serve humans all our lives.

The continuity thesis has often been presented as an alternative to the thesis that infancy is a time of extensive, rapid, and all-important learning (e.g., Haith, 1998). In fact, we suggest, these are complementary theses. If infants perceive the same world of objects as adults, then infancy is likely to be a time of extensive learning about that world. Learning in infancy can mesh smoothly with later learning, building the belief systems that guide our thoughts and actions as adults. For those who would foster human development, the infancy period could be a time when learning experiences will have lasting consequences. Understanding what infants perceive and learn therefore will be central to understanding the foundations of human knowledge.

REFERENCES

Banks, M. S., & Shannon, E. (1993). Spatial and chromatic visual efficiency in human neonates. In C. E. Granrud (Ed.), *Visual perception and cognition in infancy* (pp. 1–46). Hillsdale, NJ: Lawrence Erlbaum Associates.

Bertenthal, B. I., Campos, J. J., & Haith, M. M. (1980). Development of visual organization: The perception of subjective contours. *Child Development, 51,* 1072–1080.

Bogartz, R. S., & Shinskey, J. L. (1998). On perception of a partially occluded object in 6-month-olds. *Cognitive Development, 13,* 141–163.

Bravo, M., Blake, R., & Morrison, S. (1988). Cats see subjective contours. *Vision Research, 28*(8), 861–865.

Bushnell, I. W. R., Sai, F., & Mullin, J. T. (1989). Neonatal recognition of mother's face. *British Journal of Developmental Psychology, 7,* 3–15.

Cohen, L. B., DeLoache, J. S., & Strauss, M. S. (1971). Infant visual perception. In J. D. Osofsky (Ed.), *Handbook of infant development* (pp. 393–438). New York: Wiley.

Condry, K. F., Gentile, D., & Yonas, A. (1992, April). *Four- and seven-month-old infants' perception of kinetic illusory figures.* Poster presented at the annual meeting of the Association for Research in Vision and Ophthalmology, Sarasota, FL.

Condry, K. F., & Yonas, A. (1998). *Perception of illusory figures in 4- and 7-month-old infants.* Unpublished manuscript, University of Minnesota.

Dumais, S. T., & Bradley, D. R. (1976). The effects of illumination level and retinal size on the apparent strength of subjective contours. *Perception and Psychophysics, 19,* 339–345.

Field, D. J., Hayes, A., & Hess, R. F. (1993). Contour integration by the human visual system: Evidence for a local association field. *Vision Research, 33,* 173–193.

Friedman, S. (1972). Habituation and recovery of visual response in the alert human newborn. *Journal of Experimental Child Psychology, 13,* 339–349.

Ghim, H. R. (1990). Evidence for perceptual organization in infants: Perception of subjective contours by young infants. *Infant Behavior and Development, 13,* 221–248.

Haith, M. M. (1998). Who put the cog in infant cognition: Is rich interpretation too costly? *Infant Behavior and Development, 21,* 167–179.

Johnson, S. P., & Aslin, R. N. (1995). Perception of object unity in 2-month-old infants. *Developmental Psychology, 31,* 739–745.

Johnson, S. P., & Aslin, R. N. (1996). Perception of object unity in young infants: The roles of motion, depth, and orientation. *Cognitive Development, 11,* 161–180.

Johnson, S. P., & Náñez, J. E. (1995). Young infants' perception of object unity in two-dimensional displays. *Infant Behavior and Development, 18,* 133–143.

Kanisza, G. (1955/1987). Quasiperceptual margins in homogeneously stimulated fields (W. Gerbino, Trans.). In S. Petry & G. Meyer (Eds.), *The perception of illusory contours* (pp. 40–49). New York: Springer-Verlag.

Kaufmann-Hayoz, R., Kaufmann, F., & Walther, D. (1988). Perception of subjective contours at 5 and 8 months (abstract). *Infant Behavior and Development, 11,* 168.

Kawabata, H., Gyoba, J., Inoue, H., & Ohtsubo, H. (1999). Visual completion of partly-occluded grating in infants under 1 month of age. *Vision Research, 39,* 3586–3591.

Kellman, P. J. (1993). Kinematic foundations of visual perception. In C. E. Granrud (Ed.), *Visual perception and cognition in infancy.* Hillsdale, NJ: Lawrence Erlbaum Associates.

Kellman, P. J., & Arterberry, M. (1998). *The cradle of knowledge: Development of perception in infancy.* Cambridge, MA: MIT Press.

Kellman, P. J., & Banks, M. S. (1998). Infant visual perception. In W. Damon, D. Kuhn, & R. S. Siegler (Eds.), *Handbook of child psychology, Vol. 2: Cognition, perception, and language* (5th ed., pp. 103–146). New York: Wiley.

Kellman, P. J., & Cohen, M. H. (1984). Kinetic subjective contours. *Perception and Psychophysics, 35*(3), 237–244.

Kellman, P. J., Gleitman, H., & Spelke, E. S. (1987). Object and observer motion in the perception of objects by infants. *Journal of Experimental Psychology: Human Perception and Performance, 12,* 586–593.

Kellman, P. J., & Shipley, T. F. (1991). A theory of visual interpolation in object perception. *Cognitive Psychology, 23,* 141–221.

Kellman, P. J., & Spelke, E. S. (1983). Perception of partly occluded objects in infancy. *Cognitive Psychology, 15,* 483–524.

Lea, S. E. G., Slater, A. M., & Ryan, C. M. E. (1996). Perception of object unity in chicks: A comparison with the human infant. *Infant Behavior and Development, 19,* 501–504.

Lesher, G. (1995). Illusory contours: Toward a neurally based perceptual theory. *Psychonomic Bulletin and Review, 2,* 279–321.

Mehler, J., Jusczyk, P., Lambertz, G., Halsted, N., Bertoncini, J., & Amiel-Tison, C. (1988). A precursor of language acquisition in young infants. *Cognition, 29,* 143–178.

Michotte, A., Thines, R., & Crabbe, G. (1964). *Les complements amodaux des structures perceptives* [Amodal completion of perceptual structures]. Louvain, Belguim: Publications Universitaires de Louvain.

Needham, A. (1994). Infants' use of perceptual similarity when segregating partly occluded objects during the fourth month of life. *Infant Behavior and Development, 17*, 163 (abstract).

Needham, A. (1997). Factors affecting infants' use of featural information in object segregation. *Current Directions in Psychological Science, 6*, 26–33.

Needham, A., Baillargeon, R., & Kaufman, L. (1998). Object segregation in infancy. In C. Rovee-Collier & L. Lipsitt (Eds.), *Advances in infancy research, 11*, 1–44.

Paradiso, M. A., Shimojo, S., & Nakayama, K. (1989). Subjective contours, tilt aftereffects, and visual cortical organization. *Vision Research, 29*(9), 1205–1213.

Parks, T. E. (1986). Illusory figures, illusory objects, and real objects. *Psychological Review, 93*, 207–215.

Peterhans, E., & von der Heydt, R. (1989). Mechanisms of contour perception in monkey visual cortex. II: Contours bridging gaps. *Journal of Neuroscience, 9*, 1749–1763.

Piaget, J. (1954). *The construction of reality in the child*. New York: Basic Books.

Redies, C., Crook, J. M., & Creutzfeldt, O. D. (1986). Neuronal responses to borders with and without luminance gradients in cat visual cortex and dorsal lateral nucleus. *Experimental Brain Research, 61*, 469–481.

Regolin, L., & Vallortigara, G. (1995). Perception of partly occluded objects by young chicks. *Perception and Psychophysics, 57*, 971–976.

Schmidt, H. (1985). *The role of Gestalt principles in perceptual completion: A developmental approach.* Unpublished doctoral dissertation, University of Pennsylvania, Philadelphia, PA.

Schumann, F. (1900/1987). Some observations on the combination of visual impressions into units (A. Hogg, Trans.). In S. Petry & G. Meyer (Eds.), *The perception of illusory contours* (pp. 21–34). New York: Springer-Verlag.

Schwartz, K. (1982). *Perceptual knowledge of the human face in infancy.* Unpublished doctoral dissertation, University of Pennsylvania, Philadelphia, PA.

Shipley, T. F., & Kellman, P. J. (1992). Strength of visual interpolation depends on the ratio of physically specified to total edge length. *Perception and Psychophysics, 52*, 97–106.

Slater, A., Johnson, S. P., Brown, E., & Badenock, M. (1996). Newborn infants' perception of partly occluded objects. *Infant Behavior and Development, 19*, 147–150.

Slater, A., Johnson, S. P., Kellman, P. J., & Spelke, E. S. (1994). The role of three-dimensional depth cues in infants' perception of partly occluded objects. *Early Development and Parenting, 3*, 187–191.

Slater, A., Morison, V., Somers, M., Mattock, A., Brown, E., & Taylor, D. (1990). Newborn and older infants' perception of partly occluded objects. *Infant Behavior and Development, 13*, 33–49.

Smith, W. C., Johnson, S. P., & Spelke, E. S. (submitted). *Edge sensitivity, depth perception, and spatiotemporal integration in perception of object unity.* Manuscript under review.

Smith, W. C., Johnson, S. P., Spelke, E. S., & Aslin, R. N. (1996, April). *Edge sensitivity and temporal integration in young infants' perception of object unity.* Poster presented at the International Conference on Infant Studies, Providence, RI.

Smith, W. C., Johnson, S. P., & Spelke, E. S. (in preparation). *Four-month-olds' perception of object unity: Orientation sensitivity and temporal integration.*

Spelke, E. S. (1990). Principles of object perception. *Cognitive Science, 14*, 29–56.

Spelke, E. S., & Newport, E. (1998). Nativism, empiricism, and the development of knowledge. In R. Lerner (Ed.), *Handbook of child psychology, 5th ed., Vol. 1: Theoretical models of human development* (pp. 275–340). New York: Wiley.

Spelke, E. S., Vishton, P., & von Hofsten, C. (1995). Object perception, object-directed action, and physical knowledge in infancy. In M. S. Gazzaniga (Ed.), *The cognitive neurosciences* (pp. 165–179). Cambridge, MA: MIT Press.

Termine, N., Hrynick, R., Kestenbaum, R., Gleitman, H., & Spelke, E. S. (1987). Perceptual completion of surfaces in infancy. *Journal of Experimental Psychology: Human Perception and Performance, 13*, 524–532.

Thelen, E., & Smith, L. B. (1994). *A dynamic systems approach to the development of cognition and action.* Cambridge, MA: Bradford/MIT Press.

Trieber, F., & Wilcox, S. (1980). Perception of a "subjective" contour by infants. *Child Development, 51*, 915–917.

Tse, P. U. (1999). Volume completion. *Cognitive Psychology, 39*, 37–68.

von der Heydt, R., & Peterhans, E. (1989). Mechanisms of contour perception in monkey visual cortex. I: Lines of pattern discontinuity. *Journal of Neuroscience, 9*, 1731–1748.

Task Dependency in Infant Behavior: Toward an Understanding of the Processes Underlying Cognitive Development

Yuko Munakata
University of Denver

Infants can appear precocious or limited in almost any domain depending on the task administered to them. For example, 3.5 month-old infants demonstrate apparent sensitivity to hidden objects in violation-of-expectation experiments (Baillargeon, 1993), yet infants fail to retrieve hidden objects through 8 months (Piaget, 1954). Such simultaneous failures and successes are arguably equally important aspects of development, because the same developing system produces both the flawed and the competent behaviors. Accounting for both thus seems to be critical for understanding the origins of knowledge (see discussion in Braine, 1959; Brown, 1976; Flavell, 1985).

This chapter focuses on understanding why infant behavior is so task dependent. Why do infants simultaneously fail and succeed on different tasks meant to measure the same knowledge? What might this tell us about the nature of cognitive development? How can we understand the changes that underlie these developmental patterns? This chapter explores these questions in the context of the Piagetian notion of object permanence, the understanding that objects exist independent of our percepts of them and maintain their identity through changes in location. I contrast two approaches to these questions—principle based and process based. The more prevalent principle-based approach assumes that knowledge takes the form of generally accessible principles. Early signs of competence indicate that infants have the tested principle, so task dependencies must be attributed to deficits in ancillary systems. In contrast, the process-based approach focuses on the mechanisms underlying particular behaviors. These mechanisms are not viewed as separable from generally accessible principles, but instead as the very mechanisms that give rise to infant knowledge. Different behaviors may rely on different processing mechanisms, so task dependencies offer clues to the state of underlying knowledge.

I argue that progress on understanding task-dependent behavior requires a new focus on the *processes* underlying behavior, rather than on the attribution of *principles* to infants to describe their behavior. Findings from several areas of study (infant development, cognitive neuroscience, and neural network modeling) are used to demonstrate both the limitations of principle-based approaches and the potential of process-based approaches.

TASK DEPENDENCY IN OBJECT PERMANENCE

When Piaget (1954) attempted to measure infants' understanding of object permanence, he observed two fundamental limitations of interest here. First, infants fail to retrieve completely hidden objects until around 8 months. Second, when infants do begin to retrieve hidden objects, they still show limitations in their understanding of object permanence by making errors in the A-not-B task. When an object is hidden in one location (A), infants can retrieve it. However, when the object is then hidden in a new location (B), infants perseverate in reaching to the original hiding location (the A-not-B error). To Piaget, these limitations indicated that infants develop an understanding of object permanence over a protracted period. A full object permanence concept was attributable to infants only around 18 to 24 months. Although Piaget has been criticized for underestimating infant capabilities, replications of his empirical findings have been largely successful. For example, infants *do* fail to reach for hidden objects reliably until around 8 months, and they do reliably perseverate in the A-not-B task.

Despite the robustness of these findings, many researchers since Piaget have argued that infants are more competent than previously suspected. This argument relies on the task-dependent nature of infant behavior. Infants can appear limited on one task while simultaneously demonstrating apparent competence on another task meant to measure the same knowledge. Piaget's tasks revealed limitations; subsequent ingenious experiments have uncovered apparent competence. If only Piaget had been able to run more sensitive experiments, the argument goes, he might have given infants the credit they deserve.

For example, infants in violation-of-expectation experiments have demonstrated precocious sensitivity to physical constraints (Leslie, 1988; Spelke, Breinlinger, Macomber, & Jacobson, 1992), including the permanence of objects (Baillargeon, 1993). Perhaps the most salient difference between the Piagetian and violation-of-expectation measures is the extent to which they require active manipulation of objects. For Piaget, infants needed to retrieve hidden objects to demonstrate some understanding of the object concept. With the development of violation-of-expectation techniques, infants only need to watch events to demonstrate apparent competence. These events are typically separated into habituation or familiarization and test periods. During habituation or familiarization, infants are familiarized with the motions of objects in the display. During test, objects follow the habituated courses of motion in "impossible" or "possible" ways. The impossible events appear to violate certain physical constraints. Experimenters measure how long infants spend looking at the possible and impossible events; longer looking-times to the impossible events indicate that infants are sensitive to the tested constraints.

For example, Baillargeon (Baillargeon, 1987; Baillargeon, Spelke, & Wasserman, 1985) habituated infants to a drawbridge-like stimulus swinging back and forth. At test, a block was placed in the path of the drawbridge. In the possible event, the drawbridge swung back to the point where it would touch the block and then swung back to its starting point. In the impossible event, the drawbridge appeared to swing through the space occupied by the block before swinging back to its starting point. In both conditions, the drawbridge occluded the block as it swung toward it. Infants as young as 3.5 months looked longer at the impossible event, indicating some apparent sensitivity to the occluded block's continued existence.

Infants have also demonstrated precocious sensitivity to hidden objects in violation-of-expectation variants of the A-not-B task (Ahmed & Ruffman, 1998). In these studies, 8- to 12-month-old infants watched an experimenter hide an object at A, and after a delay the experimenter revealed the object at A or allowed infants to retrieve the object from A. The object was then hidden at B and after a delay revealed at B (the possible event) or A (the impossible event). Infants showed longer looking times to the impossible events, following delays at which they nonetheless searched perseveratively at A in the standard search version of the A-not-B task.

The Piagetian and violation-of-expectation techniques thus paint strikingly different pictures of infant competence. Researchers have documented such patterns of simultaneous successes and failures across various ages, domains, and task conditions. *That* task dependency exists has been established. The unanswered question is: Why? Focusing on this question is likely to improve our understanding of cognitive development substantially. In the next section, I contrast principle-based and process-based approaches to task dependency. I argue that the process-based approach supports a focus on task dependency in a way that the more pervasive principle-based approach does not.

PRINCIPLES VERSUS PROCESSES

Principle-based and process-based approaches to development differ in three important ways: in the presumed bases for behavior, and in turn, the types of research strategies and explanations of task dependency that are favored. I consider each of these factors in turn, first for principle-based and then for process-based approaches (see original discussion in Muna-kata, McClelland, Johnson, & Siegler, 1997).

The principle-based approach seems to govern—implicitly or explicitly—much of the study of cognitive development, particularly in infants. Within this framework, knowledge takes the form of principles in the head, such as "Objects exist independent of my percepts of them." Reasoning procedures act on these principles to produce behavior. Commonly, these principles are treated as all-or-none (see discussions in Flavell, 1971, 1984; Karmiloff-Smith, 1992, 1991; Siegler, 1993, 1989; Siegler & Munakata, 1993; Smith & Thelen, 1993; Thelen & Smith, 1994; specifically in the context of object permanence see Fischer & Bidell, 1991). In addition, these principles are often posited as if they existed in propositional form and were thus generally accessible rather than tied to specific procedures or mechanisms (Diamond, 1991; Spelke et al., 1992). In some cases, the principles are viewed as present from birth (Spelke et al., 1992). Accounts within the principle-based approach sometimes allow for the elaboration or enriching of initial concepts (Baillargeon, 1993; Spelke, 1991). However, these elaborations are often overlooked in theorizing about infant behavior. In particular, such elaborations are not used in explanations of the task-dependent nature of infant competence. In addition, such elaborations typically only follow the initial acquisition of an all-or-none concept, and the elaborative process often occurs dimension-by-dimension. For example, Baillargeon (1993) argued that infants first learn a concept of object permanence and then add to this concept the dimensions of object size and object hardness.

Within the principle-based approach, researchers can ask whether infants of a given age have certain concepts, which is to ask, do the infants "believe" or "know" the relevant principles? If infants demonstrate any sensitivity to a principle, then they must have the principle. A reasonable research strategy then, is to design the most simple task to tap sensitivity to a principle. The more simple the task, the more likely the relevant principle will be revealed if it exists. In this vein, researchers have designed many clever experiments. As a result, researchers commonly attribute a concept of object permanence to infants at an earlier age than did Piaget.

Why did Piaget observe the limitations that he did? To answer the task-dependency question within the principle-based framework, one needs to look outside the concept of object permanence, since infants are viewed as having this principle within the first few months of life. The deficit must exist in some sort of ancillary system. Several researchers (Baillargeon, Graber, DeVos, & Black, 1990; Diamond, 1991; Willatts, 1990) have argued that infants fail to retrieve hidden toys due to means—ends analysis deficits. According to this argument, infants have a concept of object permanence but lack the knowledge of how to act on one object as a means to retrieving another. The principle-based framework similarly leads to a focus on ancillary deficits to explain the A-not-B error. For example, infants' inability to inhibit the conditioned reaching response has been proposed to explain perseverative reaching (Diamond, 1985). Deficits in search behaviors and planful problem-solving abilities have also been proposed to explain the task dependency in the A-not-B task (Baillargeon & Graber, 1988; Baillargeon, DeVos, & Graber, 1989). Principles thus have privileged status. That is, although often infants do not behave in accord with such principles, the task dependency is explained by deficits in ancillary systems. The status of principles as all-or-nothing entities in the mind is preserved.

However, as my colleagues and I (Munakata et al., 1997) argued:

> Because infants seem to behave in accord with principles at times, there might be some use to describing their behavior in these terms. The danger, we believe, comes in the tendency to accept these descriptions of behavior as mental entities that are explicitly accessed and used in the production of behavior. . . . That is, one could say that infants' behavior in a looking-time task accords with a principle of object permanence, in the same way that one could say that the motions of the planets accord with Kepler's laws. However, it is a further—and we will argue, unfounded—step to then conclude that infants actually access and reason with an explicit representation of the principle itself. In the same way, one would not want to explain the motions of the planets by claiming that the planets derive their next location in space on the basis of reasoning with Kepler's laws. (p. 687)

This chapter explores an alternative approach that focuses on the processes that give rise to behavior, and in turn, the processes underlying change. One might characterize these processes as behaving in accordance with various principles (under specified conditions), but this characterization would simply serve as a shorthand description of their behavior, not a statement of the mechanism that underlies their behavior.

In the process-based approach, the knowledge underlying infants' behaviors is viewed as graded in nature, evolving with experience, and embedded in specific processes underlying overt behavior. This approach is motivated by general views of the nature and development of cognitive competence, from the frameworks of neural network modeling and cognitive neuroscience. In the neural network framework, behaviors are expressed through the activation of processing units engaged by a task (McClelland, 1989, 1992). These activations are determined by the strengths of the connections linking the processing units. Such connections are graded in nature and evolve gradually in response to experience. Graded, embedded, evolving processes are also evident across a wide variety of domains in cognitive neuroscience (e.g., Bachevalier & Mishkin, 1984; Greenough, Black, & Wallace, 1987; Morton & Johnson, 1991).

The process-based approach is also consistent with the skills approach taken by Fischer and Bidell (1991) and the dynamic systems approach detailed by Thelen and Smith (1994, Smith & Thelen, 1993). In the skills approach, behavior is the expression of skills (context-sensitive procedures) that evolve with specific practice. In the dynamic systems framework, behavior is viewed as emergent patterns of activity dependent on an individual's situation and history and embodied in physical processing systems.

Within the process-based approach, it is not so meaningful to ask whether infants of a given age *have* certain concepts. The questions are instead of the form: What are the underlying mechanisms that produce behavior? How do these mechanisms and the resulting representations change during development? Whereas the principle-based approach posits principles that describe infant behavior in limited contexts, the process-based approach would ask of these principles: What does it mean to say that infants have a concept of object permanence? How do infants know that an occluded object is still there? What form does this knowledge take? How is this knowledge accessed and used?

The simplified tasks that have revealed early competence provide constraints on process-based theorizing. However, within the process-based approach, the ability to demonstrate sensitivity in violation-of-expectation experiments does not imply that infants "have" a concept of object permanence. Infants' knowledge is not viewed as simply present or absent, disembodied from behavior. Instead, the underlying processing systems that give rise to behavior are viewed as gradually developing over time, so that infants become increasingly able to behave in ways that demonstrate sensitivity to hidden objects. Infants may initially seem "smart" only on certain tasks because these can be passed with a weak or limited sensitivity to the relevant constraints. Infants show task-dependent behavior due to the state of relevant processing systems. These processing systems are not viewed as separable from generally accessible principles, but are instead the very mechanisms that give rise to the knowledge representations governing behavior. Understanding task dependency is thus an inherent goal of the process-based approach, rather than a peripheral problem relegated to ancillary deficits.

With the distinctions between principle- and process-based approaches in mind, I now present experimental results that indicate limitations to current principle-based approaches. These data rule out what are arguably the most commonly accepted explanations of task dependency in object permanence tasks—means—ends and inhibition deficits. One specific process-based theory for understanding task dependency is considered. Although speculative, this theory indicates the potential for the process-based approach to advance our understanding of development.

EVALUATING PRINCIPLE-BASED EXPLANATIONS

To test the means—ends account for infants' failure to retrieve occluded objects, Munakata et al. (1997) trained 7-month-old infants on the means-ends abilities required for retrieving toys. The infants were then tested on the retrieval of visible and occluded toys, in tasks in which the means—ends demands were equated. If the means—ends account were accurate, and infants of this age did in fact have the concept of object permanence and were simply missing the relevant means—ends abilities, then they should have performed similarly in the visible and occluded conditions. Infants consistently performed better under visible conditions, indicating that their difficulties with occluded objects could not be attributed simply to means—ends deficits.

In the first experiment, infants were trained to pull a towel to retrieve a distant toy. Infants were then tested on trials with an opaque or transparent screen in front of the toy. Trials without toys were also included, and the difference between toy and no-toy trials in number of retrieval responses was used as a measure of toy-guided retrieval. The means—ends abilities required for toy-guided retrieval in the transparent and opaque conditions were identical, yet toy-guided retrieval was more frequent in the transparent condition.

In the second experiment, infants were trained to push a button to retrieve a distant toy. The toy sat on a distant ledge; pushing the button caused the ledge to drop so that the toy slid down a ramp to within reach. As in the first experiment, infants were tested with opaque and transparent screens, with toy and no-toy trials. This experiment tested two alternative explanations of the first experiment. Infants may have failed to retrieve occluded toys because they viewed the opaque screen as a wall or because they needed continuous feedback about the success of their towel pulling (available only in the transparent condition). In this experiment, both screens were actually rigid but the toy slid under rather than through them, so any beliefs about the screens as walls should not have affected the perceived attainability of the toy. In addition, pushing the button caused the shelf to drop immediately; there was no feedback advantage to the transparent condition. The pattern of results was similar to that from the towel experiment. Toy-guided retrieval was more frequent in the transparent condition.

A third experiment eliminated the possibility that training on the retrieval of visible toys had led infants to generalize better to the transparent condition. In this experiment, infants were trained to push the button to make the ledge drop, without toys. Equal exposure was given to the opaque and transparent screens. The pattern of results at test matched those from the first two experiments, with toy-guided retrieval more frequent in the transparent condition. Taken together, these experiments demonstrate the insufficiency of the means–ends deficit account to explain the task dependency in measures of object permanence. Infant behavior cannot be explained by positing a principle of object permanence combined with means-ends deficits.

Similarly, existing data argue against A-not-B theories that posit a principle of object permanence combined with inhibition deficits. Although such inhibition theories seem to be supported by the finding that infants occasionally show the A-not-B error even when the object is visible at location B (Bremner & Knowles, 1984; Butterworth, 1977; Harris, 1974), such visible-toy errors are likely to reflect random incorrect responding rather than perseverative responding. Using an A-not-B experiment with a third, control location, Sophian and Yengo (1985) demonstrated that infants' visible-toy errors were as likely to occur at the control location as at the previous location. Several other findings also call into question inhibition theories of the A-not-B error. Infants show the A-not-B error even after merely seeing (but not retrieving) an object hidden and revealed at the A location (Butterworth, 1974). Also, the extent to which infants show the A-not-B error is influenced by factors apparently unrelated to inhibition, such as the presence of a cover at the A location (Bremner & Knowles, 1984) and the distinctiveness of available location cues (see Wellman, Cross, & Bartsch, 1986 for meta-analysis). Additionally, looking and reaching responses presumably receive similar conditioning in the A-not-B task, and yet looking measures have revealed earlier sensitivity than reaching measures (Ahmed & Ruffman, 1998).

Means–ends and inhibition deficit accounts thus fail to account for the developmental data. Why then, do infants demonstrate sensitivity to hidden objects first in violation-of-expectation studies, then in single-location retrieval tasks, and then on the A-not-B task? How can we understand task dependency in measures of the object concept, if not through a privileged principle of object permanence together with the development of ancillary systems? The process-based framework offers alternatives that are more consistent with available data. In the following section, I detail one such alternative that posits qualitatively different processes to underlie infants' behavior in violation-of-expectation and retrieval measures of object permanence.

FACILITATED PROCESSING VERSUS MAINTAINED ACTIVITY

Theory

Researchers have typically assumed that infants look longer at impossible events with occluded objects because infants are aware of the objects during the occlusion period. From this perspective, there is a dissociation between the infants' habituation and retrieval behaviors: Why would infants fail to retrieve hidden toys when they know they are there? One possibility is that the apparent looking–reaching dissociation in measures of object permanence is illusory. That is, infants may fail to reach for hidden toys because they do not represent occluded objects up through 8 months. Early competence in looking-time measures may be based on qualitatively different kinds of processing that have nothing to do with understanding the permanence of objects. In particular, infants might form predictions about the interactions between objects when everything in the test display is visible. Infants might then show longer looking times to events that do not match these predictions, without necessarily continuing to maintain active representations of objects that become occluded.[1] Alternatively, infants might consider only the final state of the test display, and "postdict," reasoning back to what events might have led up to it; impossible events elicit longer looking times because they cannot be explained as readily as possible events. I am currently conducting violation-of-expectation experiments to distinguish whether infants predict, postdict, or maintain representations of occluded objects. In this section, I elaborate the distinct processes that may underlie prediction and maintained representations. Although speculative, this process-based account indicates how infants might recognize successful predictions before they become sensitive to the permanence of objects.

What distinguishes the processes tapped by violation-of-expectation and retrieval measures of object permanence? The facilitation–maintenance account is presented in Fig. 2.1. According to this account, habituation events in violation-of-expectation tasks familiarize infants with the motions of objects in the display. At the start of the test event, infants form predictions about upcoming events by extrapolating the visible stimulus through its habituated course of motion. These predictions cause changes in the processing system, so that when an object is occluded, infants do not need to maintain an active representation of it to exhibit sensitivity to its having been there. Subsequent processing of the possible event is facilitated from the

---

[1] I thank David Plaut for suggesting this possibility in the context of the drawbridge experiments.

Visual habituation   **Retrieval**

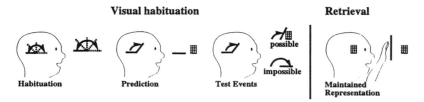

| Habituation | Prediction | Test Events | Maintained Representation |

FIG. 2.1. Proposed processes underlying infant behavior in violation-of-expectation and retrieval tasks. Habituation events familiarize infants with stimulus motions. Based on these habituated motions, infants form predictions
about visible objects at the start of test events. Subsequent processing of the
possible event is facilitated by these predictions, whereas processing of the
impossible event is not. Infants can respond to impossibility without needing
to maintain active representations of an occluded object. In contrast, retrieval
tasks require active maintenance.

earlier prediction processing, whereas processing of the impossible event
is not, leading to longer looking times. That is, infants may be able to succeed on violation-of-expectation tasks through the recognition of an event
as familiar or novel (relative to a prediction formed when everything in the
display was visible). I hypothesize that this type of facilitated processing of
familiar events emerges relatively early in development.

In contrast, according to the facilitation–maintenance account, infants
must actively maintain a representation of an occluded object to retrieve it.
That is, while the object is occluded, infants need an internal signal indicating that the object continues to exist. This signal can guide the retrieval response. Infants are not cued to their earlier processing in the way that they
are in the violation-of-expectation paradigm. In effect, longer looking times
to impossible events can be based on the violation of earlier predictions,
but reaching for hidden objects cannot rely on such recognition processes.
Infants cannot simply watch occlusion events and reach based on recognition of a match, because no such match is provided. For example, in all of
Munakata et al.'s (1997) experiments, the occlusion display looked identical
for toy and no-toy trials. I hypothesize that maintained activation emerges
relatively late.

Evidence: Monkeys

Evidence relevant to the distinction between facilitated processing and maintained activity comes from behavioral and single-cell recording data from
monkeys' stimuli (Desimone, Miller, Chelazzi, & Lueschow, 1994; Miller &
Desimone, 1994; Miller, Gochin, & Gross, 1991a; Miller, Li, & Desimone, 1991b,
1993). Monkeys were presented with series of stimuli and trained to respond
when a stimulus matched the first of the series. In the trial shown in Fig. 2.2, for
example, monkeys were rewarded for responding to the second apple stimu-

Visual Displays – Single Repeat

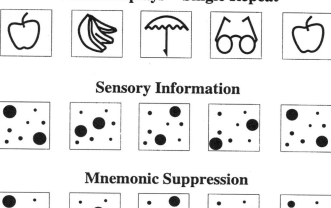

Sensory Information

Mnemonic Suppression

FIG. 2.2. Single repeat stimuli and inferotemporal (IT) neuron response. Monkeys were trained to respond to the stimulus matching the first in the series. Each dot in the schematic representation of neural activity represents a single neuron; the size of the dot indicates the neuron's activity level. IT neurons provided sensory and mnemonic information, with mnemonic neurons showing suppressed activity to matching stimuli (adapted from Desimone et al., 1994).

lus. Miller, Desimone, and colleagues recorded neurons in the inferotemporal cortex (IT) while monkeys performed this task. They found that approximately half of these neurons provided sensory information, responding with different patterns of activity to different stimuli, and showing constant activity levels to a stimulus whether it was the first presentation or a repeat. Monkeys' success in this task seemed to depend on the mnemonic processing of the remaining IT neurons recorded. As indicated in Fig. 2.2, these neurons showed no sign of maintained activity for the target stimulus during the intervening stimuli.[2] However, the majority of the mnemonic neurons that responded to the stimulus on its first presentation showed suppressed activity to the match. Monkeys appeared to simply process the first stimulus and as a result, showed facilitated processing (i.e., suppressed activity) to the repeat. Suppression of neuronal responses to familiar *spatial* locations has also been demonstrated (Steinmetz, Connor, Constantinidis, & McLaughlin, 1994). Monkeys were presented with a stimulus in various spatial locations, and trained to respond when a given location was repeated. Neurons in posterior parietal

---

[2]While IT neurons have been shown to maintain activity across delays (Fuster & Jervey, 1981; Miyashita, 1988, 1989; Miyashita & Chang, 1988), such activity appears to be abolished with the first intervening stimulus.

cortex showed reduced firing to matched locations without maintenance of activity over intervening stimuli.

Monkeys' behavioral responses in a second experiment supported the facilitated processing interpretation of suppressed neuronal responses. Miller and Desimone (1994) slightly altered their stimuli so that monkeys could not solve the task on the basis of familiarity. Half of the trials now contained embedded repeats (see Fig. 2.3), and the monkeys were trained to respond to the match to the first stimulus in the trial.

In the trial shown in Fig. 2.3, for example, monkeys were rewarded for responding to the second apple stimulus, *not* to the second banana stimulus. Interestingly, when monkeys first received the embedded repeat trials after training on the single repeat trials, they often responded to the repeated banana stimulus. These responses support the idea that monkeys were not responding based on active maintenance of the apple stimulus but instead on facilitated processing that occurred for any repeat.

The monkeys did eventually learn to respond to the match-to-first stimulus only. When monkeys were able to solve this task, maintained activity was observed in neurons in the prefrontal cortex (PFC; see Fig. 2.3). Other investigators have also documented such maintained activity in the PFC (Fuster, 1989; Goldman-Rakic, 1987). As in the single repeat task, half of the

Visual Displays – Embedded Repeat

Maintained Activity in PFC

Mnemonic Enhancement in IT

FIG. 2.3. Embedded repeat stimuli and prefrontal cortical (PFC) neuron response. Monkeys were trained to respond to the stimulus matching the first in the series. The embedded repeat prevented monkeys from solving the task on the basis of familiarity. PFC neurons showed maintained activity to the first stimulus (adapted from Desimone et al., 1994).

recorded IT neurons showed sensory responses, and the majority of the other IT neurons showed suppressed activity to any match. However, a greater proportion of neurons showed enhanced activity to matches (relative to that in the single repeat task), and this enhancement was present for the match-to-first stimulus only. Desimone et al. (1994) hypothesized that these enhancement effects were based on input from PFC. For the current arguments, the most salient findings are the maintained activity in PFC and facilitated processing in IT.

The behavioral and single-cell data distinguish between maintained activity and facilitated processing, and also indicate that monkeys do not always solve tasks in "obvious" ways. In the single-repeat task (see Fig. 2.2), monkeys could have maintained "apple, apple, apple . . ." across the trial and responded when this representation was matched. Although this might appear to be the obvious approach, monkeys actually solved the task without maintaining active representations across intervening stimuli. Similarly, in violation-of-expectation measures of object permanence, infants *could* maintain a representation of an occluded object across a trial, and respond when this representation is violated. Although this might seem to be the obvious interpretation of infants' longer looking times to impossible events, infants, like monkeys, might actually solve these tasks through facilitated processing rather than active maintenance. It is the kind of facilitated processing observed in IT that I propose underlies infants' longer looking times to impossible events. In Fig. 2.2, the first apple stimulus corresponds to infants' predictions about visible objects in the display (e.g., the prediction that the drawbridge will not complete its full trajectory). Infants process this prediction in the same way that monkeys process the apple stimulus. The intervening stimuli for the monkeys correspond to the drawbridge occlusion event. The infant is no longer receiving perceptual input about the occluded block, but the infant need not actively maintain a representation of this block during the occlusion period. The repeated apple corresponds to the possible event for infants, which is processed more readily than the impossible event due to the previously formed prediction.

In contrast, facilitated processing will not suffice for the retrieval of hidden objects; infants do not have the opportunity to respond to a match as in the violation-of-expectation experiments. Instead, it is more likely that infants must maintain a representation of the object during the occlusion period. It is the kind of maintained activity observed in PFC that I propose underlies infant's retrieval of occluded objects.

Evidence: Adult Normals and Patients

Studies on the function of PFC in adult normals and patients are consistent with the facilitation–maintenance distinction drawn earlier. The single-cell recording data in monkeys indicate that maintained activity may be subserved by the PFC. The PFC has also been implicated for active mainte-nance in humans. Numerous positron emission tomography (PET) studies have shown frontal activity for tasks requiring short-term memory for vari-ous types of stimuli (Becker, Mintun, Diehl, DeKosky, & Dobkin, 1993; Grasby, Frith, Friston, Bench, Frackowiak, & Dolan, 1993; Haxby, Horwitz, Ungerleider, Maisog, Allen, Kurkijan, Schapiro, Rapoport, & Grady, 1993; Paulesu, Frith, & Frackowiak, 1993; Petrides, Alivisatos, Evans, & Meyer, 1993; Sergent, Zuck, Levesque, & MacDonald, 1992). Studies using functional magnetic resonance imaging (fMRI) have also revealed prefrontal activa-tion during working memory tasks (Cohen, Forman, Braver, Casey, Servan-Schreiber, & Noll, 1994). In fact, the amount of prefrontal activation appears to increase monotonically with memory load (Braver, Cohen, Nystrom, Jonides, Smith, & Noll, 1997).

Neuropsychological studies of patients with PFC damage also implicate this region for human working memory (see Stuss, Eskes, & Foster, 1994 for review). Cohen and Servan-Schreiber (1992) reconciled a variety of findings on schizophrenia by positing a disturbance in prefrontal function. They used connectionist models to simulate the computational consequences of the biological abnormalities observed in schizophrenia. In particular, they demonstrated how a reduction in dopamine activity could affect PFC's abil-ity to maintain internal representations. This proposed disturbance in rep-resentations could account for schizophrenic performance in several cogni-tive tasks.

These data from adult normals and patients, like that from the monkeys, implicate the PFC for maintained activity. I suggest that infants require such maintained activity to reach for occluded objects. This type of processing may in turn depend on sufficient development of the PFC.

Although patients with frontal lobe damage show deficits in working memory, they are unimpaired in discriminating novel and familiar stimuli (see Petrides, 1989, for review). Such recognition memory might be based on facilitated processing that does not require the PFC. I suggest that in-fants may show longer looking times to impossible events based on such fa-cilitated processing. This type of processing may depend on brain regions that develop before the PFC or other relevant brain regions can support ac-tive maintenance.

Neural Network Framework

The preceding evidence suggests that qualitatively different kinds of neural processing may underlie facilitated processing and maintained activity. IT neurons can subserve facilitated processing by responding differently to a stimulus on repeat presentations, without maintaining activity for this tar-get over intervening stimuli. PFC neurons can maintain activity for a target over intervening stimuli.

The distinction between facilitated processing and maintained activity can also be made within the neural network framework. Neural networks are comprised of multiple interconnected processing units. Network activity is a function of the inputs to the units and the strength of the network's connections. In all simulations that learn, the network's experience with various inputs leads to changes in the connection weights. As a result, a given input may be processed differently on different occasions. In particular, when a network experiences a stimulus for the first time, changes will be made in the network's weights to alter the network's processing of the stimulus when it is repeated. A network could thus "recognize" a stimulus as a repeat without maintaining a pattern of activity for the stimulus between presentations. Similarly, if a network processes a prediction about a given stimulus, changes will be made to the network's weights so that the network may later recognize a match to that prediction. In this way, weight changes in the network can subserve facilitated processing.

Specific patterns of connectivity in networks can subserve maintained activity like that observed in the monkey and human PFC. Connectivity in standard feedforward networks allows activation to flow in only one direction (from input to output). In recurrent networks, units are bidirectionally connected so that activation can flow back and forth. Recurrent networks can maintain patterns of activity in the absence of input. For example, Munakata et al. (1997) trained a recurrent network to predict events with a ball and a barrier. In one event, the ball disappeared behind the barrier and then reappeared. The network quickly learned to represent the visible ball as a specific pattern of activity across the relevant processing units. In addition, the network gradually learned to maintain this pattern of activity to expect the occluded ball to reappear. That is, although the network received no input to support the representation of the ball during the occlusion period, the network's recurrent weights were adjusted so that the network maintained this representation to signal the ball's continued existence. The maintained activity observed in the brain may depend on such recurrent architectures. It is this type of maintained signal that I believe infants need to retrieve occluded objects.

Remaining Questions

The ability of the prediction theory to account for infant behavior in tasks of object permanence remains to be tested. In addition, there are many other questions that can be asked of this theory. Some of these questions and potential responses follow; more definitive responses should emerge with future experiments and simulations.

• Is it plausible to think that infants can form predictions before they can maintain representations of hidden objects? This question points to an important distinction between the monkey and patient data and the hypothesis about infant behavior. In particular, infants must do more than simply process visible stimuli; they must process predictions about visible stimuli. Although we must wait for the experimental results to evaluate whether infants can form such predictions in object permanence tasks, there is evidence that infants develop predictive abilities over the first 3 months of life that allow them to visually track objects (Aslin, 1981; Rosander & Hofsten, 1994 June) and to predict sequences (Haith, Hazan, & Goodman, 1988). In object permanence tasks, predictions might be based on habituation events, which would explain why these events are so critical to this paradigm.

• Why can't infants reach for hidden objects with the same mechanisms used for processing predictions? According to the prediction account, visible objects and predicted events cause changes in infants' processing systems so that infants can recognize matches to these objects or predictions. When a toy is presented and then an occluding screen is lowered, infants' processing systems should change as a result of the previously visible toy. Why can't infants reach based on these changes, without needing to maintain an active representation of the toy? One possibility is that these processing changes are less accessible than maintained representations. Maintained representations constitute signals that can be sent to other parts of the system. For example, maintained firing in visual object recognition neurons might activate a reaching response to a hidden object. In contrast, changes resulting from the processing of visible stimuli may be embedded within the perceptual processing systems. For example, changes in the response bias of visual object recognition neurons might allow them to respond with a different pattern of firing to repeated stimuli. However, such changes could only be realized with the subsequent processing of stimuli, and could not be accessed by the reaching system in the absence of such input. Processing changes embedded in the perceptual system thus could not guide the retrieval of occluded objects. However, processing changes *embedded within the reaching system* could affect reaching behavior.

The notion that processing changes are more embedded than maintained representations provides a coherent framework for understanding infant performance across violation-of-expectation and search paradigms, including the A-not-B task. Infants first show longer looking times to impossible events based on prediction-based processing changes in perceptual systems. Infants then begin to reach for hidden objects as they develop the ability to maintain active representations of occluded objects. As infants reach to one hiding location repeatedly, changes are made to the processing mechanisms embedded in the reaching system (see Thelen & Smith, 1994, for similar discussion of motor history). When the object is hidden in a new location, the processing changes favoring a reach to the old location compete with the newly developing ability to actively maintain a representation of the object in its new location. Continued development in the ability to actively maintain representations eventually allows infants to solve the A-not-B task (see Munakata, 1998, for a neural network simulation of this theory of A-not-B behavior).

• Can the prediction theory account for infant behavior prior to 8 months in *all* object permanence studies? Certain visual habituation experiments may not lend themselves readily to a prediction account (e.g., Wynn, 1992). It is possible that in some of these instances infants are succeeding through postdiction, or that details of the habituation procedure actually support predictive behavior. Another possible challenge to the prediction account comes from studies suggesting that infants reach for toys in the dark before they reach for occluded toys in the light (Clifton, Muir, Ashmead, & Clarkson, 1993; Clifton, Perris, & Bullinger, 1991a; Clifton, Rochat, Litovsky, & Perris, 1991b; Hood & Willatts, 1986). These findings seem to indicate that infants who fail to retrieve occluded objects can nonetheless maintain active representations, because reaching in the dark would seem to require such maintenance. However, most studies of reaching in the dark used sounding or glowing objects, allowing infants to reach based on *cued* rather than maintained representations. The single study using nonsounding, nonglowing toys (Hood & Willatts, 1986) found no difference between 5 month-old infants' reaching in toy and no-toy trials. In addition, in toy trials, infants were as likely to make their first reaches to the correct location as to an incorrect location on their opposite side. On these measures then, infants did not show advanced performance relative to expected performance on reaching for occluded toys in the light. When all reaches over the 25 second trials were analyzed, infants did reach more to the correct location for a toy than to the incorrect location. However, given infants' lack of discrimination on the toy/no-toy and first-reach measures, it is unclear whether this overall reach difference was driven by maintained representations.

• If maintained activity is required for reaching for hidden objects, why do monkeys with frontal lesions succeed with single-hiding location tasks? Diamond and Goldman-Rakic (1989) demonstrated that frontal lesions impair performance on the A-not-B task. Of course, to show the A-not-B error, prefrontal monkeys must first succeed when an object is first hidden at A. Where is the maintained activity that governs these initial successes when PFC is lesioned? One possibility is that neural substrates other than PFC (e.g., IT) are responsible for active maintenance for single location hidings. Alternatively, nonlesioned areas of PFC may subserve this maintained activity. Finally, it is possible that any preserved processing in the lesioned area of PFC may be sufficient to maintain activity for a simple single location task. In any case, it is important to note that this question challenges one particular neural substrate of the prediction account, and not the theoretical distinction between maintained activity and facilitated processing.

Although the prediction theory is clearly speculative at this point, I present the theory here to demonstrate the kinds of questions and possible answers that emerge when one considers the *processes* underlying behavior. The distinction between maintained activity and facilitated processing would be meaningless within a principle-based approach to object permanence. I would even argue that it is not critical whether this particular theory turns out to be correct in all of its details. In fact, I have actively explored two alternative process-based approaches for understanding task dependency in object permanence: one based on graded representations with stronger representations needed for retrieval than for perceptual expectations, the other based on two distinct representational systems for perception and action (Munakata et al., 1997). Whichever (if any!) of these accounts turn out to be true, I believe we will advance our understanding of development substantially by exploring such process-based possibilities, rather than focusing on the existence of disembodied principles that fail to account for the full range of behavior. In the spirit of this volume, I close with some process-based considerations for language development and imitation.

LANGUAGE DEVELOPMENT AND IMITATION

The process-based framework poses interesting questions to theories of language development and imitation. For example, consider Kuhl's theory of speech production (chap. 6, this volume). Kuhl presents evidence for the development of phonetic attractors for speech perception and production. These attractors pull members of a category toward the best instances. To explain these findings, Kuhl suggests that infants store representations of speech based on the ambient language, and then use these representations as targets for their own speech production. Kuhl and Meltzoff (1994) demonstrated that infants as young as 12-weeks can use targets to alter their vowel productions. Infants were recorded as they heard one of three vowel sounds for 15 minutes over 3 days. For each vowel sound, infants who were exposed to the sound produced more utterances like the vowel than did infants exposed to either of the other vowel sounds.

How do infants represent these targets from laboratory exposure and ambient language? As patterns of activation? If so, do infants actively maintain these target patterns, produce sounds that result in additional patterns, and then compare these maintained patterns? If 12-week-old infants can maintain such representations to learn language, why can't they maintain representations to allow them to reach for hidden objects for at least 20 more weeks? Is speech special? Or can infants only maintain representations for a limited time, which is sufficient for learning speech but not for retrieving hidden objects? Or do infants receive more relevant exposure to language than to objects? Another possibility is that infants cannot actively maintain target representations until around 8 months, when they will reach for occluded objects; their stored representations of speech may be based on facilitated processing.

According to this facilitated processing account, changes are made to infants' perceptual processing systems based on the phonetic distinctions they experience. Such changes result in facilitated processing of familiar sounds, and may underlie the attractor effects documented by Kuhl (1991). Infants can use these changes in their perceptual systems for "goodness" signals for shaping their own speech production. In babbling, infants may begin by producing speech sounds randomly, without particular targets in mind. Infants perceive the sounds that are similar to sounds in the ambient language as good, because these undergo facilitated processing. This positive feedback from the perceptual system reinforces the production of sounds resembling those in the ambient language, resulting in identical phonetic attractors for speech perception and production. That is, rather than trying to match particular target sounds that are actively maintained, infants may simply repeat sounds that result in facilitated processing. Their development of phonetic attractors in production may be based on the perceptual feedback they receive about the processing of their own productions. In the case of infants imitating vowel sounds (Kuhl & Meltzoff, 1994), infants may have formed a new perceptual attractor for the single speech sound that was presented repeatedly. When they then vocalized, the infants exposed to a given vowel may have been more likely to reinforce the production of this sound than infants exposed to a different vowel. Thus, according to this facilitated processing account, infants learn to produce speech based on the way their speech productions are processed by their perceptual systems. Good speech sounds are recognized through ease of processing, rather than through a match to specific targets that are actively maintained. In the same way, the monkeys in Miller and Desimone's (1994) experiments recognized target stimuli by the way the visual system responded to them, rather than by actively maintaining representations of these targets. Similarly, infants might recognize impossible events because they are difficult to process due to previously formed predictions, without actively maintaining a representation of objects occluded in the events.

How would infants begin to shift from facilitated processing to maintained representations? The ability to cue representations may be a precursor to the ability to maintain representations. As previously mentioned, Clifton et al. (1991b) demonstrated that 6.5 month infants could use sounds to cue representations of objects in the dark. Meltzoff and Moore (chap. 10, this volume) demonstrated that younger infants seem to be able to use cued representations for deferred imitation. In one experiment (Meltzoff &

Moore, 1994), 6-week-old infants watched a person modeling a particular facial behavior. Infants then imitated the behavior the next day when presented with the person making a neutral face. The infants seemed to be able to form a representation of the person carrying out the behavior and could later use the person's neutral face as a cue to activate this representation, which led them to imitate. These early representational abilities raise the question of why infants cannot cue representations of hidden objects to retrieve them (see Meltzoff, 1990 for some discussion of the relation between imitation and hidden object tasks). Why doesn't the visible lump in the cloth cue infants to the hidden toy? Do infants need a relatively direct match between cues to representations (neutral face to tongue-protruding face, or sound of toy to shape of toy) which is missing in the case of lump-in-cloth to toy? Would infants younger than 8 months reach for objects completely occluded in the light, given more direct cues? The process-based framework encourages exploration of these kinds of questions and links between findings from different areas. In this framework, there are no principles of object permanence that are separable from principles of imitation; instead, it is likely there are common processes underlying infant behavior in both types of tasks, and the goal is to understand these processes.

CONCLUSIONS

In this chapter, I have posed many questions regarding the processes underlying infant development in the first year of life. In posing these questions together with potential answers, I hope to have provided a sense of the promise of the process-based approach for advancing our understanding of development. *Principles* do not provide a satisfying account of infant behavior, which is highly task dependent; we must understand the processes—mental, neural, computational, environmental—governing infants' responses in different tasks. Whether any of the process-based theories put forth here will hold true remains to be seen. But a shift from principle-based to process-based accounts focuses our attention on the nature of the representations underlying infants' understanding, and the mechanisms responsible for change, which should in turn bring us closer to understanding cognitive development.

ACKNOWLEDGMENTS

Preparation of this chapter was supported by McDonnell-Pew grant 93-29. I thank Jay McClelland, Randy O'Reilly, and Liz Spelke for many useful comments and discussions.

REFERENCES

Ahmed, A., & Ruffman, T. (1998). Why do infants make A not B errors in a search task, yet show memory for the location of hidden objects in a non-search task? *Developmental Psychology, 34*, 441–453.

Aslin, R. (1981). Development of smooth pursuit in human infants. In D. Fisher, R. Monty, & E. Senders (Eds.), *Eye movements: Cognition and visual perception* (pp. 31–51). Hillsdale, NJ: Lawrence Erlbaum Associates.

Bachevalier, J., & Mishkin, M. (1984). An early and a late developing system for learning and retention in infant monkeys. *Behavioral Neuroscience, 98*(5), 770–778.

Baillargeon, R. (1987). Object permanence in 3.5- and 4.5-month-old infants. *Developmental Psychology, 23*, 655–664.

Baillargeon, R. (1993). The object concept revisited: New directions in the investigation of infants' physical knowledge. In C. Granrud (Ed.), *Visual perception and cognition in infancy: Carnegie Mellon symposia on cognition* (pp.). Hillsdale, NJ: Lawrence Erlbaum Associates.

Baillargeon, R., DeVos, J., & Graber, M. (1989). Location memory in 8-month-old infants in a non-search AB task: Further evidence. *Cognitive Development, 4*, 345–367.

Baillargeon, R., & Graber, M. (1988). Evidence of location memory in 8-month-old infants in a non-search AB task. *Developmental Psychology, 24*, 502–511.

Baillargeon, R., Graber, M., DeVos, J., & Black, J. (1990). Why do young infants fail to search for hidden objects? *Cognition, 36*, 255–284.

Baillargeon, R., Spelke, E., & Wasserman, S. (1985). Object permanence in five-month-old infants. *Cognition, 20*, 191–208.

Becker, J., Mintun, M., Diehl, D., DeKosky, S., & Dobkin, J. (1993). Functional neuroanatomy of verbal memory as revealed by word list recall during PET scanning. *Society for Neuroscience Abstracts* (Vol. 19, p. 1079). Washington, DC: Society for Neuroscience.

Braine, M. D. S. (1959). The ontogeny of certain logical operations: Piaget's formulation examined by nonverbal methods. *Psychological Monographs, 73*(Whole No. 475).

Braver, T. S., Cohen, J. D., Nystrom, L. E., Jonides, J., Smith, E. E., & Noll, D. C. (1997). A parametric study of frontal cortex involvement in human working memory. *NeuroImage, 5*, 49–62.

Bremner, J. G., & Knowles, L. S. (1984). Piagetian stage IV errors with an object that is directly accessible both visually and manually. *Perception, 13*, 307–314.

Brown, A. L. (1976). Semantic integration in children's reconstruction of narrative sequences. *Cognitive Psychology, 8*, 247–262.

Butterworth, G. (1974). *The development of the object concept in human infants.* Unpublished doctoral dissertation, University of Oxford.

Butterworth, G. (1977). Object disappearance and error in Piaget's stage IV task. *Journal of Experimental Child Psychology, 23*, 391–401.

Carey, S., & Gelman, R. (Eds.). (1991). *The epigenesis of mind.* Hillsdale, NJ: Lawrence Erlbaum Associates.

Clifton, R. K., Muir, D. W., Ashmead, D. H., & Clarkson, M. G. (1993). Is visually guided reaching in early infancy a myth? *Child Development, 64*, 1099–1110.

Clifton, R. K., Perris, E., & Bullinger, A. (1991). Infants' perception of auditory space. *Developmental Psychology, 27*(2), 187–197.

Clifton, R. K., Rochat, P., Litovsky, R. Y., & Perris, E. E. (1991). Object representation guides infants' reaching in the dark. *Journal of Experimental Psychology: Human Perception and Performance, 17*, 319–323.

Cohen, J. D., Forman, S. D., Braver, T. S., Casey, B., Servan-Schreiber, D., & Noll, D. C. (1994). Activation of the prefrontal cortex in a nonspatial working memory task with functional MRI. *Human Brain Mapping, 1*, 293–304.

Cohen, J. D., & Servan-Schreiber, D. (1992). Context, cortex, and dopamine: A connectionist approach to behavior and biology in schizophrenia. *Psychological Review, 99*(1), 45–77.

Desimone, R., Miller, E. K., Chelazzi, L., & Lueschow, A. (1994). Multiple memory systems in the visual cortex. In M. S. Gazzaniga (Ed.), *The cognitive neurosciences* (pp. 475–486). Cambridge, MA: MIT Press.

Diamond, A. (1985). Development of the ability to use recall to guide action, as indicated by infants' performance on $A\overline{B}$. *Child Development, 56,* 868–883.

Diamond, A. (1991). Neuropsychological insights into the meaning of object concept development. In S. Carey & R. Gelman (Eds.), *The epigenesis of mind* (pp. 67–110). Hillsdale, NJ: Lawrence Erlbaum Associates.

Diamond, A., & Goldman-Rakic, P. S. (1989). Comparison of human infants and rhesus monkeys on Piaget's $A\overline{B}$ task: Evidence for dependence on dorsolateral prefrontal cortex. *Experimental Brain Research, 74,* 24–40.

Fischer, K. W., & Bidell, T. (1991). Constraining nativist inferences about cognitive capacities. In S. Carey & G. Gelman (Eds.), *The epigenesis of mind* (pp. 199–236). Hillsdale, NJ: Lawrence Erlbaum Associates.

Flavell, J. H. (1971). Stage-related properties of cognitive development. *Cognitive Psychology, 2,* 421–453.

Flavell, J. H. (1984). Discussion. In R. J. Sternberg (Ed.), *Mechanisms of cognitive development.* New York: Freeman.

Flavell, J. H. (1985). *Cognitive development.* Englewood Cliffs, NJ: Prentice-Hall.

Fuster, J. (1989). *The prefrontal cortex* (2nd ed.). New York: Raven Press.

Fuster, J., & Jervey, J. (1981). Inferotemporal neurons distinguish and retain behaviorally relevant features of visual stimuli. *Science, 212,* 952–955.

Goldman-Rakic, P. S. (1987). Circuitry of primate prefrontal cortex and regulation of behavior by representational memory. F. Plum, & V. Mountcastle (Eds.), *Handbook of physiology: The nervous system V* (pp. 373–417). Bethesda, MD: American Physiological Society.

Granrud, C. (Ed.). (1993). *Visual perception and cognition in infancy: Carnegie Mellon symposia on cognition.* Hillsdale, NJ: Lawrence Erlbaum Associates.

Grasby, P., Frith, C., Friston, K., Bench, C., Frackowiak, R., & Dolan, R. (1993). Functional mapping of brain areas implicated in auditory-verbal memory function. *Brain, 116,* 1–20.

Greenough, W. T., Black, J. E., & Wallace, C. S. (1987). Experience and brain development. *Child Development, 58,* 539–559.

Haith, M. M., Hazan, C., & Goodman, G. (1988). Expectation and anticipation of dynamic visual events by 3.5-month-old babies. *Child Development, 59,* 467–479.

Harris, P. L. (1974). Perseverative search at a visibly empty place by young infants. *Journal of Experimental Child Psychology, 18,* 535–542.

Haxby, J. V., Horwitz, B., Ungerleider, L. G., Maisog, J., Allen, D. G., Kurkijan, M., Schapiro, M. B., Rapoport, S. I., & Grady, C. L. (1993). Lateralization of frontal lobe activity associated with working memory for faces changes with retention interval: A parametric PET-rCBF study. *Society for Neuroscience Abstracts* (Vol. 19, p. 1284). Washington, DC: Society for Neuroscience.

Hood, B., & Willatts, P. (1986). Reaching in the dark to an object's remembered position: Evidence for object permanence in 5-month-old infants. *British Journal of Developmental Psychology, 4,* 57–65.

Karmiloff-Smith, A. (1991). Beyond modularity: Innate constraints and developmental change. In S. Carey & R. Gelman (Eds.), *The epigenesis of mind* (pp. 171–197). Hillsdale, NJ: Lawrence Erlbaum Associates.

Karmiloff-Smith, A. (1992). *Beyond modularity: A developmental perspective on cognitive science.* Cambridge, MA: MIT Press.

Kuhl, P. K. (1991). Human adults and human infants show a "perceptual magnet effect" for the prototypes of speech categories, monkeys do not. *Perception & Psychophysics, 50,* 93–107.

Kuhl, P. K., & Meltzoff, A. N. (1994). Infant vocalizations in response to speech: Vocal imitation and developmental change. *Journal of Acoustical Society of America, 100*, 2425–2438.

Leslie, A. (1988). The necessity of illusion: Perception and thought in infancy. In L. Weiskrantz (Ed.), *Thought without language* (pp. 185–210). Oxford, England: Clarendon Press.

McClelland, J. L. (1989). Parallel distributed processing: Implications for cognition and development. In R.G. M. Morris (Ed.), *Parallel distributed processing: Implications for psychology and neurobiology* (pp. 8–45). Oxford, England: Oxford University Press.

McClelland, J. L. (1992). *The interaction of nature and nurture in development: A parallel distributed processing perspective* (Parallel Distributed Processing and Cognitive Neuroscience PDP. CNS. 92. 6). Carnegie Mellon University, Department of Psychology.

Meltzoff, A. N. (1990). Towards a developmental cognitive science: The implications of cross-modal matching and imitation for the development of representation and memory in infancy. In A. Diamond (Ed.), *The development and neural bases of higher cognitive functions* (pp. 1–37). New York: New York Academy of Sciences Press.

Meltzoff, A. N., & Moore, M. (1994). Imitation, memory, and the representation of persons. *Infant Behavior and Development, 17*, 83–99.

Miller, E. K., & Desimone, R. (1994). Parallel neuronal mechanisms for short-term memory. *Science, 263*, 520–522.

Miller, E. K., Gochin, P. M., & Gross, C. G. (1991a). Habituation-like decrease in the responses of neurons in inferior temporal cortex of the macaque. *Visual Neuroscience, 7*, 357–362.

Miller, E. K., Li, L., & Desimone, R. (1991b). A neural mechanism for working and recognition memory in inferior temporal cortex. *Science, 254*, 1377–1379.

Miller, E. K., Li, L., & Desimone, R. (1993). Activity of neurons in anterior inferior temporal cortex during a short-term memory task. *The Journal of Neuroscience, 13*, 1460–1478.

Miyashita, Y. (1988). Neuronal correlate of visual associative long-term memory in the primate temporal cortex. *Nature, 335*(6193), 817–820.

Miyashita, Y. (1989). How is the visual associative memory represented in neurons of the primate temporal cortex? In M. Ito (Ed.), *Neural programming*, Tanigushi Symposia on Brain Sciences No. 12 (pp. 149–161). Tokyo: Japan Scientific Societies Press.

Miyashita, Y., & Chang, H.-S. (1988). Neuronal correlate of pictorial short-term memory in the primate temporal cortex. *Nature, 331*(6151), 68–70.

Morton, J., & Johnson, M. H. (1991). CONSPEC and CONLERN: A two-process theory of infant face recognition. *Psychological Review, 98*, 164–181.

Munakata, Y. (1998). Infant perseveration and implications for object permanence theories: A PDP model of the $A\overline{B}$ task. *Developmental Science, 1*, 161–184.

Munakata, Y., McClelland, J. L., Johnson, M. H., & Siegler, R. (1997). Rethinking infant knowledge: Toward an adaptive process account of successes and failures in object permanence tasks. *Psychological Review, 104*(4), 686–713.

Paulesu, E., Frith, C., & Frackowiak, R. (1993). The neural correlates of the verbal component of working memory. *Nature, 362*, 342–345.

Petrides, M. (1989). Frontal lobes and memory. In F. Boller, & J. Grafman (Eds.), *Handbook of neuropsychology* (Vol. 2 , pp. 75–90). New York: Elsevier.

Petrides, M., Alivisatos, B., Evans, A., & Meyer, E. (1993). Dissociation of human mid-dorsolateral from posterior dorsolateral frontal cortex in memory processing. *Proceedings of the National Academy of Sciences USA, 90*, 873–877.

Piaget, J. (1954). *The construction of reality in the child.* New York: Basic Books.

Rosander, K., & Hofsten, C. v. (1994, June). *Developing an ability to stabilize gaze during body motion and/or motion of the visual field.* Presented at the Ninth Biennial International Conference for Infant Studies, Paris, France.

Sergent, J., Zuck, E., Levesque, M., & MacDonald, B. (1992). Positron emission tomography study of letter and object processing: Empirical findings and methodological considerations. *Cerebral Cortex, 80*, 68–80.

Siegler, R. (1989). Mechanisms of cognitive development. *Annual Review of Psychology, 40*, 353–379.

Siegler, R. (1993). Cheers and lamentations. In C. Granrud (Ed.), *Visual perception and cognition in infancy: Carnegie Mellon Symposia on cognition* (pp.). Hillsdale, NJ: Lawrence Erlbaum Associates.

Siegler, R., & Munakata, Y. (1993). Beyond the immaculate transition: Advances in the understanding of change. *SRCD Newsletter, Winter Issue.*

Smith, L. B., & Thelen, E. (Eds.). (1993). *A dynamic systems approach to development: Applications.* Cambridge, MA: MIT Press.

Sophian, C., & Yengo, L. (1985). Infants' search for visible objects: Implications for the interpretation of early search errors. *Journal of Experimental Child Psychology, 40*, 260–278.

Spelke, E. (1991). Physical knowledge in infancy: Reflections on Piaget's theory. In S. Carey & R. Gelman (Eds.), *The epigenesis of mind* (pp. 133–170). Hillsdale, NJ: Lawrence Erlbaum Associates.

Spelke, E., Breinlinger, K., Macomber, J., & Jacobson, K. (1992). Origins of knowledge. *Psychological Review, 99*, 605–632.

Steinmetz, M., Connor, C., Constantinidis, C., & McLaughlin, J. (1994). Covert attention suppresses neuronal responses in area 7a of the posterior parietal cortex. *Journal of Neurophysiology, 72*(2), 1020–1023.

Stuss, D., Eskes, G., & Foster, J. (1994). Experimental neuropsychological studies of frontal lobe functions. In F. Boller, & J. Grafman (Eds.), *Handbook of neuropsychology* (Vol. 9, pp. 149–185). Amsterdam: Elsevier.

Thelen, E., & Smith, L. B. (1994). *A dynamic systems approach to the development of cognition and action.* Cambridge, MA: MIT Press.

Wellman, H. M., Cross, D., & Bartsch, K. (1986). Infant search and object permanence: A meta-analysis of the A-Not-B error. *Monographs of the Society for Research in Child Development, 51*(3, Serial No. 214).

Willatts, P. (1990). Development of problem-solving strategies in infancy. In D. F. Bjorklund (Ed.), *Children's strategies: Contemporary views of cognitive development* (pp. 23–66). Hillsdale, NJ: Lawrence Erlbaum Associates.

Wynn, K. (1992). Addition and subtraction by human infants. *Nature, 358*, 749–750.

3

Infants' Initial "Knowledge" of the World: A Cognitive Neuroscience Perspective

Mark H. Johnson
Birkbeck College
University of London

Spelke (1994) observed that the initial knowledge of the infant tends to capture the most fundamental properties of the world (see also chap. 1, this volume). In her view, this is the case for either of two reasons. The first reason is that certain "principles" relating to the structure of the world are prespecified in the mind at birth or are triggered by maturation shortly thereafter. These principles serve to enable the infant to interpret information arriving through sensory channels, and are the result of evolutionary selection. The second reason is that the most fundamental properties of the world are simply those easiest to learn. By this view, powerful learning mechanisms in the infant's mind extract invariances from the information impinging on their sensory systems. The most fundamental properties of the world are argued to be also the lowest order invariances, and therefore those extracted most rapidly by these learning mechanisms. In contrast to the acquisition of prespecified principles by the species through evolution, by this latter view each infant acquires information about the basic structure of the world anew. Behavioral studies of young infants' cognitive abilities have been interpreted as consistent with both these views. (see Spelke and Munakata, chap. 1, this volume). In this chapter I turn to evidence from the development of the brain, and particularly the cerebral cortex, to argue for a perspective that incorporates aspects of both viewpoints outlined by Spelke.

Brain development, like all other forms of development, may be viewed in terms of the increasing restriction of fate of component elements (such as neurons, and neural circuits). In other words, as development proceeds, neurons and circuitry become increasingly specialized and dedicated to particular functions and less capable of change. A point of interest is that many brain circuits have not restricted their fate entirely by the time of birth (i.e., they retain some degree of "plasticity"). Furthermore, even within the same region of the brain some aspects of structure can be relatively fixed (and therefore relatively impervious to interactions with the world outside the organism), while other aspects of the same neural circuitry remain comparatively unspecified (and consequently open to influence by interaction with the external world). In this chapter I examine some consequences of the fact that not all parts of the vertebrate brain are on the same time course of fate restriction, and explore some consequences of this observation for theories of cognitive and behavioral change in young animals, including the human infant.

To anticipate the argument put forward in this chapter, I show that although there is evidence for prespecified representations in subcortical circuits, much recent neurobiological and neuropsychological data support the conclusion that there are few, if any prespecified representations that relate to higher cognition intrinsic to the cerebral cortex. In other words, regions of cortex do not appear to contain prespecified representations to support functions such as face recognition and language processing. Rather, the appropriate representations emerge through the infant's interaction with its environment. In this sense, the infant is a participant in guiding its own postnatal brain development. I argue that the types of representations that emerge within regions of cortex are highly constrained by the action of subcortical circuits in structuring the organism's interaction with the external world, the statistical regularities latent in the external world, and the complex internal cytoarchitectonics of neural networks in the neocortex and other brain regions. To illustrate these sources of constraint, I review evidence from two domains of infancy research: face recognition and the planning of eye movements. First, I provide an overview of some neurobiological and neuropsychological evidence concerning the development and plasticity of the mammalian cerebral cortex.

THE DEVELOPMENT, STRUCTURE, AND PLASTICITY OF THE CEREBRAL CORTEX: A BRIEF OVERVIEW

The cerebral cortex, along with the hippocampus, are generally considered to be the slowest parts of the mammalian brain to develop, with changes occurring in the prefrontal portion of cortex in man as late as the teenage years. The cerebral cortex is also the part of the brain commonly associated with higher cognitive functions in many species, and damage to this part of the brain in adults can result in a range of specific cognitive deficits. For the remainder of this chapter I focus on the development of the cortex and its relation to certain subcortical structures.

The cerebral cortex may be thought of as an extensive sheet possessing two dimensions of structure: "areal" and "layered." The layered structure is tangential to the surface of the cortex and is relatively constant in structure (cell numbers, etc.) across both regions of cortex and different mammalian species. The areal structure (division into "areas") can vary in both extent (total area of the sheet) and divisions into regions between species, and even between different individuals of the same species. For example, although the layered structure of most of human cortex is roughly similar to that of cats (about the same number and types of cells), we have a much greater extent (total surface area) of cortex. Thus, as Killackey (1990) and others have argued, having hit on a good computational machine, evolution has merely generated more *quantity* of the same. This leads us to the surprising conclusion that there is unlikely to be particular neural circuitry unique to our own species. Instead, we have to look for the difference between humans and other species in terms of the activity-dependent development of cortex, and to the greater areal surface of cortical tissue available.

The layered structure of the cortex consists of, roughly speaking, six layers (see Fig. 3.1). Each layer possesses characteristic combinations of cell types (although the upper layer contains no cells, only fibers) and characteristic connectivity patterns. In human infants virtually all cortical cells are already in place at birth, and most postnatal development concerns the extent of their dendritic fields, myelinisation, and synaptic density. Although most of the cells are in place at birth, the lack of development of dendritic fields and synaptic contacts undoubtedly makes the cortex, at best, only partially functional. For example, in the visual cortex the main inputs from the retina (via the lateral geniculate) may not reach their normal termination sites in layers 2 and 3 until several months after birth (e.g., Conel, 1939/1967). Another postnatal structural change in the cerebral cortex is synaptic density, the number of contacts between neurons. Synaptic density in the primate cortex goes through a characteristic rise and fall, with density increasing to levels approximately double that observed in the adult for most cortical regions. The peak is probably reached at different postnatal ages for different regions of cortex, but a process of synaptic loss leads to density returning to adult levels sometime between the end of the first year of life (for visual cortex in humans) to the end of the first decade (for frontal cortex; see Huttenlocher, 1990, 1994). This phase of synaptic loss has been associated with the refining of cortical representations (Changeux, 1985; Edelman, 1987).

Divisions in the areal structure of cortex commonly reflect boundaries between regions with different representations. By representations here I

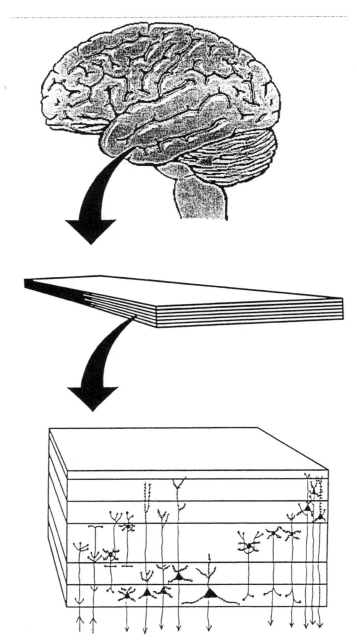

FIG. 3.1. Schematic figure illustrating that the neocortex is a layered flat sheet. Each layer contains particular cell types and has characteristic connectivity.

simply refer to the fact that clusters and groups of cells share common response properties, such as only responding to moving visual stimuli, or to particular combinations of sensory input and motor output. These specialized response properties reflect the detailed patterns of input and interconnectivity between cells (Elman, Bates, Johnson, Karmiloff-Smith, Parisi, & Plunkett, 1996). Commonly, the arrangement of cells and their response properties is topographic, with neighboring cells maximally responding to closely related inputs (such as line orientation selectivity, or the frequency and intensity of sound input). A number of lines of evidence indicate that representations are not prespecified within particular areas of cortex, and that at least some of the areal divisions observed in the adult cortex emerge as a result of postnatal experience (Elman et al., 1996; Johnson, 1997). In other words, there is currently no strong evidence for a genetic "protomap" that ensures particular circuits support particular types of representations, such as those involved in face recognition or language.

Some of the evidence consistent with this view includes the following:

- Transplants in which one area of neocortex is displaced to a different spatial location in foetal rodents results in the displaced region of cortex taking on the functions associated with its new location, rather than that of its site of origin.[1]
- Manipulating the extent of thalamic input to a region of cortex early in life (in primates) changes the size of the area corresponding to that input. For example, Rakic (1983) reduced the projection from the lateral geniculate nucleus to the primary visual cortex and observed that the extent of this area reduced correspondingly due to a change in the border with V2. This experiment demonstrates that even in the primary visual cortex any prespecification is modifiable.
- Functional neuroimaging studies show evidence for cortical specialization for such stimuli as pronounceable English words. Such specializations are obviously not prespecified, and result as a consequence of experience with a particular language.
- Projections from the thalamus to the cortex do not appear to be selectively attracted to particular cortical areas, but rather to cortical tissue as a whole (Molnar & Blakemore, 1991).

---

[1]It should be noted that this type of evidence for cortical plasticity involves experiments conducted mainly with rodents. Thus, it remains possible that primate cortex is more prespecified around the time of birth. This appears to be true of at least one area of primate cortex, the primary visual cortex, a distinctive area of cortex that shows differences from other cortical regions as early as the prenatal stage of cell generation. Another possibility is the entorhinal cortex (the cortical "gateway" to the hippocampus) which shows some areal differentiation by the 10th prenatal week in the human infant (Kostovic, Petanjek, & Judas, 1993). However, there is as yet little or no evidence for such prespecification in other cortical areas in the human.

This, and other evidence, raises what I have referred to as the *"paradox of plasticity"* (Johnson, Oliver, & Shrager, 1998): Although cortical representations do not appear to be intrinsically prespecified, in most normal adults similar types of representations emerge in roughly similar areas of cortex. The issue may be dissociated into the *type* of representations developed on the one hand, and the *location* within the cortex on the other. I only deal here with type of representations developed, because this issue is of more interest to psychologists. The issue of the constraints that operate on the cortical location of a particular type of representation are, as yet, poorly understood, but some of the factors involved have been discussed elsewhere (Elman et al., 1996, Johnson, 1997, 2000).

The paradox of plasticity can be resolved by considering three sources of constraints on the types of representations that emerge within cortex: the role of subcortical circuitry in structuring the organisms interaction with the external world; the statistical regularities present in the structure of the external world; and the complex general cytoarchitectonics of the cortex. In the rest of this chapter I discuss two examples from infancy research in which these three sources of constraint on cortical plasticity can be illustrated: the development of face recognition and the development of visual orienting. The development of face recognition provides an example from perception, whereas visual orienting provides an example from a relatively simple form of action planning.

Example 1: Face and Species Recognition

The first example comes from my work with a vertebrate species other than our own, the domestic chick. I do argue later, however, that the findings from the chick may be extrapolated to the human infant. Chicks make exceptionally good subjects for studies of behavioral development for a variety of reasons, but they are of particular interest here because the part of their forebrain that corresponds to the mammalian cortex is much simpler in structure. These studies with chicks are concerned with neural basis of filial imprinting. Filial imprinting is the process by which newly hatched chicks (and the young of other species) develop a strong attachment to a particular individual member of their own species, normally their mother. Being able to recognize mother on the basis of her visual features is, of course, a necessity for the young of many species including our own. A number of studies with the chick have provided evidence that at least two independent brain systems contribute to the establishment of filial preferences in this species. Most of these studies are conducted using standard laboratory techniques in which day-old chicks are exposed to (trained on) one of a variety of naturalistic object (such as a stuffed hen) or inanimate objects (such as a rotating illuminated red box). Studies on the neural basis of imprinting have employed autoradiographic, biochemical, lesion, and electrophysiological techniques to establish that a particular localized region of the chick forebrain, known as the Intermediate and Medial part of the Hyperstriatum Ventrale (IMHV) is crucially involved in visual imprinting (for reviews, see Horn, 1985, Horn & Johnson, 1989). For example, lesions to IMHV placed before or after training on an object severely impairs preference for that object in subsequent choice tests, but does not affect several other types of visual and learning tasks (Johnson & Horn, 1986, 1987; McCabe, Cipolla-Neto, Horn, & Bateson, 1982). Similar size lesions placed elsewhere in the chick forebrain do not result in significant impairments of imprinting preference (Johnson & Horn, 1987; McCabe et al., 1982).

Although the avian forebrain lacks the layered structure of mammalian cortex (but see Karten & Shimizu, 1989), the relation of the forebrain to subcortical structures is similar, following a basic higher vertebrate brain design (Ebbesson, 1980; Nauta & Karten, 1970). The evidence from a variety of vertebrate species supports the suggestion that this region of the brain is a site of plasticity, and not the location of inbuilt, automatic, systems for controlling behavior (Ewert, 1987; MacPhail, 1982).

Figure 3.2 illustrates the location of IMHV within the chick brain. It is worth noting that this region corresponds to, or overlaps with, regions critical for auditory imprinting and song learning (e.g., Maier & Schiech, 1983).

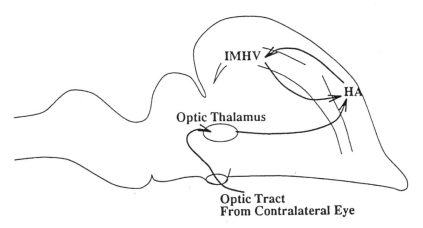

FIG. 3.2. Visual inputs to IMHV from the thalamic pathway. Shown is a saggital view (strictly diagrammatic, as some areas are out of the plane with others) of the chick brain, with visual information coming in through the optic tract, which then synapses in the optic nucleus of the thalamus. This then projects to area HA (hyperstriatum accessorium), which connects reciprocally with IMHV. This pathway may correspond to the retina to LGN to V1 pathway in mammals. There are other routes of visual input to IMHV, which are not shown in this figure (see Horn, 1985). The brain of a 2-day-old chick is approximately 2 cm long.

The area occupies about 5% of total forebrain volume. Its main inputs come from visual projection areas (Hyperstriatum accessorium and the optic tectum) and some of its projections go to regions thought to be involved in motor control (such as the archistriatum). Thus, the area is well placed to integrate visual inputs and motor outputs.

Although regions of the avian forebrain may have analogous functions to the mammalian cerebral cortex (Horn, 1985), cytoarchitectonic studies of IMHV have revealed that it is much simpler in structure. In contrast to the 6-layered structure with many cell types found in the mammalian cerebral cortex, there is no clear laminar structure of IMHV, and, to date, only four distinctive types of cells have been classified (Tombol, Csillag, & Stewart, 1988). Figure 3.3 illustrates the basic intrinsic microcircuit described by Tombol et al. (1988).

O'Reilly and Johnson (1994) built a neural network model based on two characteristics of the cytoarchitectonics of IMHV: the existence of positive feedback loops between the excitatory principle neurons (PNs), and the extensive inhibitory circuitry mediated by the local circuit neurons. They argued that these properties of the basic intrinsic microcircuit of the region lead to a hysteresis of the activation state of PNs in IMHV, a feature that contributes to the development of translation invariant object-based representations within the region. The detailed architecture of the O'Reilly and

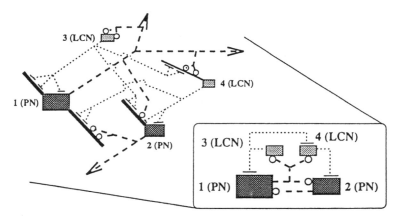

FIG. 3.3. Schematic drawing summarizing the circuitry of IMHV at two levels of detail (simplified version in the box). Excitatory contacts are represented by open circles, and inhibitory ones by flat bars. Shown are the local circuit inhibitory neurons (LCN) and their reciprocal connectivity with the excitatory principal neurons (PN), and the recurrent excitatory connectivity between the principal neurons. In the detailed version, the thick solid lines are dendrites, while the axons are dashed or dotted lines. Both the inhibition and recurrent excitatory connectivity are used in the simplified model to produce hysteresis in the activation state of the IMHV (adapted from Tömböl et al., 1988).

Johnson (1994) model is designed around the anatomical connectivity of IMHV and its primary input area, the Hyperstriatum Accessorium (HA), and is shown in Fig. 3.4.

Training in the model consisted of presenting a set of feature bits (assumed to correspond to a given object) in different random spatial locations in the input layer, and adjusting the weights between all units in the system according to an associative Hebbian learning rule once the activation state of the network had reached equilibrium for each position. The general properties of a learning rule that are important for this model (and most other self-organizing models) are that it have both a positive and a negative associative character, which work together to shape the receptive fields of units both toward those inputs that excite them, and away from those that don't. The degree of hysteresis (the influence of previous activation states on subsequent ones) was controlled by a decay parameter, which reset the activations to a fraction of their equilibrium values for the previous object position. The hysteresis caused units in the model that were active for a given position of a simulated object to remain active for subsequent positions. In combination with the Hebbian associative learning

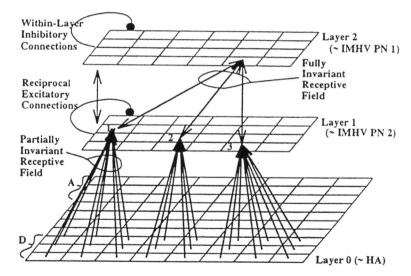

FIG. 3.4. Network architecture used for the simplified model of IMHV, showing the three layers (Layer 0 represents HA, Layer 1 represents IMHV PN Type 2, Layer 2 represents IMHV PN Type 1), and their interconnectivity. The network is shown being trained on stimulus D, and the 3 different units numbered 1–3 in Layer 1 have partially invariant fields that capture local invariance over portions of the different positions of stimulus D. These different units project reciprocally to the Layer 2 unit, which has a fully invariant representation of stimulus D by combining the partially invariant fields from Layer 1.

rule, this resulted in the emergence of units that would respond to a particular set of features in any of a certain range of different locations (or views of the object if it had been rotating), depending on how long that unit was able to remain active. Hysteresis in the activation states comes from the combined forces of lateral inhibition (which prevents other units from becoming active), and recurrent, excitatory activation loops, which cause whatever units are active to remain active through mutual excitation. These two forms of neural interaction are known to be present in IMHV, as was discussed earlier.

With this model a range of phenomena associated with imprinting in the chick have been successfully simulated, such as "self-terminating" sensitive periods, reversibility effects, and temporal blending effects (see O'Reilly & Johnson, 1994). For the purposes of this discussion, however, the important point is that the model illustrates two of the sources of constraints discussed earlier. First, the statistical structure of the information coming into the network (the input) has a major effect on the nature of the representation that emerges. This can be illustrated by a simulation (of a chick experiment by Chantrey, 1974) in which the network was either trained with two different training stimuli in rapid succession (equivalent to alternating the presentation of the stimuli every few seconds) or trained for the same time on the two stimuli but in blocks (equivalent to alternating the presentation of the training stimuli every several minutes). When the network is exposed to the rapidly alternating stimuli, units in the top layer learn to respond to both stimuli. In other words, the network develops a "blended" representation of the two objects. In contrast, the other training condition results in units in the top layer of the network responding to one or other of the training stimuli. In this case the network develops independent representations of the two stimuli. Thus, despite the features of the stimuli being identical in the two training conditions, in this case the temporal properties of the input influences type of representation that emerges.

The second source of constraint illustrated by the model (and by inference the chick forebrain) is that the a combination of a particular basic network architecture and learning rule constrains the type of representations that emerges such that a spatially invariant object representation develops, and not, for example, a location-dependent stimulus representation.

Although the structure of the network, in a combination with a particular learning rule, can constrain the type of representation that emerges, a third source of constraint mentioned earlier concerns the role of subcortical circuitry in structuring the organisms interaction with its environment. It is to this source of constraint that I now turn. The microcircuitry found in IMHV makes it an especially powerful mechanism for acquiring certain types of object representations. In the laboratory a wide range of objects such as red boxes and blue balls are as effective for imprinting as more naturalistic stimuli such as a moving stuffed hen. However, in the wild, precocial birds such as chicks invariably imprint on their mother, and not on other passing objects. In other words, representations of mother tend to emerge within IMHV. A clue as to why this happens came from a series of experiments in which striking stimulus-dependent effects of IMHV lesions were found (Horn & McCabe, 1984; Johnson, Bolhuis, & Horn, 1985). While groups of chicks trained on an artificial stimulus such as a red box were severely impaired by lesions to the IMHV placed either before or after training, groups of chicks trained on a stuffed hen were only mildly impaired. Other neuro-physiological manipulations also showed differences between the hen-trained and box-trained birds. For example, administration of a drug that depletes the level of certain neurochemicals (the noradrenergic neurotoxin DSP4) results in a severe impairment of preference in chicks trained on a simple artificial stimulus, a rotating red box, but only a mild impairment in birds trained on a stuffed hen (Davies, Horn, & McCabe, 1985). In contrast, levels of the hormone testosterone correlate with preference for a stuffed hen, but not preference for a red box (Bolhuis, McCabe, & Horn, 1986).

These results led us to seek experimental evidence for an earlier sugges-tion (Hinde, 1962) that naturalistic objects such as hens may be more effec-tive at eliciting attention in young chicks than are other objects. Johnson and Horn (1988) conducted a series of experiments in which dark-reared chicks, which had not been exposed to any training stimulus, were pre-sented with a choice between an intact stuffed hen and a variety of test stimuli created from cutting up and jumbling the pelt of a stuffed hen. Re-sults of these experiments led to the conclusion that chicks have a sponta-neous tendency to attend toward characteristics of the head and neck re-gion of the hen. Although this untrained preference seemed to be specific to the correct arrangement of features of the face or head, it was not spe-cific to the species. For example, the head of a duck was as attractive as that of a hen (Johnson & Horn, 1988).

The results of these and other experiments led to the proposal that there are two independent neural systems that underlie filial preference in the chick (Horn, 1985; Johnson et al., 1985). The first is a specific predisposi-tion for the young chick to orient toward objects resembling conspecifics. In contrast to nonspecific color and size preferences in the chick (see John-son & Bolhuis, 1991), the predisposition system appears to be specifically tuned to the correct spatial arrangement of elements of the head and neck region (Johnson & Horn, 1988). Although the stimulus configuration trigger-ing the predisposition is not species or genus specific, it is sufficient to pick out the mother hen from other objects the chick is likely to be exposed to in the first few days after hatching. The second system acquires information about the objects to which the young chick attends and is subserved by the brain region IMHV. In the natural environment, we argued, the first system ensures that the second system acquires information about the particular individual mother hen by orienting it toward such objects. Biochemical, electrophysiological, and lesion evidence all support the conclusion that the two systems have largely independent neural substrates (for review, see Horn, 1985). For example, selective lesions to IMHV impair preferences acquired through exposure to an object, but do not impair the predisposition (Johnson & Horn, 1986).

To conclude, we have seen that the representations that emerge as a result of the imprinting experience in the chick are constrained in a number of ways. First, the biasing of input through the action of the predisposition. Second, the nature of the statistical regularities present in the input to the network. Third, the basic architecture of the learning mechanism (in combination with the learning rule) biases the network to extract certain types of invariances from the input (in this case spatially invariant object representations). I now turn to our own species, and present some preliminary evidence that similar constraints operate on the emergence of representations for face processing in the human infant.

Johnson and Morton (1991; Morton & Johnson, 1991) have argued, by analogy with the chick studies, that there are two relatively independent processes involved in the recognition of mother in our species also. To briefly review the evidence for this contention, several studies have shown that newborn infants track faces further than they do a variety of scrambled face stimuli (Goren, Sarty, & Wu, 1975, Johnson, Dziurawiec, Ellis, & Morton, 1991). There are a number of reasons for believing that this preferential tracking of faces observed in newborns is subcortically mediated. One is the time course that the response shows: It declines between 4 and 6 weeks after birth, an age at which several newborn reflexes disappear. Another reason is that the newborn face preferences are only found in the temporal, and not the nasal, visual field (Johnson et al., 2000).

Johnson and Morton argued that later developing face preferences commonly studied by preferential looking methods reflect the developing cortical representations utilized in face processing. I hypothesize that these representations emerge constrained by the three sources discussed earlier. First, the newborn bias to orient to faces structures its interaction with the external world and ensures that a common input to developing cortical circuits are faces. Second, the presence of faces in the early environment of the infant (note that, in the absence of faces, the newborn bias would not be effective), and third, the complex internal cytoarchitectonics of the cortex. The latter source of constraint is still poorly understood with the cerebral cortex, but I hypothesize that the major constraints from this source recur throughout the cortex in the same way.

Example 2: The Development of Visual Attention and Saccade Planning

Saccadic eye movements in infants merit study for a number of reasons, including the fact that they are a relatively simple form of action (e.g., eye movements involve many less muscles and degrees of freedom than reaching), and they are present and easy to elicit from birth. In visual orienting, as in face recognition, there is evidence for the involvement of both cortical and subcortical circuits. A gross characterization of the distinction is that subcortical saccades tend to be rapid, automatic, and less accurate in character, whereas cortical saccades are slower, and directed by volitional and attentional factors. I argue that while subcortical saccades are present from birth, cortical saccades are controlled by representations that emerge during interactions with the external environment. These initial interactions with the external world are structured by subcortical control in the sense that subcortical saccades provide approximate saccades to a target, and possibly also a source of error signal for the training of cortical representations that later control saccades. I illustrate the point that cortical representations for action are generated through interaction with the environment by presenting evidence that over the first 6 months of life, and in association with the development of cerebral cortex, different types of representations become available for planning saccades.

The parietal cortex is a region of the primate cortex that has been implicated in aspects of saccade planning in monkey cellular recording studies, human functional neuroimaging studies, and neuropsychological studies of brain damaged patients. It is also a region of cortex that undergoes marked developmental changes between ages 3 and 6 months as demonstrated in both neuroanatomical studies of postmortem brains (e.g., Conel, 1939/1967), and resting PET (glucose uptake) studies (Chugani, Phelps, & Mazziotta, 1987). According to the cellular recording studies of Andersen and colleagues, many cells in the parietal cortex code for saccades within an eye or head-centered frame of reference. In other words, their receptive fields respond to combinations of eye or head position on the one hand, and retinal distance from the fovea to the target on the other. This is in contrast to subcortical structures involved in oculomotor control in which cells commonly respond according to the retinal distance and direction of the target from the fovea.

A question that remains is whether the postnatal anatomical changes observed in the parietal cortex are maturationally determined, or whether they reflect the increasing specialization of microcircuitry in response to experience. Zipser and Andersen (1988) and Andersen and Zipser (1988) presented a connectionist model in which the hidden layer units developed response properties that closely resembled those observed within regions of the primate parietal cortex. The model is a three-layered net with the input layer divided into two components, input from the "retina" (gaussian function) and input information about the position of the eye within the head (monotonic). The retinal input is gaussian to simulate the point where a target falls on the retina, while the eye position input is monotonic corresponding to the neurons found to code eye position in the parietal cortex. Training consists of presenting several hundred patterns of random eye position and retinal input to the network, and adjusting the weights between nodes in the layers according to the backpropagation algorithm (Rumelhart & McClelland, 1986). In some simulations the trained output is the eye-position independent, head-centered location of the target stimulus, or the "shift of the eyes" necessary to bring the stimulus into the center of the retina. Zipser and Andersen (1988) reported that after several hundred trials the network becomes very accurate at making the appropriate "saccades." After training, the response patterns of nodes in the hidden layer strikingly resembled those of cells found in regions of the parietal cortex, Area 7a and LIP. Further, "microstimulation" of these nodes produced types of saccades closely corresponding in type and frequency to cells in the same regions of cortex (Goodman & Andersen, 1989). This model is thus a demonstration that head or eye-centered representations for saccade planning could be acquired through an interaction between the structure of the network, on the one hand, and the information entering it on the other. It might be objected that the Andersen and Zipser network uses a learning algorithm, backpropagation, in which the network is "tutored" with the correct answer until its errors are reduced. This problem is especially acute because there are no obvious correlations between eye position and retinal location. In other words, there is a wide range of possible combinations of eye position and retinal location, and the network is trained on the complete set in random sequence. However, the types of representations that emerge in the hidden layer of backpropagation nets are often very similar to those that appear in a similar network that uses self-organizing (e.g., Hebbian) learning rules. Further, there may be structure in the relation between eye position and retinal location that is not present in the simplified model. Johnson and Gilmore (1996) suggested that such correlations may lie in the fact that during gaze shifts, the retinal vector and the eye position undergo transition at the same time. Thus, temporal coincidence could be used to relate information from the two sources. Interestingly, this arrangement would require that some ability to make saccades precedes the training of the parietal cortex network. I speculate that this is the role played by subcortical (automatic) saccades.

Whereas Andersen and colleagues have focused on the properties of the fully trained model, I have run simulations designed to investigate the emergence of representations during the training process. The model shows a number of properties characteristic of phases of the development of visual attention and orienting, such as hypometric saccades, and "obligatory attention." For the purposes of the present argument, however, the important question is whether there is any evidence that infants only develop the ability to use extraretinal coordinates to plan saccades during postnatal life. If they do, this would be consistent with the assumption underlying the model. Namely, that representations controlling eye or head-centered action need to be constructed postnatally, and result from constraints imposed by network structure, and the interaction with the external environment "scaffolded" by subcortical saccades.

In collaboration with Rick Gilmore, I have conducted several experiments designed to ascertain whether the ability of infants to use extraretinal frames of reference to plan saccades emerges over the first few months of life. In one of these experiments we exposed 4- and 6-month-old infants to two simultaneously flashed targets on a large monitor screen. The targets were flashed so briefly that they were gone before the infant started to make a saccade to them. We then studied the saccades that infants made in response to these targets (see Fig. 3.5). In many trials they made two saccades, the first of these being to the location of one of the two targets. Having made a saccade to one of the two targets, we examined whether the second saccade was to the actual location of the second target, or whether it was to the retinal location (the location on the retina at which that target had originally appeared; see Fig. 3.5). To make the second

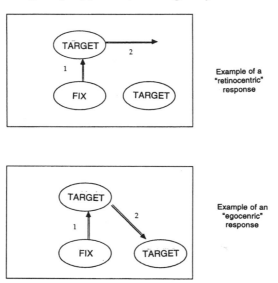

FIG. 3.5. The two types of responses seen in infants. In retinocentric responses infants fail to integrate the retinal vector with their initial eye movement, and thus make their second saccade to an "error" location.

saccade to the correct spatial location requires infants to be able to take into account the fact that their eyes had shifted position, and then compute the saccade necessary given the new eye position. The results indicated that for 4-month-olds the majority of second saccades were directed to the retinal location in which the target had appeared. In contrast, for the 6-month-olds, the majority of second saccades were made to the correct spatial location for the other target. These results suggest that the ability to use extraretinal cues to plan saccades emerges through the first 6 months of life. However, saccades based on retinal location (and thought to be subcortical in origin) are present from birth.

A variety of other experiments have demonstrated that the ability of infants to use acquired information to direct saccades also develops over the first 6 months of life (e.g., Gilmore & Johnson, 1995; Johnson et al., 1991). However, many of these tasks involve more classical learning situations, such as the association of a particular central stimulus with a particular reward location. The foregoing experiment is more relevant to the claims of this chapter inasmuch as the same three sources of constraint on the emergence of representations are evident. First, the structure of the network model (and the learning rule), while much simpler than the real cortex, ensured that representations were generated which combined eye position and retinal location in a particular way. Second, it was suggested that statistical regularities between the inputs (eye position and retinal location), such as temporal coincidence of changes, could contribute to the representations that emerge. The third, and interrelated, source of constraint comes from the subcortical saccadic control system, which could provide the "tutor" signal, necessary for computing error, and initiate the saccade shifts necessary for the temporal correlation just described.

CONCLUSIONS

In two domains—the development of face recognition and the development of saccade planning—I have reviewed evidence consistent with the view that while subcortical brain systems are present from birth and automatic in nature, the representations within the cerebral cortex result from several factors, including the interaction between the organism and its environment, biases imposed by subcortical circuits, and constraints operating from the intrinsic structure of the cortex. For face recognition, the subcortical system serves to bias the input to developing cortical circuitry, causing it to generate appropriate representations for processing faces. In visual orienting, subcortical circuits provide a basic foundation upon which more advanced cortical representations can be constructed.

This general view of the infant's initial "knowledge" of the world has a number of implications for issues such the nature–nurture debate and species differences. First, regarding species differences, our own species appears to have no new structures or parts of the brain relative to other mammals. Rather, we have a greater extent of cortical tissue (and related thalamic regions). What is the effect of having a greater extent of cerebral cortex, and how does it influence the three constraints mentioned earlier? First, the structural constraints imposed by the cortex will be more complex as they will involve not only constraints imposed by the basic architecture of cortical columns (six layers, certain cell types in each layer, etc.), but an expanded cortical surface means that the inputs to "association" (as opposed to sensory) areas of cortex is more complex and may involve pathways with processed information from other cortical regions (see Shrager & Johnson, 1995). The second way in which an expanded cortex would influence the constraints on the emergence of representations is that higher order invariances can be extracted from the input. That is, if first-order correlations latent in the input can be mapped in sensory or motor areas, then other parts of cortex still available for maintaining representations that receive the filtered output from these regions can extract higher order regularities (see Johnson, 1997; Shrager & Johnson, 1995). Thus, along with an expanded cortex we would expect protracted postnatal development, more representational maps for a given domain, and an ability to extract higher order representations from input (or input–output mapping). It is possible that the role of subcortical circuits early in life would be even more important in species with a larger extent of cortex, because there is a greater variety of representations that could emerge in a larger extent of tissue (greater representational space), and therefore a greater number of ways that it could deviate from the normal trajectory.

Turning to the nature–nurture issue, the question with which I began this chapter was why does the initial knowledge of the infant capture the most fundamental properties of the world? We have seen that the two possible answers suggested by Spelke are not exclusive alternatives. Instead, I have suggested that the infants knowledge of the fundamental properties of the world is the result of a complex combination of factors some of which are intrinsic to the infant, some of which are due to the structure of the world, and others of which are due to the interaction between the two. Hopefully, over the next decade we will be able to move beyond the simple dichotomies that have dominated infant psychology, and move to a more integrated and constructivist view of the emergence of knowledge.

ACKNOWLEDGMENTS

Thanks are due to the participants of the Grangärde meeting for their discussion of the verbal version of this paper, and to Annette Karmiloff-Smith for detailed comments on the written version which was prepared in 1994.

I acknowledge financial support from MRC (Programme Grant G97 155 87) and Birkbeck College.

REFERENCES

Andersen, D. A., & Zipser, D. (1988). The role of the posterior parietal cortex in coordinate transformations for visual-motor integration. *Canadian Journal of Physiology & Pharmacology, 66,* 488–501.

Bolhuis, J. J., McCabe, B. J., & Horn, G. (1986). Androgens and imprinting. Differential effects of testosterone on filial preferences in the domestic chick. *Behavioral Neuroscience, 100,* 51–56.

Changeux, J. P. (1985). *Neuronal man: The biology of mind.* New York: Pantheon.

Chantrey, D. (1974). Stimulus pre-exposure and discrimination learning by domestic chicks: Effect of varying interstimulus time. *Journal of Comparative Physiological Psychology, 87,* 517–525.

Conel, J. L. (1939–1967). *The postnatal development of the human cerebral cortex.* Cambridge, MA: Harvard University Press.

Davies, D. C., Horn, G., & McCabe, B. J. (1985). Noradrenaline and learning: the effects of noradrenergic neurotoxin DSP4 on imprinting in the domestic chick. *Behavioral Neuroscience, 99,* 652–660.

Ebbesson, S. O. (1980). The parcellation theory and its relation to interspecific variability in brain organization, evolutionary and ontogenetic development, and neuronal plasticity. *Cell and Tissue Research, 213,* 179–212.

Edelman, G. M. (1987). *Neural Darwinism.* New York: Basic Books.

Elman, J., Bates, E., Johnson, M. H., Karmiloff-Smith, A., Parisi, D., & Plunkett, K. (1996). *Rethinking Innateness: A connectionist perspective on development.* Cambridge, MA: MIT Press.

Ewert, J. -P. (1987). Neuroethology of releasing mechanisms: Prey-catching in toads. *Behavioral and Brain Sciences, 10*(3), 337–405.

Gilmore, R. O., & Johnson, M. H. (1995). Working memory in infancy: Six-month-olds performance on two versions of the oculomotor delayed response task. *Journal of Experimental Child Psychology, 59,* 397–418.

Goodman, S. J., & Andersen, R. A. (1989). Microstimulation of a neural network model for visually guided saccades. *Journal of Cognitive Neuroscience, 1,* 317–326.

Goren, C. C., Sarty, M., & Wu, P. Y. K. (1975). Visual following and pattern discrimination of face-like stimuli by newborn infants. *Pediatrics, 56,* 544–549.

Hinde, R. A. (1962). Some aspects of the imprinting problem. *Symposia of the Zoological Society of London, 8,* 129–138.

Horn, G. (1985). *Memory, imprinting, and the brain: An inquiry into mechanisms.* Oxford, England: Clarendon Press.

Horn, G., & Johnson, M. H. (1989). Memory systems in the chick: Dissociations and neuronal analysis. *Neuropsychologia, 27,* 1–22.

Horn, G., & McCabe, B. J. (1984). Predispositions and preferences. Effects on imprinting of lesions to the chick brain. *Brain Research, 168,* 361–373.

Huttenlocher, P. R. (1990). Morphometric study of human cerebral cortex development. *Neuropsychologia, 28,* 517–527.

Huttenlocher, P. R. (1994). Synaptogenesis, synapse elimination, and neural plasticity in human cerebral cortex. In C. A. Nelson (Ed.), *Threats to optimal development: The Minnesota symposia on child psychology* (Vol. 27, pp. 35–54). Hillsdale, NJ: Lawrence Erbaum Associates.

Johnson, M. H. (1997) *Developmental cognitive neuroscience: An introduction.* Oxford, England: Blackwell.

Johnson, M. H. (2000). Functional brain development in infants: Elements of an interactive specialization framework. *Child Development, 71*, 75–81.

Johnson, M. H., Bolhuis, J. J., & Horn, G. (1985). Interaction between acquired preferences and developing predispositions during imprinting. *Animal Behaviour, 33*, 1000–1006.

Johnson, M. H., Dziurawiec, S., Ellis, H. D., & Morton, J. (1991). Newborns' preferential tracking of face-like stimuli and its subsequent decline. *Cognition, 40*, 1–19.

Johnson, M. H., Farroni, T., Brockbank, M., & Simon, F. (2000). Preferential orienting to faces in 4 month olds. *Developmental Science, 3*, 41–45.

Johnson, M. H., & Gilmore, R. O. (1996). Developmental cognitive neuroscience: A biological perspective on cognitive change. In R. Gelman & T. Au (Eds.), *Handbook of perception and cognition: Perceptual and cognitive development* (pp. 333–372). Orlando, FL: Academic Press.

Johnson, M. H., & Horn, G. (1986). Dissociation of recognition memory and associative learning by a restricted lesion of the chick forebrain. *Neuropsychologia, 24*, 329–340.

Johnson, M. H., & Horn, G. (1987). The role of a restricted region of the chick forebrain in the recognition of individual conspecifics. *Behavioural Brain Research, 23*, 269–275.

Johnson, M. H., & Horn, G. (1988). The development of filial preferences in the dark-reared chick. *Animal Behaviour, 36*, 675–683.

Johnson, M. H., & Morton, J. (1991). *Biology and cognitive development: The case of face recognition.* Oxford, England: Blackwell.

Johnson, M. H., Oliver, A., & Shrager, J. (1998). The paradox of plasticity: Constraints on the emergence of representations in the neocortex. *Journal of the Japanese Cognitive Science Society, 5*, 5–24.

Karten, H. J., & Shimizu, T. (1989). The origins of neocortex: Connections and lamination as distinct events in evolution. *Journal of Cognitive Neuroscience, 1*, 291–301.

Killackey, H. P. (1990). Neocortical expansion: An attempt toward relating phylogeny and ontongeny. *Journal of Cognitive Neuroscience, 2*, 1–17.

Kostovic, I., Petanjek, Z., & Judas, M. (1993). The Earliest areal differentiation of the human cerebral cortex: Entorhinal area. *Hippocampus, 3*, 447–458.

MacPhail, E. M. (1982). *Brain and intelligence in vertebrates.* Oxford, England: Clarendon Press.

Maier, V., & Scheich, H. (1983). Acoustic imprinting leads to differential 2-deoxy-D-glucose uptake in the chick forebrain. *Proceedings of the National Academy of Sciences, USA, 80*, 3860–3864.

McCabe, B. J., Cipolla-Neto, J., Horn, G., & Bateson, P. P. G. (1982). Amnesic effects of bilateral lesions placed in the hyperstriatum ventrale of the chick after imprinting. *Experimental Brain Research, 48*, 13–21.

Molnar, Z., & Blakemore, C. (1991). Lack of regional specificity for connections formed between thalamus and cortex in coculture. *Nature, 351*, 475–477.

Morton, J., & Johnson, M. H. (1991). CONSPEC and CONLERN: A two-process theory of infant face recognition. *Psychological Review, 98*(2), 164–181.

Nauta, W. J. H., & Karten, H. J. (1970). A general profile of the vertebrate brain with sidelights on the ancestry of the cerebral cortex. In F. O. Schmitt (Ed.), *The neurosciences: Second study program.* New York: Rockefeller Press.

O'Reilly, R., & Johnson, M. H. (1994). Object recognition and sensitive periods: A computational analysis of visual imprinting. *Neural Computation, 6*, 357–390.

Rakic, P. (1983). Geniculo-cortical connections in primates: Normal and experimentally altered development. *Progressive Brain Research, 58*, 393–404.

Rumelhart, D. E., & McClelland, J. L. (Eds.). (1986). *Parallel distributed processing: Explorations in the microstructure of cognition. Vol. 1: Foundations.* Cambridge, MA: MIT Press.

Shrager, J., & Johnson, M. H. (1995). Waves of growth in the development of cortical function: A computational model. In I. Kovacs & B. Julesz (Eds.), *Maturational windows and cortical plasticity.* Santa Fe, NM: The Santa Fe Institute Press.

Spelke, E. (1994). Initial knowledge: Six suggestions. *Cognition, 50*, 431–446.

Tombol, T., Csillag, A., & Stewart, M. G. (1988). Cell types of the hyperstriatum ventrale of the domestic chicken, gallus domesticus: A golgi study. *Journal fur Hinforschung, 29,* 319–334.

Zipser, D., & Andersen, R. A. (1988). A back-propagation programmed network that simulates response properties of a subset of posterior parietal neurons. *Nature, 331,* 679–684.

4

On the Early Development of Action, Perception, and Cognition

Claes von Hofsten
Uppsala University

Infants come into this world endowed with action capabilities. As a result, they are able to sustain life in their new environment and prepared to explore and adapt to it. Neonates smell, look, listen, and feel. They root to suck, orient their heads toward interesting sounds, extend their arms forward toward attractive objects, and may even imitate facial gestures. All developing perception and cognition are in one way or another founded on these early capabilities. In this chapter I discuss the origins and development of actions and the possible role they play for the early development of perception and cognition.

INFORMATION FOR ACTIONS

It is important to make a distinction between the information motivating an action and the information controlling it. The affordances of an object, that is, the kind of action it invites to, may be different from the information used to control the action in question. For instance, the information that defines an apple as eatable has little to do with the control of eating it, let alone the act of reaching for the apple and grasping it.

Actions applied to objects reveal new affordances or make already detectable affordances more salient to the perceiver. It is also important to note that affordances do not just refer to stable properties of objects but also to how that object relates to the perceiver. For instance, although a far away object may invite looking, the same object at a closer distance may attract reaching and grasping, and when it is really close it may invite sucking. Learning to discriminate the useful affordances of objects and events is an important aspect of perceptual development.

Controlling an action requires information about what is going to happen next. There are several reasons why this is so. First of all, there is a lag between the time information enters into the system and the time that adjustments are made. The inertia of the system introduces a mechanical lag. In addition, muscles exert limited force and it may take a second or more between the time a reach is launched and the time the hand secures the object in a grasp. These lags will introduce interruptions in the flow of action if adjustments are not prepared. It is evident that the motor system could not function on an ad hoc basis, because movements would then be discontinuous and jerky.

There are at least three kinds of basic problems to be solved in the production of movements. They have to do with controlling the body part to be moved, maintaining posture and balance, and interacting with the outer world. First, several different active and passive forces act on the limb or body segment during a movement. They need to be kept under control by the adjustments of active muscular contractions ahead of time. During purposeful movement, the equilibrium of the body needs to be maintained and a stable orientation relative to the environment. This requires the forces induced by the movement to be counterbalanced ahead of time.

The third set of problems involves the coordination of movements with the external world. As the environment exists independent of us, adaptive coordination is possible only if we can adjust our actions relative to properties of the environment and time them relative to the external events encountered. This holds true whether we are walking in a cluttered terrain, chopping wood, catching a baseball, riding a horse, or engaging in social communication. All these skills rely on our ability to perceive what is going to happen next.

THE ORIGINS OF ACTION

The basic action systems serving important functions for an animal have profound phylogenetic roots. This is most clearly seen in the morphology of the body, which is frequently adjusted to better serve action goals. Thus, feet are made for walking, hands for grasping, and wings for flying. The perceptual system is frequently adjusted in order to provide better information for controlling action. It has made the visual system sensitive to motion and change and made animals able to extract optical information about upcoming encounters with external objects and surfaces (Lee, 1992). In manually skilled animals, the adjustment of the visual system to manual action in is expressed in the forward direction of the eyes and the development of binocularity.

The constraints set up by phylogeny will selectively sponsor the growth and structuring of pathways in the nervous system, that are parts of functional systems that the animal needs at birth (Anokhin, 1964). As a consequence of this selective, accelerated growth, neonates are prepared to sustain life in their new environment and to explore and adapt to it. Anokhin (1964) gave a number of examples of such accelerated growth. For instance, although the facial nerve is an isolated structure, it shows a marked disproportion of maturation of separate fibers at a certain stage in development. The fibers projecting to M. orbicularis oris, providing the most important movement in sucking, are already myelinated and the contacts with the muscle fibers established at a stage when no other facial muscles have such marked organization. Similar accelerated growth can be observed in the medulla oblongata. The parts related to the functional system of sucking are already completely differentiated, while, for instance, the parts that are the source of the frontal branches of the N. facialis, are just beginning to differentiate. The fact that the development of the nervous system follows primarily functional rules rather than structural ones was called "the principle of systemogenesis" by Anokhin (1964).

NEONATAL ACTIONS

The behavior of the neonate has traditionally been discussed in terms of reflexes rather than actions. According to Sherrington (1906), a reflex is a hardwired sensorimotor loop organized at a spinal or paraspinal level. Although reflexes may serve important functions for the subject, they are generally conceived of as reactions to specific stimuli. They are elicited rather than guided and once launched, they run their predetermined course. In other words, they are not goal directed and subject to learning as actions are.

The variety of movements performed by the neonate may be small, but the task specificity and goal directedness demonstrated by these movements warrants referring to at least some of them as actions rather than reflexes. The neonate is clearly prepared for interacting with the external world and to adapt to it.

Take rooting behavior, for instance, which refers to the infant's search for the nipple of the breast. Mechanical stimulation in the area around the mouth makes the infant move his or her mouth toward the point of stimulation (Prechtl, 1958). However, rooting is more than a simple reflex. Odent

(1979) showed that rooting does not just involve movements of the head and mouth but seems to include explorative movements of the whole body with all the senses involved. This requires a common spatial reference system for these sensory systems.

Sucking is another good example of an action system functioning at birth. Skilled sucking relies on a complex interaction of muscle contractions that are prospective in nature. Within a few days of birth the sucking system functions with amazing accuracy (Craig & Lee, 1999). Apart from using this behavior to acquire food, neonates are also able to use sucking as a means to get access to the mother's voice (deCasper & Fifer, 1980) or to regulate a visual event (Kalnins & Bruner, 1973). DeCasper and Fifer found that 1-day-old neonates would alter their sucking rate in order to get assess to their mothers voice. Kalnins and Bruner found that 5-week-old infants would use sucking as a means to focus a picture. When high-frequency sucking resulted in a clear focus, the subjects quickly detected this contingency and increased their sucking rate. When sucking resulted in a blur, sucking rate dropped instead. This shows that neonates can separate the perceived affordance of an event and the action used to fulfill what it invites. In other words, actions can be flexibly applied to various problems.

Neonates have been reported to imitate facial gestures. Meltzoff and Moore (1977; chap. 10, this volume) reported that neonates imitate, for example, mouth opening and tongue protusion. These observations have been replicated several times (see e.g., Heimann, Nelson, & Schaller, 1989; chap. 11, this volume). The results show that neonates have a visual acuity good enough to identify the mouth among other facial features and can discriminate different mouth movements. The fact that they themselves tend to perform mouth movements similar to the ones just seen also shows that they have the embryo of a social communication system based on facial gestures. It also indicates that neonates have a capability to learn about affordances by observing the actions of others.

It is important to point out that perceptual systems are also action systems and that perceiving also involves body movements. For instance, the visual system is built to scan the world, focus on objects and events, and track them over the visual field. The development of oculomotor control is as important to vision as the development of the receptor function itself. If a subject cannot control his or her eye movements, the visual system is useless. Neonates' have some ability to direct gaze toward interesting parts of the optical array, toward parts containing much optical change, and toward certain specific stimuli like faces and moving objects (Johnson & Morton, 1991). Therefore, it can be said that neonates are prepared to explore their surrounding. They can also coordinate the movements of both eyes to some degree and converge them toward the object on which they are fixating (Haineline, Riddell, Grose-Fifer, & Abramov, 1992).

There are, however, important restrictions to the use of the oculomotor system. Kremenitzer, Vaughan, Kurtzman, and Dowling (1979) found that neonates would smoothly track a 12° black disc, but only with low relative amplitude and only approximately 15% of the time. Small targets were only followed with discrete saccadic steps. Bloch and Carchon (1992) used a red transparent ball covering 4° of visual angle and found only saccadic tracking in neonates. Similar findings were reported by Aslin (1981) who used a black bar 2° wide and 8° high moving sinusoidally in a horizontal path. Head movements are used in orienting gaze toward salient objects and events in the environment. For instance, neonates turn their head toward a human voice and other complex sound sources (Alegria & Noirot, 1978; Field, Muir, Pilon, Sinclair, & Dodwell, 1979; Mendelsson & Haith, 1976). They also have a tendency to use head movements in the tracking of an attractive target (Bloch & Carchon, 1992).

Although successful reaching does not typically appear until age 4 months, the link between eye and hand is already established in the neonate. Von Hofsten (1982, 1984) studied arm and hand movements of neonates in the presence and absence of a large, colorful, and slowly moving object: A tuft made of yarn. It was found that the newborn infants performed proportionally more forward extended arm movements in the presence of this object. Quantitative analyses of these movements showed that when the object was fixated, the forward extended arm movements of the infants were aimed toward it. The immediate function of this reaching behavior cannot be to manipulate objects, because the infant cannot yet individually control arm and hand (von Hofsten, 1984). Getting the hand into the visual field and toward the focus of attention, however, closes the visual–manual loop.

Viewing their hands seems attractive in itself for neonates, and van der Meer, van der Weel, and Lee (1995) showed that neonates made an effort to continue to view their hand if they have it in sight. When both hands of the neonate were gently pulled downwards, he or she counteracted this pulling but only for the hand they could see. This was true whether the hand was in the direction in which they turned the head or whether it was in the opposite direction and could only be seen through a TV monitor.

ACTION DEVELOPS THROUGH ACTIONS

An action system is established in development when its efferent and afferent parts form a loop. This is also a necessary condition for developing the system further. When an aspect of an action is controllable, however crudely, it opens up a window for experience to tailor and refine it. In other words, the phylogenetic adaptations are primarily focused on setting up minimal conditions for activating the system. Thereafter the activity of the system itself becomes the primary source of structuring and adaptation. This seems to be a rather general principle in the ontogenesis of the nervous system.

Let's take the embryogenesis of the visual system as an example. First, an abundance of axons originating at the retinal level migrate to the Lateral Geniculate Nucleus (LGN) and the superior colliculus under guidance of genetically determined chemical gradients where they will form topographies crudely corresponding to the retinal one (Retaux & Harris, 1996). The resulting projections and connections exceed by far what will be useful for the functional network. The mapping is very crude and of little use for extracting specific information about the world. This stage is followed by a second stage of fine mapping during which the system becomes active. Structured activity at the retinal level will cause connections to be modulated through competitive interactions (van der Malsburg & Singer, 1988) that will shape the initial crude mapping into a detailed correspondence between the retinal and the receiving structures at the LGN and the superior colliculus. The structured activity on the retina could be determined by structured light after birth. If this was the case, the neonate would be unable to use vision in any practical way. A simple but crucial change in the epigenetic process, however, has enabled the fine structuring to start much before birth. Shatz (1992) and colleagues showed in prenatal cats that ordered waves of activity move back and forth over the retina. This is quite sufficient for launching the fine mapping process that makes the neonate ready to extract information from the outside world.

The same general principles that apply to the mapping of the visual system also seem relevant to the organization of action systems. Phylogenetic adaptations set up minimum conditions for closing the sensorimotor loop and enabling the system to be activated, but it is through its own activity that the action system will finally organize. For instance, the neonate is endowed with a rather primitive system for controlling arm and hand movements. Because of synergistic constraints, it does not allow the infant to grasp attractive objects in its surrounding. However, it fulfills certain basic requirements that make it possible to move the hand to the mouth, into the visual field, and toward a target. This is precisely what is needed for developing the system. It makes it possible for the infant to explore the relationship between commands and movements, between vision and proprioception, and to discover the possibilities and constraints of manual movements

However, nothing will be done without motives. Motives both foresee future conditions and provide the driving force to get there. They make infants try to do things they have not yet mastered. For instance, one might say it is the urge to grasp objects that gets the reaching system assembled. Around age 3 to 4 months, a normal infant will work systematically to get the hand to an object and grasp it. To start with, the attempts are not very successful but that doesn't seem to make much of a difference. The infants stubbornly continue.

Explorative Actions

From the beginning of life, infants are deeply engaged in exploring the external world and their ability to act in it. This is clearly reflected in their cognitive development. It has even been suggested that cognitive development should be divided into phases characterized by the emergence of new means for exploring the world: looking, reaching, and locomotion (Gibson, 1988). While the infant is engaged in mastering a certain action, perception and other cognitive activities related to that action show rapid development.

Exploratory actions have traditionally been thought of as being focused on the external world and on objects and events in it, but they may just as well be focused on one's own actions. It seems quite clear that the way to learn about one's own movement capabilities is to move. This is how infants learn about the properties that change and those that remain invariant during the execution of an action, depending on the posture of the body and how the movements are performed, and this is how they learn about problems that arise when coordinating with the external world (von Hofsten, 1993). During the early months of life, infants devote much of their daily activity to exploring their action possibilities. Movements are performed again and again with slight alternations. This was observed by Piaget (1953) who named several of the early developmental stages he described as stages of circular reactions.

CONTROLLING ACTIONS

Knowledge about upcoming events is necessary for controlling our actions. We need to know what is going to happen next in order to plan our activities and to coordinate our movements. To be able to predict what is going to happen next, we have to rely on the regularities or invariances of the events in the world like physical laws, mobility constraints, rules of social relations and communication, and the specific opportunities and constraints of the task.

Predictions can be achieved perceptually. Events obeying the law of physics do not only tell us what has already happened but, more importantly, how they are going to evolve in the imminent future. By watching the ongoing motion of an object it is possible to perceive it's next step (Pavel, 1990). Such perceived extrapolations of events have their limitations, however. They are confined to short time intervals. As the distance into the future increases, the relation between parameters in the sensory array and the upcoming events becomes less direct. If a moving object is occluded for a very short period as when it passes behind a tree, we are utterly surprised if it does not reappear on the other side. If the moving object is occluded for several seconds during its motion, its reappearance is much less certain and we are not very surprised if it does not turn up on the other side. Predicting what is happening behind the occluder relies on knowledge of the rules that govern events. Some of the rules like the laws of physics are very general and invariant over many tasks, whereas other rules, indeed most of them, are much more heuristic and task dependent. Next, I discuss predictions in two specific domains: looking and reaching.

Gaze Control

The most basic visual action is directing and stabilizing gaze. The development of gaze control is of utmost importance for the development of visual perception. Controlling gaze may involve both head and eye movements and is guided by at least three types of information: visual, vestibular, and proprioceptive.

A stable gaze is accomplished by smooth and continuous adjustments of eye direction. Such eye movements are called smooth pursuit to distinguish them from saccades. To avoid slippages of the retinal image and to keep the target of interest within the foveal area of the retina, the smooth pursuit must predict the motion of the target. In addition to the smooth pursuit eye movements, head movements may be involved as well. These head movements must be coordinated with the eye movements so that they add up to the target motion. What makes things complicated is that the head also moves for other reasons and those movements must to be compensated for by appropriate compensatory eye movements. In adults, eye movements simultaneously serve both compensatory and pursuit functions making it possible to move around while fixating a moving target.

Rosander and myself (von Hofsten & Rosander, 1996, 1997) have studied the development of gaze stabilization in a situation where the infant could freely move eyes and head. We found that a large target was pursued at 1 month of age with a combination of eye and head movements. The eye movements were partly smooth. For an intermediate sized target moving back and forth at 0.2 or 0.4 Hz, we found that smooth pursuit was very well established at 2 months of age. To investigate the development of predictive tracking, we used two kinds of target motions, one with smoothly changing velocity (a sinusoidal motion), and one with constant velocity that abruptly reversed at the end points (a sawtooth motion). The important difference between these two motions is that the next step of a smoothly changing motion is directly perceivable, whereas this is not true for an abruptly changing one. The constant velocity of the sawtooth motion does not reveal where or when the object is going to turn. This can only be derived from the periodicity of the motion. Figure 4.1 shows the smooth component of the eye movements of a 3-month-old infant when tracking these two kinds of motions. Note the consistent lag in the tracking of the sawtooth motion.

One-month-old infant's tracking of a sinusoidal target shows a substantial lag which is much reduced at 2- and 3-months-of-age indicating the development of some kind of predictive ability (see Fig. 4.2). These extrapolations are most probably perceptually based, because the lag for the sawtooth motion at age 2 and 3 months was still large. At 5 months, the eyes

Smooth pursuit

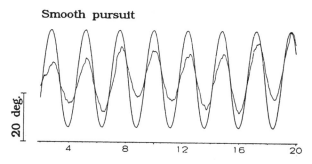

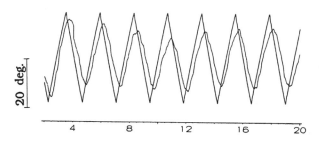

Time (sec)

FIG. 4.1. Examples of smooth pursuit position profiles after the saccades had been removed. The examples are from a single 3-month-old subject tracking a sinusoidal (upper graph) and a sawtooth motion (lower graph) at 0.4 Hz. The smooth pursuit gains were 0.52 and 0.71 for the sinusoidal and the sawtooth motions, respectively. The lag of the smooth pursuit for the sawtooth motion was substantial (max r = 0.97 at a lag of 277 ms) while it was modest for the sinusoidal motion (max r = 0.96 at a lag of 80 ms).

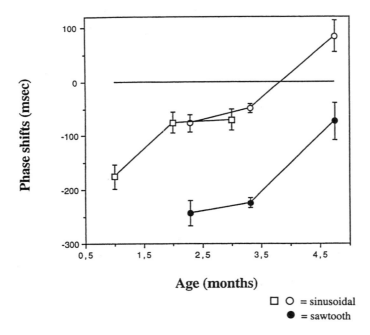

FIG. 4.2. Average time lags and standard errors for the tracking of targets moving according to a sinusoidal (open symbols) or a triangular (filled symbols) motion function. The diagram combines data from von Hofsten & Rosander (1996, squares) and from von Hofsten & Rosander (1997, circles).

were leading the sinusoidally moving target and the lag for the sawtooth motion was very much reduced (see Fig. 4.2). The development is parallel for the two kinds of motions. This indicates that a new kind of prediction is introduced based on the global aspects of the motion. This is in line with research performed by Haith and associates (Canfield & Haith, 1991; Haith, Hazan, & Goodman, 1988) who demonstrated that 4-month-old infants will predict where and when the next picture in a left–right sequence is going to be shown, by moving the eyes there, just before the picture appears.

Catching

The early development of prediction can also be observed in the catching of moving objects. At an age when infants first start to successfully grasp stationary objects, they also catch moving ones (von Hofsten, 1980). They do it by initiating their arm and hand motions before the object is within reaching distance, aiming ahead of the object's current position toward a place where the paths of the object and the hand will intersect. Aiming was found to be accurate on the first attempted reach for a fast moving object

(30 cm/s). These findings indicate that young infants can reach predictively without trial and error learning over the course of the experimental session. The prospective nature of the action becomes very clear once the motion is suddenly perturbed by, for instance by stopping it (see Fig. 4.3).

Reaching for moving objects includes an element of tracking, but in addition it involves approaching the target of interest. Von Hofsten (1983) described catching as a combination of two tasks: tracking the target and approaching it. If the tracking vector corresponds to the object motion, the resultant reaching vector, defined as the vector sum of tracking and approach, will always be directed toward a meeting point with the object. In other words, successful catching in terms of this model relies on perceiving and extrapolating the motion of the target.

The model, however, is insufficient for explaining predictive reaching, if the object is only within reach at a specific region of its trajectory, as it was in von Hofsten (1980, 1983) and in von Hofsten, Vishton, Spelke, Feng, and Rosander (1998). Successful catching must then be planned so as to make the hand intercept the object within this region (see Fig. 4.4). This is exactly

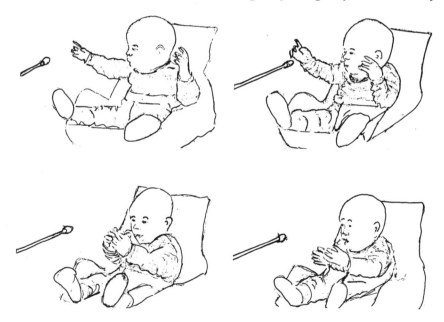

FIG. 4.3. An 8-month-old infant reaching for an object that moves at 60 cm/s and stops 500 ms into the reach. (Upper left) 300 ms into the reach. (upper right) 500 ms into the reach; the object stops. (Lower left) the end of the reach; the infant grasps at the position the object would have occupied if it had continued to move. (Lower right) 300 ms later; the infant redirects attention toward the object's true position (after von Hofsten and Rosander, unpublished, 1993, Umeå University, Umeå, Sweden).

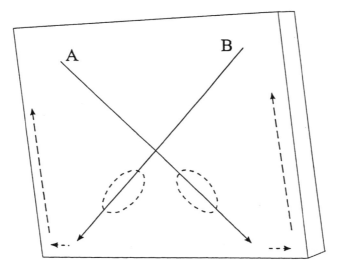

FIG. 4.4. A schematic view of the display screen showing the four different motion paths used in the experiments. The dashed ellipses indicate the reaching areas for each path.

what infants did, in those studies. These findings indicate that the reaches predicted future positions of the target right from their very onset and were not just online extrapolations.

What rules may guide the planning of these predictive reaches? When objects continued to move at a certain speed and along a specific trajectory reaches were well timed and catching successful. However, when the object abruptly turned before entering the area where it was reachable, the infants continued to direct their reaches toward the area that the object would pass if it had continued on a straight path. This was true even after 12 trials on which the object turned (von Hofsten et al., 1998). The results suggest that reaches were guided by a rule stating that an object moving at a certain speed would maintain that speed. It is a reasonable assumption within a small time window and follows from the law of inertia that states that objects continue their ongoing motion in the absence of forces and change their motion smoothly when forces are present. It is possible that infants also learn other basic rules at an early age for how objects move in a world governed by physical laws; rules that may guide their actions toward moving objects.

Such rules become important when moving objects temporarily disappear from view behind an occluder. Studies by Munakata, Jonsson, von Hofsten, and Spelke (1996) and by Jonsson and von Hofsten (1998) show that when objects move in a straight path behind an occluder, 6-month-old infants will turn their head toward the reappearance point before the object arrives there. If the object reappears at a different place, 6-month-old infants will learn this over an experimental session (von Hofsten, Feng, & Spelke, 2000), thus incorporating a new rule of prediction.

AFFORDANCES

An important part of the biological preparation for development has to do with affordances. Closing the sensorimotor loop is necessary but not sufficient for the development of actions. There must be some minimum ability to apply actions appropriately.

Let us consider face perception. Goren, Sartu, and Wu (1975) found that neonates, only a few minutes old, showed a greater tendency to track a schematic face than a scrambled face or a blank head outline. These results were replicated by Johnson and Morton (1991) who suggested the existence of an underlying mechanism, a "conspec," attracting gaze to facial patterns. Similar mechanisms attract neonates to a human voice toward which they turn their head and to a moving nearby object toward which they may extend their arms.

As Johnson and Morton (1991) pointed out, the conspec could be a very simple receptor, essentially reacting to any configuration of three high-contrast areas corresponding to the eyes and mouth. A few such mechanisms will direct attention toward important aspects of the surrounding world which the neonate is prepared to act on. Such an arrangement provides optimal conditions for learning. If the perception–action loop is in the right ballpark, it opens up a window for experience to explore and differentiate the perceived affordances in a very efficient way.

Coupled with this differentiation of affordances is a differentiation of actions. Together they will weave an increasingly complex web of relationships with the outside world. Both perception and action are necessary parts of such a knowledge structure. This insight was excellently brought out and discussed by Piaget (1953, 1954).

THE RELATIONSHIP BETWEEN ACTION AND COGNITION

Before language emerges, children's awareness of the world and their ability to reflect on it can only be expressed through their actions. To begin with, actions are tightly coupled with perception, but with age the coupling will be less direct as children begin to use acquired knowledge and symbolic thought to regulate their actions. Piaget (1953, 1954) saw continuity between the knowledge structure of the infant consisting of perception–action relationships and the more abstract structure of the older child. He believed that all knowledge was originally based on sensorimotor schemes. Today, another view has stepped forward, which states that the development of cognition and the development of actions are different but parallel developmental processes (Mandler, 1988).

Representations are associated with meaning and meaning with actions. All actions, even those of neonates, are geared to the future. It can thus be argued that even neonatal actions carry referential meaning and entail a minimal degree of consiousness (Zelazo, 1996). It is within this context that early cognition develops. The infant needs to know what is going to happen next in order to plan its actions and coordinate its movements. To be able to predict what is going to happen next, they have to rely on the regularities or invariances of the events in the world like physical laws, mobility constraints, rules of social relations and communication, and the specific opportunities and constraints of the task. There is reason to believe that basic cognitive activities like perceiving, attending, remembering, feeling, and thinking originally evolved to enable organisms to utilize these rules in order to prepare and organize their behavior for future events and activities.

It does not seem reasonable that cognition should develop isolated from the actions it is designed to serve. Data on early cognition rather support the opposite view that knowledge expands in the context of specific tasks and is embedded in multiple systems of representation (Spelke, 1994). For instance, studies of infants reaching for moving objects provide evidence for an extrapolation of the object motion on linear paths, in accordance with the principle of inertia (von Hofsten et al., 1998). In contrast, infants fail to extrapolate linear object motion in preferential looking experiments (Spelke, Katz, Purcell, Ehrlich, & Breinlinger, 1994; Spelke, Kestenbaum, Simons, & Wein, 1995). There are even arguments that cognitive development should be divided into phases characterized by the emergence of new means for action: looking, reaching, and locomotion (Gibson, 1988). It is after the child masters reaching and grasping that object permanence starts to appear, and after crawling begins do they grow fearful of heights and evolve a concept of allocentric space (Bertenthal & Campos, 1991).

In the development of actions, increasingly complex relationships between meanings arise, and this process leads to an increasing detachment of meaning from the immediate situation and from the immediate action (Vygotsky, 1978). Both Vygotsky and Piaget underestimated the rate at which such symbolic representational knowledge emerges. Already during the first 6 months of life, infants seem to begin reflecting on events that they perceive as external and independent of themselves.

It is important, however, to point out that actions are not just confined to manipulation and locomotion. Looking is an earlier developing action skill, much used as an index of early cognition in the infant. By looking at external events, infants learn about the rules that govern them. This is of direct relevance for their looking actions, because it tells them where to look next.

There are, of course, also some general differences between the way knowledge is used in motor movements and in symbolic thinking. The most critical difference has to do with time. The closer one gets to the implementation of the action the more important becomes timing and the more crucial becomes direct access to information about the future without the involvement of consciousness. When performing the motor task, even thinking of the rules often disrupts performance. The reason is that explicit thinking is too slow. Therefore, action knowledge often becomes implicit rather than explicit. Just because I can ride a bike does not mean that I can explain how I do it. Just because someone tells me the rules of tango, doesn't mean that I can dance. The rules have to be incorporated into the action patterns themselves before one masters the action. However, this difference concerns the application of knowledge rather than how it evolves. It gives further credit to the view that cognition originally emerges in the tasks it serves.

REFERENCES

Alegria, J., & Noirot, E. (1978). Neonate orientation behavior towards human voice. *International Journal of Behavioral Development, 1*, 291–312.

Anokhin, P. K. (1964). Systemogenesis as a general regulator of brain development. *Progress in Brain Research, 9.*

Aslin, R. N. (1981). Development of smooth pursuit in human infants. In D. F. Fisher, R. A. Monty, & J. W. Senders (Eds.), *Eye Movements: Cognition and Visual Perception.* Hillsdale, NJ: Erlbaum.

Bloch, H., & Carchon, I. (1992). On the onset of eye-head co-ordination in infants. *Behavioural Brain Research, 49*, 85–90.

Bertenthal, B. I., & Campos, J. J. (1991). A systems approach to the organizational effects of self-produced locomotion during infancy. In C. Rovee-Collier & L. Lipsitt (Eds.), *Advances in infant research. Vol. 6* (pp. 1–60). Norwood, NJ: Ablex.

Canfield, R. L., & Haith, M. M. (1991). Young infants' visual expectations for symmetric and asymmetric stimulus sequences. *Developmental Psychology, 27*, 198–208.

Craig, C. M., & Lee, D. N. (1999). Neonatal control of sucking pressure: Evidence from an intrinsic tau-guide. *Experimental Brain Research, 124*, 371–382.

deCasper, A. J., & Fifer, W. P. (1980). Of human bonding: Newborns prefer their mothers' voices. *Science, 208*, 1174–1176.

Field, J., Muir, D., Pilon, R., Sinclair, M., & Dodwell, P. (1979). Infants' orientation to lateral sounds from birth to three months. *Child development, 51*, 295–298.

Gibson, E. J. (1988). Exploratory behavior in the development of perceiving, acting and the acquiring of knowledge. *Annual Review of Psychology, 39*, 1–41.

Goren, C. G., Sartu, M., & Wu, P. Y. K. (1975). Visual following and pattern discrimination of face-like stimuli by newborn infants. *Pediatrics, 56*, 544–549.

Haineline, L., Riddell, P., Grose-Fifer, J., & Abramov, I. (1992). Development of accomodation and convergence in infancy. *Behavioural Brain Research, 49*, 33–50

Haith, M., Hazan, C., & Goodman, G. S. (1988). Expectation and anticipation of dynamic visual events by 3.5-month-old babies. *Child Development, 59,* 467–479.

Heimann, M., Nelson, K. E., & Schaller, J. (1989). Neonatal imitation of tongue protrusion and mouth opening: Methodological aspects and evidence of early individual differences. *Scandinavian Journal of Psychology, 30,* 90–101.

Johnson, M. H., & Morton, J. (1991). *Biology and cognitive development: The case of face recognition.* Oxford, England: Blackwell.

Jonsson, B., & von Hofsten, C. (1998, April). *Predictive head movements in 6 -month old infants.* XIth International Conference on Infant Studies, Atlanta, GA.

Kalnins, I. V., & Bruner, J. S. (1973). The coordination of visual observation and instrumental behavior in early infancy. *Perception, 2,* 307–314.

Kremenitzer, J. P., Vaughan, H. G., Kurtzberg, D., & Dowling, K. (1979). Smooth-pursuit eye movements in the newborn infant. *Child Development, 50,* 442–448.

Lee, D. N. (1992). Body–environment coupling. In U. Neisser (Ed.), *Ecological and interpersonal knowledge of the self.* Cambridge, England: Cambridge University Press.

Mandler, J. (1988). How to build a baby: II. Conceptual primitives. *Psychological Review, 99,* 587–604.

Meltzoff, A. N., & Moore, M. K. (1977). Imitation of facial and manual gestures by human neonates. *Science, 198,* 75–78.

Mendelsson, M. J., & Haith, M. M. (1976). The relation between audition and vision in the human newborn. *Monographs of the Society for Research in Child Development, 41*(No. 167)

Munakata, Y., Jonsson, B., von Hofsten, C., & Spelke, E. S. (1996, April). *When it helps to occlude and obscure: 6-month-old's predictive tracking of moving toys.* Xth International Conference on Infant Studies, Providence, RI.

Odent, M. (1979). The early expression of the rooting reflex. In L. Carneza & L. Zichella (Eds.), *Emotion and reproduction, Vol. 20B.* London, England: Academic Press.

Pavel, M. (1990). Predictive control of eye movement. In E. Kowler (Ed.), *Eye movements and their role in visual and cognitive processes: Reviews of oculomotor research, Vol. 4* (pp. 71–114). Amsterdam: Elsevier.

Piaget, J. (1953). *The origins of intelligence in the child.* New York: Routledge.

Piaget, J. (1954). *The construction of reality in the child.* New York: Basic Books.

Prechtl, H. F. R. (1958). The directed head turning response and allied movements of the human infant. *Behaviour, 13,* 212–242.

Retaux, S., & Harris, W. A. (1996). Engrailed and retinotectal totgraphy. *Trends in Neuroscience, 19,* 542–546.

Shatz, C. J. (1992). The developing brain. *Scientific American,* September, 35–41.

Sherrington, C. S. (1906). *The integrative action of the nervous system.* New Haven, CT: Yale University Press.

Spelke, E. S. (1994). Initial knowledge: Six suggestions. *Cognition, 50,* 431–445.

Spelke, E. S., Katz, G., Purcell, S. E., Ehrlich, S. M., & Breinlinger, K. (1994). Early knowledge of object motion: Continuity and inertia. *Cognition, 51,* 131–176.

Spelke, E. S., Kestenbaum, R., Simons, D., & Wein, D. (1995). Spatio-temporal continuity, smoothness of motion and object identity in infancy. *British Journal of Developmental Psychology, 13,* 113–142.

van der Meer, A. L. H., van der Weel, F. R., & Lee, D. N. (1995). The functional significance of arm movements in neonates. *Science, 267,* 693–695.

van der Malsburg, C., & Singer, W. (1988). Principles of cortical network organisations. In P. Rakic & W. Singer (Eds.), *Neurobiology of the neocortex* (pp. 69–99). London, England: Wiley.

von Hofsten, C. (1980). Predictive reaching for moving objects by human infants. *Journal of Experimental Child Psychology, 30,* 369–382.

von Hofsten, C. (1982). Eye-hand coordination in newborns. *Developmental Psychology, 18,* 450–461.

von Hofsten, C. (1983). Catching skills in infancy. *Journal of Experimental Psychology: Human Perception and Performance, 9,* 75–85.

von Hofsten, C. (1984). Developmental changes in the organization of pre-reaching movements. *Developmental Psychology, 20,* 378–388.

von Hofsten, C. (1993). Prospective control: A basic aspect of action development. *Human Development, 36,* 253–270.

von Hofsten, C., Feng, Q. & Spelke, E. S. (1999). Object perception and predictive action in infancy. *Developmental Science, 3,* 193–205.

von Hofsten, C., & Rosander, K. (1996). The development of gaze control and predictive tracking in young infants. *Vision Research, 36,* 81–96.

von Hofsten, C., & Rosander, K. (1997). Development of smooth pursuit tracking in young infants. *Vision Research, 37,* 1799–1810.

von Hofsten, C., Vishton, P., Spelke, E. S., Feng, Q., & Rosander, K. (1998). Predictive action in infancy: Tracking and reaching for moving objects. *Cognition, 67,* 255–285.

Vygotsky, S. (1978). *Mind in society.* Cambridge, MA: Harvard University Press.

Zelazo, P. D. (1996). Towards a characterization of minimal consciousness. *New Ideas in Psychology, 14,* 63–80.

5

Auditory and Articulatory Biases Influence the Initial Stages of the Language Acquisition Process

Francisco Lacerda
Ulla Sundberg
Stockholm University

Following the pioneering work of Ferdinand de Saussure, the Prague School introduced the notion of "contrast" as central to phonological descriptions. The suggestion that language can be seen as a system of contrasts conveyed by acoustic differences between speech sounds obviously captures an essential aspect of the adult speech communication system in a powerful and intuitive manner. From both the phonological and from the information theory perspective as well, the possibility of building discrete sequences of differentiated speech sounds clearly plays a central role in the communication process.

Acoustically, however, speech sounds are produced in the continuous fashion colorfully illustrated by Hockett's Easter Eggs analogy, and are thus not nearly as crispy and distinct units as when they are described in terms of the adult language's phonological structure. In fact, the long debated "variance–invariance issue" exposes the paradoxes raised by, on the one hand, the "within-phoneme acoustic variability" and, on the other hand, by the "acoustic similarity of distinct phonemic categories." The variance–invariance issue clearly uncovers what seems to be an intrinsic fuzziness in the correspondence between the logical (phonological) and the biological (phonetic) components of the speech communication process. All of a sudden, the notion of contrast becomes problematic: How is *phonemic contrast* expressed in acoustic terms? How does the listener partition the perceptual space so that sometimes acoustically distinct speech sounds can be interpreted as phonemically equivalent whereas equally large acoustic differences in other regions of the space are mapped in clearly different phonemic categories?

In broad terms, language acquisition can be viewed as a structuring (or re-structuring) process of the infant's perceptual and articulatory spaces. Perception and production of speech sounds must allow reliable recognition and articulation of sounds that are relevant in the ambient language's inventory. However, as experiments in adult speech perception demonstrate, listeners adjust for tempo, age, and gender differences of the speaker in such a way that the same acoustic signal can be perceived in different ways depending on the contextual information that is provided by the carrier sentence. Recall, for instance, the classical example provided by the perception of a synthetic /ba/-syllable in carrier sentences pronounced with different speech tempo (Miller & Liberman, 1979). Because a crucial acoustic dimension signaling a bilabial stop consonant is F_1 transition speed, inserting the syllable in a carrier sentence produced with high speech tempo tends to shift /b/ into /w/. The synthetic syllable is then perceived as /wa/ in a high speech tempo context. In addition, as demonstrated by Pisoni, Aslin, Perey, and Hennessy (1982), the category boundaries can even be relocated through training, strongly suggesting that the acoustic characteristics of the speech signal are not firmly anchored on specific locations along the physical dimensions. A competent listener makes use of virtually all the available acoustic information in the speech signal, as Diehl and Kluender (1987) expressed it. Obviously, the young language learner is at odds with the acoustic variability of the speech signal that seems to hide the relevant linguistic information. In the absence of additional information, the infant's discovery of the underlying linguistic structure in its ambient language seems impossible. Therefore, nativistic suggestions, assuming that linguistic information is present from the onset of the process, are an appealing short cut toward language. But because language is used in a consistent fashion, other sources of information are also available to the infant and the necessity of a genetic program toward language is somewhat degraded given the ecologically relevant language development contexts.

These issues have been addressed by well-known theories, such as the motor theory of speech perception (Liberman, Cooper, Shankweiler, & Studdert-Kennedy, 1967; Liberman & Mattingly, 1985), the quantal theory of speech (Stevens, 1972) or the action theory (Fowler, 1986), but these theories are strongly biased by the adult perspective and seem to take phonemes for granted. From the ontogenetic perspective, such a phonematic assumption is not easily motivated. How does the infant know "phonemes"? Is that knowledge conveyed genetically or is it the result of the infant's experience with the ambient language?

Clearly, these genetic and functional behavioristic approaches are not necessarily incompatible. Nature and nurture are two aspects of the same reality, where behavior is both influenced by and modulates the organism's genetic potential. Behavior's contribution to the establishment of phoneme categories cannot simply be dismissed a priori as irrelevant and the fact that infants learn their ambient language clearly indicates that there is a good degree of plasticity in the genetically determined neurological structures. Thus, the processes by which the phonetic continuum is linguistically structured deserves to be a primary focus of interest and addressed in the search for independent motivation to the infant's initial speech perception and production propensities.

In this chapter we use infant speech perception data to illustrate how the vowel space might be structured during the early stages of the language acquisition process and speculate on the possible impact that those initial propensities may have for language development in general.

Our approach to language acquisition emphasizes the role of global exposure to the spoken language, specifically the importance of multisensory input and memory factors, suggesting that although our experimental data are collected during controlled laboratory studies, their implications must necessarily be integrated in the infant's broad developmental frame.

One pertinent aspect of the normal language acquisition process is the infant's initial capacity to perceive and detect relevant acoustic characteristics of the speech sounds. "Initial perceptual capacities" are likely to influence the acoustic characteristics picked up by the newborn infants and can therefore bias the early stages of speech perception toward auditorily motivated contrasts. However, under the pressure of increasingly larger amounts of information, the initial role of psychoacoustic biases in the organization of the perceptual system may be traded by more global optimization constraints (Castro-Caldas, Petersson, Reis, Stone-Elander, & Ingvar, 1998; Merzenich, 1998; Zohary, Celebrini, Britten, & Newsome, 1994).

ASSESSING THE INFANT'S LINGUISTIC DEVELOPMENT

Psychoacoustic experiments with young infants indicate that performance generally is poorer than the adults' (Werner, 1992). Pure tone frequency discrimination, for instance, demands changes of 2% to 3% for 6-month-old infants and 3% to 4% for 3-month-olds whereas adults discriminate frequency shifts of typically less than 1%. The same type of pattern is also observed for absolute thresholds where the detection thresholds for 6-month-old infants are about 30 to 40 dB higher than corresponding adult thresholds. Similar relations between infant and adult performance were also found for gap-detection and forward masking—young infants typically need longer durations to detect gaps and the effect of a masker lasts longer for infants than for adults. Incidentally, it should be noted that 6-month-olds and adults displayed about the same frequency resolution pattern in a pulsation threshold experiment, whereas 3-month-olds evidenced cruder frequency discrimination in the 4 kHz region than their older peers (Werner, 1992). A question in line is how infants can display such good speech discrimination ability like the capacity to discriminate foreign speech contrasts that adults tend to miss (Werker & Tees, 1984) and at the same time have poorer psychoacoustic performance than the adult?

When addressing these questions it is convenient to have in mind the procedures used in infant speech perception research and the specially designed research techniques that are suited to the infant's response capacities. Most behavioral techniques currently used in infant speech perception research—high-amplitude sucking (Jusczyk, 1985; Lacerda, 1992a), head-turn technique (Kuhl, 1985), visual preference looking (Jusczyk & Aslin, 1995) or variants of these—are operant-conditioning paradigms exploring the infant's curiosity and ability to derive operation rules from specific examples. The methods were originally used to assess the infant's ability to discriminate speech sounds but have subsequently been applied to the study of equivalence classes or word recognition tasks. The data typically reflect behavioral changes that are assumed to be contingent on the manipulation of the acoustic stimuli. The infant's first task in an experimental situation is to infer the "rules of the game"—a basic requirement inasmuch as traditional "adult instructions" are clearly ineffective in this context. Success in this initial task clearly indicates that infants are competent and quick at picking up the rules implicit in a series of examples. Further implications of specific experimental results may be less obvious. Because the situations created in experimental setups typically involve simplifications of the natural contexts in which language acquisition takes place, relevant generalizations to real life must be done with caution and integrated in an overall coherent theoretical frame. In contrast with adult speech perception research, there is no explicit way of carrying out a posttest assessment of infant's strategies during the experiment. Also, whereas adult behavior may be characterized by a goal-oriented strategy, relying on the subject's vast previous problem-solving experiences, the infant's behavior is more likely to be determined by local, immediate, or even spurious variables. Thus, the relevance that the speech signal has for the subject may clearly affect the experimental results.[1] In addition, because the proportion of new information relative to the infant's life experience is extremely large in the beginning of life and

---

[1]For instance, discussing Kuhl's (1991) results showing that the perceptual-magnet effect occurs for humans but not for monkeys, Lacerda (1995) suggested the results may be a consequence of the fact that stimuli used by Kuhl (1991) were not made relevant for the monkeys. This notion is further supported by Kluender, Lotto, Holt, and Bloedel (1998) perception experiments with quails, where the effect was observed probably because the stimuli were made relevant for the avian subjects.

the infant's responses are highly plastic, the experimental outcome will generally reflect the interplay between basic sensitivities and the infant's cognitive and linguistic development.

In this chapter we focus on one aspect of the early organization of the infant's perceptual space for vowels. We review perception data from our previous work that indicates that young infants discriminate better vowel contrasts that are conveyed by F_1 than vowel contrasts associated with corresponding F_2 changes and attempt to integrate this experimental evidence into a broader theoretical model involving also production and interactive components.

Asymmetries in the Infant's Representation of Vowel Sounds

The First Six Months of Life. Some years ago we investigated how 1- to 4-month-old Swedish infants managed to discriminate the front/back open vowel contrast between [ɑ] and [a] (Lacerda, 1992b). The vowels were generated by a four-formant serial speech synthesizer and differed only in their F_2 values (see Fig. 5.1). The results indicated that the infants were unable to show reliable discrimination between [ɑ] and [a] when the contrast was

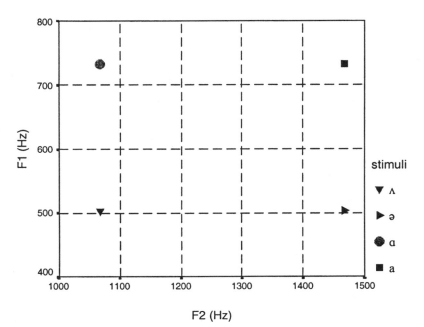

FIG. 5.1. F_1 and F_2 frequencies of the target vowel-like stimuli and their approximate phonetic labels.

solely conveyed by the vowel's F_2 (1067 Hz and 1467 Hz, respectively).[2] This outcome was surprising because American 2-month-olds, who had been tested by Jusczyk and his colleagues (Jusczyk, Bertoncini, Bijeljac-Babic, Kennedy, & Mehler, 1990) with the same paradigm (High-Amplitude Sucking), evidenced discrimination on a similar vowel contrast[3] ([ba] vs. [bʌ]).

To rule out the possibility that the lack of discrimination of the [ɑ] vs. [a] stimuli might be due to idiosyncrasies in our particular subject sample, we ran an additional series of experiments with additional subjects. The infants were now tested with both the original [ɑ] vs. [a] stimuli and with an additional [ɑ] vs. [ʌ] contrast (Lacerda, 1993a, 1993b). The [ʌ] stimulus was synthesized by incrementing the original [ɑ] F_1 by the same amount, in Bark, that had initially been applied to the [ɑ] vs. [a] stimuli's F_2. As reported in Lacerda (1993a, 1993b), the results corroborated the perceptual dominance of the contrasts involving F_1 differences. Further data were collected, this time using CV syllables generated by a hardware speech synthesizer (Infovox). The infants were assigned to three different conditions—a control condition where the same syllable was presented throughout the session, a [bɑ] vs. [bʌ] contrast and a [bɑ] vs. [ba] contrast. A total of 113 infants participated in 237 sessions. Roughly half of the sessions were successful, as indicated in Table 5.1.

One of these 122 sessions was also rejected because the sucking rate during the 2 minutes before the shift was momentarily below 10 sucks per minute. The average age of the 113 infants was 98 days and the standard deviation 33 days (range 11 to 193 days). The age range of infants that actually contributed the final data was 23 to 193 days. This age distribution has a very wide range, is slightly skewed (0.275), and broader than a normal distribution (kurtosis = 0.245). Thus, to assess the influence of the age variable on the results, data were first analyzed by age groups—a group up to 2 months, a group of 3-month-olds, and a group of infants starting at 4 months. Because no interaction was found between experimental condition (control, [bɑ] vs. [bʌ] or [bɑ] vs. [ba]) and age groups [$F_{(4,112)} = 1.116$, $p < 0.353$] the data were pooled for all ages. Pooling the data blurred the picture somewhat because the variance of the older infants (25% of the whole population) was slightly higher than for the infants in the first two age groups. The results are displayed in Fig. 5.2.

ANOVA of these data provided less clear results than those reported earlier (Lacerda, 1993a, 1993b), essentially because of the larger variance that

---

[2]The actual formant values were adjusted to meet the requirements of the Infovox text-to-speech card that was used to create the initial versions of the stimuli.

[3]The formant difference in F_1 between [a] and [ʌ] is of about the same magnitude as that in F_2 between [a] and [ɑ] when measured in Barks.

TABLE 5.1
Distribution of "Infant Status" After Each Session

	Count	Column %
bowl	7	3.0%
cry	7	3.0%
error	23	9.7%
fussy	18	7.6%
refused	45	19.0%
sleep	12	5.1%
vocalize	2	.8%
vomit	1	.4%
ok	122	51.5%
Group Total	237	100.0%

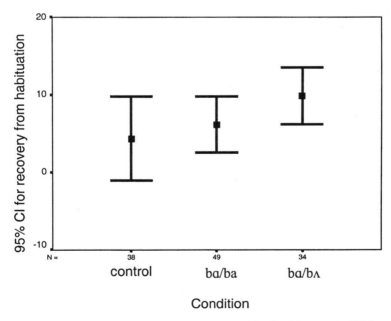

FIG. 5.2. Recovery from habituation as measured by the difference in #HAS during the first postshift minute and the last preshift minute.

was now observed for the control group. Nevertheless the perceptual dominance of the F_1 over the F_2 manipulations persists. In fact, the significance
level for the contrast between the control group and the [bɑ] vs. [ba] group
was only $p < 0.532$, whereas between the control group and the [bɑ] vs. [bʌ]
group the level was $p < 0.087$.

The Second Six Months of Life. Although the perceptual anisotropy for
the low back region of the vowel space was confirmed by the results, there
still is the possibility of an artifact due to the influence that F_1 has on the
overall intensity of vowels produced by serial speech synthesizer. In fact,
the F_1 shift associated with [bɑ] vs. [bʌ] has an impact of about 8 dB on the
vowel intensities, whereas the F_2 shift corresponding to [bɑ] vs. [ba] difference introduces only a 3.4 dB change in intensity. Adult listeners are known
to compensate for the intensity fluctuations introduced by F_1 variations in
natural vowels. They tend to perceive the speaker's effort, rather than the
vowel's physical intensity (Ladefoged & McKinney, 1963). However, if this is
an acquired behavior it is possible that the prelinguistic infant may not yet
have learned to disregard intensity differences, in which case the infant's
responses may simply reflect fluctuations in the vowels' intrinsic intensity
instead of the intended target dimension, F_1. To examine this possibility, the
vowel discrimination experiments were repeated using an equivalent set of
stimuli, this time generated by a parallel speech synthesizer. In addition, to
investigate the effect of developmental changes, a new group of infants in
the age range 6 to 12 months was studied. This also allowed us to use the
head-turn procedure to assess the infant's differential performance on both
F_1 and F_2. The stimuli used in the perception test are listed in Table 5.2. V_{00}
was the reference vowel sound (background) and the variants were named
V_{11}, V_{21}, and V_{31}. F_1 was lowered by 1.8 Bark for V_{11}, relative to the reference
vowel V_{00}. Between V_{00} and V_{21} F_2 was increased by 2.0 Bark and the difference between V_{00} and V_{31} includes both a 1.8 Bark lowering of F_1 and a 2.0
Bark increase in F_2.

Before the test phase, the infants went through a conditioning phase in
which they were acquainted with the procedure. The stimuli in the conditioning phase involved larger changes in F_1 and F_2 frequencies ($\Delta F_1 = 2.8$
bark; $\Delta F_2 = 3.0$ bark) than those to be used in the test proper. During the
conditioning phase the reference vowel, V_{00}, was presented against a target
vowel that differed from the reference in both F_1 (2.8 bark lower) and F_2 (3.0
bark higher). In this phase, all trials were test trials. To proceed to the criterion phase, the infants were requested to produce three consecutive correct positive discriminations. Two targets were used in the criterion phase.
One of the targets had a lower F_1 than reference vowel, V_{00}, and the other
differed from the reference by a higher F_2. The criterion phase included
both *control* and *test* trials. The criterion was defined as 7 correct responses

TABLE 5.2
Formant Frequency Specifications and Approximate IPA Symbols for the Vowel-Like Stimuli Used
in the Tests

Stimulus	IPA	F_1	F_2	F_3	F_4
V_{00}	ə	733	1067	2467	3200
V_{11}	ʌ	503	1067	2467	3200
V_{21}	a	733	1467	2467	3200
V_{31}	ɐ	503	1467	2467	3200

Note. cf. Fig. 5.1

(both in control and in test trials) out of 8 consecutive trials. The condition phase was run with 129 infants. Of these, 83 (64.3%) met the requirement to proceed to the criterion phase. A total of 30 infants (37%) went through the criterion phase and qualified for the test phase. Finally, data could be collected from 29 Swedish infants (one infant dropped out from the test phase) in the age range 6 to 12 months.

The results of this experiment are displayed in Fig. 5.3, where the average head-turns and the corresponding 95% confidence intervals are displayed for the false alarms (catch-trials) and for each of the target vowels involving changes in F_1, in F_2, or in both F_1 and F_2. The data were treated as a

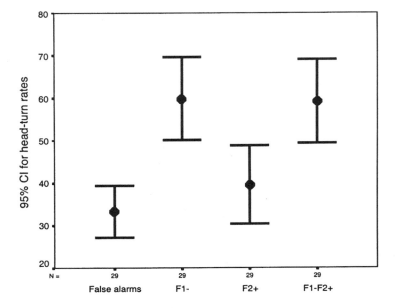

FIG. 5.3. Confidence intervals for the average head-turn rates observed for the different type of stimuli.

TABLE 5.3
Vowel Contrasts and Respective Significance Levels of Discrimination

Contrast	F(1,28)	Significance
V_{11} vs. V_{00}	23.574	.000
V_{21} vs. V_{00}	1.603	.216
V_{31} vs. V_{00}	19.958	.000

set of repeated measures, in which each subject's performance on V_{11}, V_{21}, and V_{31} was compared to the false alarm rates produced when listening to the reference vowel, V_{00}. The analysis of variance revealed a very significant overall effect of the formant manipulations [$F_{(3,84)} = 12.709$, $p < 0.000$]. An assessment of the within-subjects contrasts between the responses to each of the target vowel stimuli and the reference gave the following results (Table 5.3). In addition, the contrast between the discrimination levels for V_{11} and V_{21} also revealed a very significant difference [$F_{(1,28)} = 17.752$, $p < .000$], confirming the advantage of the F_1 changes against F_2. Thus, it appears that, everything else being equal, in this region of the vowel space, a change in F_1 is perceptually much more salient for the infants than a change in F_2.

Is the Infant's Vowel Space Anisotropic? The perceptual asymmetry reported earlier might be associated with the particular region of the vowel space that was explored. There is the possibility that the reference vowel's proximity to the low-back border of the vowel space might have an impact on the discrimination performance of the infants. To answer this question, other regions of the vowel space have to be analyzed to establish whether or not the observed asymmetry still is observed in those regions. To help us evaluate the generality of our finding, Kuhl submitted the vowel discrimination data from the American/Swedish study (Kuhl, Williams, Lacerda, Stevens, & Lindblom, 1992) to an analysis of the errors committed by the infants, to expose possible asymmetries in the infant's discrimination of F_1 and F_2 differences. Her analysis (Kuhl, personal communication, November, 1992) indicated that all groups of infants had poorer discrimination for the variants along the F_2 vector than along the F_1, although the difference only reached statistic significance for the Swedish infants listening to both the Swedish /y/ [$F_{(1,15)} = 7.3$, $p < 0.016$] and to the American /i/ [$F_{(1,15)} = 14.78$, $p < 0.002$].

To investigate further this apparent perceptual asymmetry, a new study was carried out using a schwa vowel as reference. The paradigm was again the head-turn procedure and the stimuli were produced by a parallel speech synthesizer. In the conditioning phase, the infants were to discriminate the reference schwa vowel W_{00} (see Table 5.4) from two other vowels. One of the target vowels differed from the reference by a 3 Bark increase in F_2 and

TABLE 5.4
Formant Frequencies of the Vowels Used in the Perception Tests

Vowel		F_1	F_2	F_3	F_4
W_{00}	Ref	500	1500	2700	3200
W_{01}	F_{2-}	500	1290	2700	3200
W_{21}	F_{1-}	390	1500	2700	3200
W_{41}	F_{2+}	500	1750	2700	3200
W_{61}	F_{1+}	610	1500	2700	3200

the other differed from the reference by a 2 Bark decrease in F_2 plus a 2 Bark increase in F_1. In the criterion phase, there were four variant vowels and the differences between these variants and the reference schwa vowel was reduced to 2 Bark only. Each of these variants differed from the reference by a ±2 Bark shift in either F_1 or F_2. For the test phase the stimuli had the same structure as that of the criterion phase, except that the shift was only of ±1 Bark. The full set of stimuli used in the test phase is given in Table 5.4.

An initial group of 134 infants participated in the condition phase. Of these, 84 (63%) infants qualified to proceed to the criterion phase but two of them dropped out before going through criterion phase. Of the remaining 82 subjects, 30 (36%) met both the criterion and successfully completed the test phase. Their age range extended from 6 to 12 months. The results of this perception test are displayed in Fig. 5.4. The ordinate shows the percentage of average head turns produced in response to the different kinds of stimuli. The corresponding 95% confidence intervals are displayed by the error bars. The labels on the ordinate indicate the variation in the F_1 and F_2 relative to the reference schwa vowel. The overall difference in performance for all the stimuli was very significant [$F_{(4,26)} = 6.903$, $p < 0.001$]. The within-subjects contrasts between the responses to each of the variants and to the schwa vowel also reached significance for all but the F_2+ contrast (Table 5.5). Although in this case the magnitude of the formant deviations relative to the reference vowel was only 1 Bark, there still is an asymmetry in the processing of F_1 and F_2 manifested by the systematically lower significance levels associated with F_2 manipulations. The asymmetry is particularly clear for the contrasts involving increases in F_1 and F_2.

In summary, these studies clearly indicate that the Swedish infants' perceptual space is more sensitive to changes along the F_1 dimension than for F_2.

Integrating the Data Into a Theoretical Framework

Perceptual Aspects. In line with the assumption that auditory sensitivity may bias the initial selection of speech sound systems, we attempted to investigate how these vowel discrimination data might predict the structure of nat-

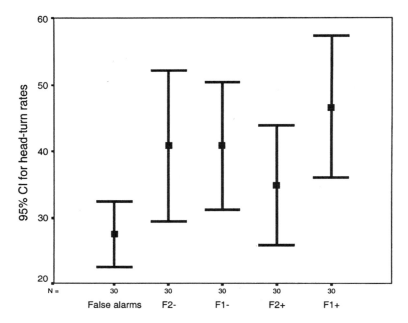

FIG. 5.4. Confidence intervals for the average head-turns generated by the different stimuli.

TABLE 5.5
Formant Frequencies of the Vowels Used in the Perception Tests

Contrast	Ref.	F(1,29)	Significance
W_{01} vs. W_{00}	F_{2-}	6.351	.017
W_{21} vs. W_{00}	F_{1-}	10.325	.003
W_{41} vs. W_{00}	F_{2+}	3.589	.068
W_{61} vs. W_{00}	F_{1+}	15.326	.001

ural vowel systems. Using the available data, we estimated areas of discrimination in the neighborhood of the [ɑ] and [ʌ] vowels used in the perceptual experiments. We also used the data in Kuhl et al. (1992) to estimate the asymmetries in F_1 and F_2 discrimination in the neighborhood of an /y/ vowel. The overall results are displayed in Fig. 5.5. The four filled circles indicate the locations of /i/, /u/, /ɑ/, and /a/ in that space. The ellipses are estimates of equal discrimination contours for d' = 0.5. This discrimination sensitivity leads to rather plausible vowel systems when used to infer the perceptual partitioning of the vowel space. Predictions based on the direct application of the discrimination contours suggest that the vowel space may be partitioned in more levels along the high–low dimension than along the front–back dimension. In ad-

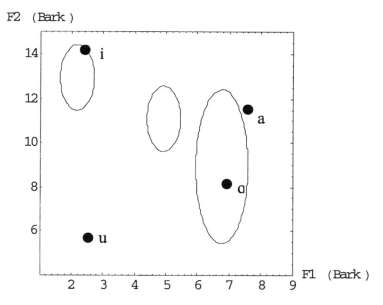

FIG. 5.5. Estimated iso-discrimination contours (d' = 0.5). The filled circles indicate the locations of /i/, /u/, /ɑ/, /a/. Formant from Catford (1988, p. 161).

dition, the proportions of the axis of the discrimination ellipses obtained at different locations of the vowel space suggest that the perceptual room may be larger for front–back contrasts among high vowels than for contrasts in frontness involving low vowels. It is interesting, for instance, that Liljencrants and Lindblom's (1972) numerical simulations of vowel quality systems would be improved by including a perceptual asymmetry of this kind in their distance computations.

But our suggestion of a perceptual dominance of the high–low dimension is obviously difficult to prove experimentally because perception, in spite of its importance, is only one of the factors influencing the early development of speech categories. Production preferences and the ambient language's historical evolution are clearly factors that will have to be taken into account when describing the ontogenetic development.

From the typological perspective, this asymmetry is compatible with the available evidence. In natural vowel systems, the high–low dimension actually tends to accommodate more levels of phonological distinctions than the front–back dimension. Besides, front–back contrasts are often accompanied by "default" rounding of the back-vowel series, as if "pure frontness" needed to be underlined by rounding in order to increase perceptual distinction (Liljencrants & Lindblom, 1972; Maddieson, 1984). Thus, to the extent that the infants' vowel-discrimination performance can be taken as an indicator of the initial perceptual biases, we would expect languages to display just the kind of vowel typology that they indeed do.

To be sure, although the observed patterns in natural vowel systems are compatible with the perceptual asymmetries already described, perceptual salience is clearly not the only criterion influencing natural sound systems. Clicks, for instance, are apparently salient for young infants (Best, McRoberts, & Sithole, 1988) but do not seem to be included in natural sound systems to the extent that their relative perceptual salience would suggest. As pointed out by Lindblom (1990), a possible reason for the rather low frequency of occurrence of clicks in natural sound systems may indeed be due to the relatively high articulatory costs involved in their production. However, as far as the partition of the vowel space is concerned, the domination of the high–low dimension seems to emerge as a natural consequence of both articulatory and perceptual factors. Because vowels are "low cost" speech sounds, easy to produce but difficult to target, perceptual tuning may play a relatively larger role in this class of sounds.

Articulatory and Interactive Aspects. Within a framework of multisensory development, this dominance of F_1 over F_2 makes good sense and is also compatible with production and interaction data underlying the effect of the perceptual asymmetry. Davis and MacNeilage (1994, 1995) indicate, for instance, that young infants display a higher degree of articulatory precision along the open–close vocalic dimension than along the front–back dimension and suggest that this may be a consequence of the infant's tongue following passively the jaw movements. To address the question of how the vocalic output may be related to the young infant's articulatory abilities we put together a crude acoustic–articulatory model of the young infant's vocal tract. To allow direct comparisons with adult data, we created an upscaled model where the infant's vocal tract is mapped onto an equivalent 17 cm acoustic tube comprised of 20 tube sections (Fant, 1960). The proportions between pharynx and mouth cavity characteristic of the human infant at different ages were preserved in the model. Also, to generate a crude approximation of the jaw movement, the infant's jaw was represented by two segments, one corresponding to the ramus and the other to the body of the mandible. At this stage of the model development, we simply assumed that the body would be 2.3 times longer than the ramus[4] and that the tongue would rest on the mandible, lying level with the teeth. Thus, our calculations were carried out for a tongue with no degrees of freedom.

---

[4]The lengths of the body and the ramus were estimated from an adult skull. The body length was obtained by extending a line along the base of the teeth, from the lower incisors to intersection with the back of the ramus; the ramus length was measured from this intersection up to the top condylar process. These proportions will have to be subsequently readjusted to match actual anatomic data from infants.

A pharyngeal constriction arises in this model because lowering of the jaw involves a backward swing of the ramus, as illustrated by the right panels in Fig. 5.6.

The results of the model calculations are shown in Fig. 5.7. The top panels display the formant path on a $F_1 \times F_2$ plane obtained for jaw openings when the position of the larynx is high, corresponding to an infant's vocal tract. The bottom panels display the paths resulting from the same jaw opening gesture but with a lower larynx position, as in the adult vocal tract. As indicated by this crude model, identical jaw opening gestures lead to different phonetic consequences depending on the length of the pharynx. In accordance with the observations by Davis and MacNeilage (1995), when the length of the pharynx is short, the model predicts that opening gestures with the tongue locked to the jaw generates series of vowels with constant

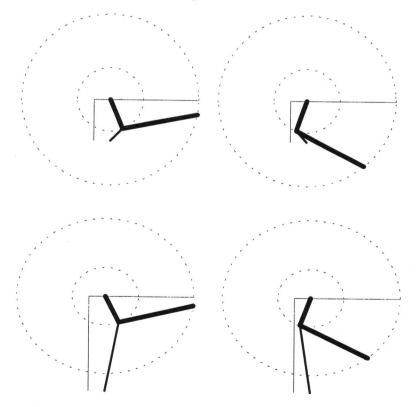

FIG 5.6. Model representation of jaw movements. Configurations for the maximum closure (left panels) and maximum opening (right panels) computed by the model. The top row represents the schematic jaw movement for a young infant. The bottom represents the movements of an adult jaw. The jaw movements are identical except for the lowering of the larynx.

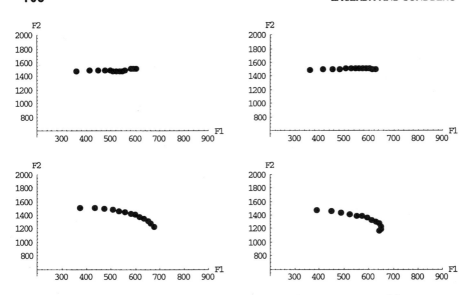

FIG. 5.7. Formant trajectories produced by identical jaw openings, at different pharyngeal lengths. The length of the pharynx is relative to the ramus length (top left, 1.3 the ramus; top right, 1.5, ramus; bottom left, 2.3 ramus; bottom right, 3.3 ramus).

F_2, while F_1 is directly related to the degree of jaw aperture. In contrast, when the larynx reaches its adult position (e.g., Aronson, 1990, p. 40), the same jaw opening movement leads to formant trajectories involving both F_1 and F_2 changes (see bottom panels in Fig. 5.7). These model predictions are interesting also in the context of adult judgments of vocalic sounds produced by young infants. In fact, these predictions are supported by data reported by Lacerda and Ichijima (1995). The authors asked a group of nonexpert Japanese and Swedish students of Phonetics (basic level) to estimate the tongue positions that presumably had been used by two Japanese infants to produce a random sample of 107 vowel-like sounds. The vowel-like portions of the infants' utterances were selected from a series of 30-minute sessions recorded every other week and covering an age range from 17 to 78 weeks. The students' task was to mark the tongue position for each vocalization in a height by frontness pseudo-articulatory space, with 5 levels in each dimension. Figure 5.8 displays contours reflecting the level of agreement across adult subjects, when judging vowel-like sounds produced before and after 8 months of age. The contours indicate that untrained adult listeners tend to have more differentiated height than frontness judgments when listening to vowel-like sounds produced by infants under 8 months of age. In addition, considering that adults do change the phonetic characteristics of the speech they direct to infants in face-to-face conversational situations,

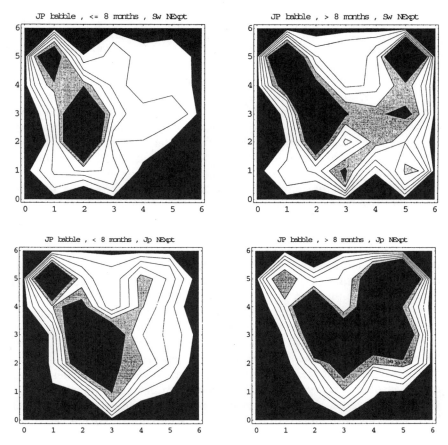

FIG. 5.8. Distribution of adult estimates of the tongue height and frontness used by two babbling Japanese infants. The results were pooled for the samples obtained before and after 8 months of age.

the infant is virtually "constrained" into converging toward its ambient language (Kuhl et al., 1997; Sundberg, 1998).

CONCLUSIONS

The speech perception data reported here support the notion that vowel contrasts conveyed by F_1 are perceptually more salient than contrasts generated by equal shifts in F_2. On the basis of these data, it may be expected that, when everything else is equal, infants have a bias toward high–low vowel contrasts. The dominance of this dimension is further underlined by formant measurements of vowel-like sounds produced by infants showing a higher degree of precision along the opening degree dimension than along the front–back dimension (Davis & MacNeilage, 1995). The bias toward F_1 dominance relative to F_2 becomes even stronger as their data is linked to the predictions of the acoustic–articulatory model outlined earlier in this chapter. In fact, the model suggests that opening and closing movements of the jaw during early infancy impact mainly on F_1 values, due to the infant's short pharyngeal length. The bias toward F_1 dominance becomes even stronger when the adult–infant interaction is taken into account. In data presented by Lacerda and Ichijima (1995), the adult judgments of infants' tongue body positions tend to be more consistent along the opening degree dimension than along frontness. As this interactive component is added to the infant's perceptual and articulatory biases, an overall picture of dominance of the high–low contrasts emerges.

In a very broad perspective, it may be speculated that the cumulative effect of these relatively small factors may eventually appear both as long-term determinants of the early stages of language development and even of the dominance of high–low contrasts observed in natural languages. If language acquisition is seen as a specialization process in the context of the infant's general development, biases like those mentioned earlier will influence the selection of vowel contrasts to be included in the infant's repertoire. And the plasticity of the infant's developing representational system further suggests that the establishment of links across different perceptual modalities may emerge from such recurrent, or otherwise salient intermodal associations. Eventually, the information pressure imposed on the young language learner and the system's plasticity will override the initial biases and allow the infant to restructure the perceptual space. Yet, it still is tempting to speculate that a possible impact of such initial biases may have contributed to the popularity of high–low contrasts in vowel systems, giving a biological perspective to the Prague School's notion of contrast.

REFERENCES

Aronson, A. (1990). *Clinical voice disorders*. New York: Thieme Inc.

Best, C., McRoberts, G., & Sithole, N. (1988). Examination of perceptual reorganization for nonnative speech contrasts: Zulu click discrimination by English-speaking adults and infant. *Journal of Experimental Psychology: Human Perception and Performance, 14*, 345–360.

Castro-Caldas, A., Petersson, K. M., Reis, A., Stone-Elander, S., & Ingvar, M. (1998). The illiterate brain: Learning to read and write during childhood influences the functional organization of the adult brain. *Brain, 121*, 1053–1063.

Catford, J. (1988). *A practical introduction to phonetics*. Oxford, England: Oxford University Press.

Davis, B., & MacNeilage, P. (1994). Organization of babbling: A case study. *Language and Speech, 37*, 341–355.

Davis, B., & MacNeilage, P. (1995). The articulatory basis of babbling. *Journal of Hearing and Speech Research, 38*, 1199–1211.

Diehl, R., & Kluender, K. (1987). On the categorization of speech sounds. In S. Harnard (Ed.), *Categorical perception: The groundwork of cognition* (pp. 226–253). Cambridge, England: Cambridge University Press.

Fant, G. (1960). *Acoustic theory of speech production.* The Hague: Mouton.

Fowler, C., (1986). An event approach to the study of speech perception from a direct-realist perspective. *Journal of Phonetics, 14*, 3–28.

Jusczyk, P. (1985). The high amplitude sucking technique as a methodological tool in speech perception research. In G. Gottlieb & N. Krasnegor (Eds.), *Measurement of audition and vision in the first year of postnatal life: A methodological overview* (pp. 195–221). Norwood, NJ: Ablex.

Jusczyk, P., & Aslin, R. (1995). Infant's detection of sound patterns of words in fluent speech. *Cognitive Psychology, 29*, 1–23.

Jusczyk, P., Bertoncini, J., Bijeljac-Babic, R., Kennedy, L., & Mehler, J. (1990). The role of attention in speech perception by young infants. *Cognitive Development, 5*, 265–286.

Kluender, K., Lotto, A., Holt, L., & Bloedel, S. (1998). Role of experience for language-specific functional mappings of vowel sounds. *Journal of the Acoustical Society of America, 104*, 3568–3582.

Kuhl, P. (1985). Methods in the study of infant speech perception. In G. Gottlieb & N. Krasnegor (Eds.), *Measurement of audition and vision in the first year of postnatal life: A methodological overview* (pp. 223–251). Norwood, NJ: Ablex.

Kuhl, P., Andruski, J., Chistovich, I., Chistovich, L., Kozhevnikova, E., Ryskina, V., Stolyarova, E., Sundberg, U., & Lacerda, F. (1997). Cross-language analysis of phonetic units in language addressed to infants. *Science, 277*, 684–686.

Kuhl, P., Williams, K., Lacerda, F., Stevens, K., & Lindblom, B. (1992). Linguistic experience alters phonetic perception in infants by 6 months of age. *Science, 255*, 606–608.

Lacerda, F. (1992a). Young infants' discrimination of confusable speech signals. In M. E. Schouten (Ed.), *The auditory processing of speech: From sounds to words* (pp. 229–238). Berlin: Mouton.

Lacerda, F. (1992b). Young infants prefer high/low vowel contrasts *(Tech. Rep. 10)*. Department of Information Theory, Chalmers University of Technology, Göteborg, 75–78.

Lacerda, F. (1993a, May). Dominance of sonority contrasts in young infants' vowel perception. *125th Meeting of the Acoustical Society of America*, Ottawa, Canada.

Lacerda, F. (1993b). Sonority contrasts dominate young infants' vowel perception. *PERILUS* XVII, Stockholm University, 55–63.

Lacerda, F., & Ichijima, T. (1995). Adult judgements of infant vocalizations. In K. Elenius & P. Branderud (Eds.), *Proceedings of the ICPhS 95* (Vol. 1, pp. 142–145). Stockholm.

Ladefoged, P., & McKinney, N. (1963). Loudness, sound pressure and sub-glottal pressure. *Journal of the Acoustical Society of America, 35*, 454–460.

Liberman, A., Cooper, F., Shankweiler, D., & Studdert-Kennedy, M. (1967). Perception of the speech code. *Psychological Review, 74*, 431–461.

Liberman, A., & Mattingly, I. (1985). The motor theory of speech perception revised. *Cognition, 21*, 1–36.

Liljencrants, J., & Lindblom, B. (1972). Numerical simulation of vowel quality systems: The role of perceptual contrast. *Language 48*, 839–862.

Lindblom, B. (1990). On the notion of 'possible speech sound'. *Journal of Phonetics, 18*, 135–152.

Maddieson, I. (1984). *Patterns of sound.* Cambridge, England: Cambridge University Press.

Merzenich, M. (1998). Long-term change of mind. *Science, 282*, 1062–1063.

Miller, J., & Liberman, A. (1979). Some effects of later-occurring information on the perception of stop consonant and semivowel. *Perception & Psychophysics, 25*, 457–465.

Pisoni, D., Aslin, R., Perey, A., & Hennessy, B. (1982). Some effects of laboratory training on identification and discrimination of voicing contrasts in stop consonants. *Journal of Experimental Psychology: Human Perception and Performance, 8*, 297–314.

Stevens, K. (1972). Quantal nature of speech. In E. David & P. Denes (Eds.), *Human communication: A unified view* (pp. 67–84). New York: McGraw Hill.

Sundberg, U. (1998). Mother tongue—Phonetic aspects of infant-directed speech. *PERILUS XXI*. Doctoral dissertation. Stockhom: Stockholm University.

Werker, J., & Tees, R. (1984). Cross-language speech perception: Evidence for perceptual reorganization during the first year of life. *Infant Behavior and Development, 7,* 49–63.

Werner, L. (1992). Interpreting developmental psychoacoustics. In L. Werner & E. Rubel (Eds.), *Developmental psychoacoustics* (pp. 47–88). Washington, DC: American Psychological Association.

Zohary, E., Celebrini, S., Britten, K., & Newsome, W. (1994). Neuronal plasticity that underlies improvement in perceptual performance. *Science, 263,* 1289–1292.

6

Speech, Language, and Developmental Change

Patricia K. Kuhl
University of Washington, Seattle

NATURE, NURTURE AND DEVELOPMENTAL CHANGE

In the 1960s, there was a historical confrontation between a strong nativist and a strong learning theorist. Chomsky's (1957) reply to Skinner's (1957) *Verbal Behavior* had just been published, reigniting the debate on the nature of language. On Chomsky's (1965, 1981) nativist view, universal rules encompassing the grammars and phonologies of all languages were innately specified. Language input served to trigger the appropriate subset of rules, and developmental change in language ability was viewed as biological growth akin to other bodily organs, rather than learning. In the Skinnerian view, language was explicitly learned. Language was brought about in the child through a process of feedback and reinforcement (Skinner, 1957).

Both views made assumptions about three critical parameters: the biological preparation that infants bring to the task of language learning; the nature of language input; and the nature of developmental change. Chomsky asserted, through the "poverty of the stimulus" argument, that language input to the child is greatly underspecified. Critical elements are missing; thus the necessity for innately specified information. Skinner viewed speech as simply another operant behavior, shaped through parental feedback and reinforcement like all other behaviors.

In the decades that have passed since these positions were developed, the debate has been played out at the syntactic, semantic, and phonological levels of language. In this chapter, I concentrate on the phonetic level, because it provides both a strong test of the opposing views and is amenable to detailed empirical manipulations.

Speech is readily accessible. One can study infants' perceptual abilities at birth to assess the initial state of their knowledge about speech perception, and examine at various points in development the results of nature's experiment—infants from various cultures who have been raised listening to vastly different languages. Adults from different cultures can be tested to assess the endstate of learning. Moreover, nonhuman animals can be tested to examine evolutionary constraints on sound perception and production. These studies have produced a great deal of data about the initial state of infant speech perception, the nature of developmental change that infants undergo in speech perception as they are exposed to a specific language, and the agent of developmental change, language input to the child.

The new data, demonstrating the effects of early language experience on infants, suggest a theoretical revision. At age one—prior to the time infants begin to master higher levels of language, such as sound-meaning correspondences, contrastive phonology, and grammatical rules—infants' perceptual and perceptual–motor systems have been altered by linguistic experience. Phonetic perception has changed dramatically to conform to the native-language pattern, and language-specific speech production has emerged. According to the model developed here, this developmental change is caused by a complex "mapping" of linguistic input. This account is different in two respects from traditional views: (a) Language input is not conceived of as triggering innately provided options, nor as parameter setting, and (b) the kind of developmental change that occurs does not involve traditional Skinnerian learning, in which change is brought about external through feedback and reinforcement.

CONCEPTUAL DISTINCTIONS: "DEVELOPMENT" AND "LEARNING"

In human language, as well as in the development of species-typical behavior in animals, the relation between "development" (processes that cause change over time independent of experience) and "learning" (processes that depend on activity/experience of some kind) is key to understanding the contribution of the organism and the environment. Are development and learning independent, and if not, how do they interact?

Four alternatives are conceptually illustrated in Fig. 6.1. Development and learning could be thought of as completely separable processes (Fig. 6.1 A). Development follows a strict maturational course, and learning neither follows from nor leads to changes in the preestablished course of development. Alternatively, the two processes could be viewed as identical, so inseparable that we cannot pull them apart, even conceptually (Fig. 6.1 B).

Conceptual relations between development and learning

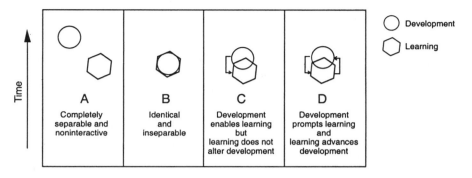

FIG. 6.1. Conceptual relations between development and learning (from Kuhl, 1999).

More commonly, development and learning are thought of as separate and distinguishable processes that interact in one way or another (Fig. 6.1 C–D). Developmental psychologists, neuroscientists, and neurobiologists largely agree that interaction occurs between development and learning (Bonhoeffer & Shatz, 1998; Doupe, 1998; Faneslow & Rudy, 1998; Gopnik & Meltzoff, 1997; Kuhl, 1994). At issue, however, is exactly how the two systems interact, and particularly whether the interaction between development and learning is bidirectional.

Among the interactionist views, one model is that development enables learning, but that learning does not change the course of development, which unfolds more or less on its own timetable (Fig. 6.1 C). Learning is seen as capitalizing on the achievements of development, and cannot occur unless a certain level of development has been achieved. The interaction is unidirectional, however. Development is not impacted by learning. In classical developmental psychology, this position is closest to the view of Piaget (1954). In modern neurobiology, the notion that there are constraints on learning, that development both prepares the organism and sets limits on learning, is consistent with this model (see Marler, 1974, and Doupe, 1998). Greenough and Black's (1992) "experience-expectant" plasticity, wherein changes in neural development are thought to precede and prepare an organism to react to a reliably present environmental stimulus, provides a detailed example of this model. In each of these cases, development is conceived of as both enabling and limiting learning, but learning does not alter the course of development.

There is an alternative interactionist view. This model describes development and learning as mutually affecting one another (Fig. 6.1 D). Development enables and even prompts learning, and learning in turn advances development. This view is closest to that developed by Vygotsky (1979). Vygotsky's theory, the zone of proximal development (ZPD), described development at two levels. One was the infant's actual developmental level, the level already achieved. The second was the level that was just within reach. The ZPD was the difference between the two. In Vygotsky's view, environmental stimulation slightly in advance of current development (in the ZPD) resulted in learning and, when this occurred, learning prompted development. A recent theory proposed by developmental psychologists to account for a wide variety of cognitive and linguistic tasks, also provides a detailed model of mutual interaction between development and learning (Gopnik & Meltzoff, 1997; see also Gopnik, Meltzoff, & Kuhl, 1999).

In linguistic theory, Chomsky's classic view that the growth of language is largely determined by a maturational process, fits Model C. Experience plays a role, but it is seen as triggering prespecified options, or as setting innately determined parameters, rather than creating the form of language in any fundamental way. In contrast, the data reviewed here at the phonetic level of language come closer to the mutual interaction of Model D. In the model of speech development I describe, language input plays a significant role. Language input is mapped in a complex process that appears to code its subtle details. Input thus goes beyond simply triggering a prespecified option. Moreover, early mapping of the perceptual regularities of language input is argued to allow infants to recognize words and phrases, thus advancing development.

In summary, there is a great deal of support for interactionist views (Models C and D) over noninteractionist views (Models A and B). Although the relations between learning and development may differ across species and systems, there is an emerging consensus across diverse disciplines including neurobiology, psychology, linguistics, and neuroscience, that development and learning are not separate and distinct entities. The form of the interaction between the two remains a question, with a cutting-edge issue being whether (and how) learning can alter development. The model I here propose on the basis of recent research on speech development goes some distance toward addressing this issue.

DEVELOPMENTAL CHANGE IN SPEECH PERCEPTION

One of the puzzles in language development is to explain the orderly transitions that all infants go through during development. Infants the world over achieve certain milestones in linguistic development at roughly the same time, regardless of the language they are exposed to. Moreover, developmental change can also include cases in which infants' early skills exceed their later ones. Explaining these transitions is one of the major goals of developmental linguistic theory.

One of these transitions occurs in *speech perception*. At birth, infants discern differences between all the phonetic units used in the world's languages (Eimas, Miller, & Jusczyk, 1987). All infants show these universal skills, regardless of the language environment in which they are being raised. Data on nonhuman animals' perception of speech suggest that the ability to partition the basic building blocks of speech is one delivered by evolution (Kuhl, 1991a).

When do infants from different cultures begin to diverge? Infants' initial "language-general" abilities are highly constrained just one year later. By the end of the first year, infants fail to discriminate foreign-language contrasts they once discriminated (Werker & Tees, 1984), resembling the adult pattern. Adults often find it difficult to perceive differences between sounds not used to distinguish words in their native language. Adult native speakers of Japanese, for example, have great difficulty discriminating American English /r/ and /l/ (Best, 1993; Strange, 1995), and American English listeners have great difficulty hearing the difference between Spanish /b/ and /p/ (Abramson & Lisker, 1970). Infants' abilities change over a 4-month period. A recent study in Japan shows, for example, that at 7 months of age Japanese infants respond to the /r-l/ distinction and are as accurate in perceiving it as American 7-month-old infants. By 11 months, Japanese infants' performance has declined, even though American infants at that same age have become better at discriminating the two sounds (Kuhl et al., submitted).

A similar transition occurs in *speech production*. Regardless of culture, all infants progress through a set of universal stages during the first year (Ferguson, Menn, & Stoel-Gammon, 1992). By the end of the first year, however, the utterances of infants reared in different countries begin to diverge, reflecting the ambient language (de Boysson-Bardies, 1993). In adulthood, the speech motor patterns that we initially learned contribute to our "accents" when attempting to speak another language.

These transitions in speech present one of the most intriguing problems in language acquisition. What causes these changes? The thesis developed here is that linguistic experience produces a special kind of developmental change. Language input alters the brain's processing of speech, resulting in the creation of complex mental maps for speech. The mapping "warps" underlying acoustic dimensions, altering perception in such a way as to highlight native-language categories while making foreign-language categories less discriminable. This mapping is not like traditional learning. It does not depend on external reinforcement, and appears to be unconscious and long-lasting.

LANGUAGE EXPERIENCE ALTERS PERCEPTION

Language experience produces a mapping that alters phonetic perception. A research finding that helps explain how this occurs is called the "perceptual magnet effect." It is observed when tokens perceived as exceptionally good representatives of a phonetic category (prototypes) are used in tests of speech perception (Kuhl, 1991b). Our results show that phonetic prototypes function like *perceptual magnets* for other sounds in the category. When listeners hear a phonetic prototype and attempt to discriminate it from sounds that surround it in acoustic space, the prototype displays an attractor effect on the surrounding sounds (Fig. 6.2). It perceptually pulls other members of the category toward it, making it difficult to hear differences between the prototype and surrounding stimuli. Poor instances from the category (nonprototypes) do not function in this way. A variety of experimental tasks produce this result with both consonants and vowels (Iverson & Kuhl, 1995, 1996; Sussman & Lauckner-Morano, 1995). Other studies confirm listeners' skills in identifying phonetic prototypes and show that they are language specific (Kuhl, 1992; Miller, 1994; Willerman & Kuhl, 1996).

Developmental tests revealed that the perceptual magnet effect was exhibited by 6-month-old infants for the sounds of their native language (Kuhl, 1991b). Moreover, cross-language experiments demonstrated that the magnet effect is the product of linguistic experience (Kuhl, Williams, Lacerda, Stevens, & Lindblom, 1992). In the cross-language experiment, infants in the United States and Sweden were tested. The infants from both countries were tested with two vowel prototypes, an American English vowel prototype, /i/ (as in "peep"), and a Swedish vowel prototype, /y/ (as in "fye"). The

A

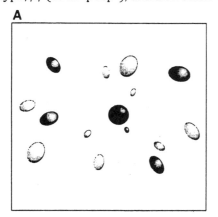

B

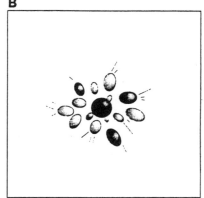

FIG. 6.2. The *perceptual magnet effect.* When a variety of sounds in a category surround the category prototype (A), they are perceptually drawn toward the prototype (B). The prototype appears to function like a magnet for other stimuli in the category (from Kuhl, 1998).

results demonstrated that the perceptual magnet effect in 6-month-old infants was affected by exposure to a particular language. American infants demonstrated the magnet effect only for the American English /i/; they treated the Swedish /y/ like a nonprototype. Swedish infants showed the opposite pattern, demonstrating the magnet effect for the Swedish /y/ and treating the American English /i/ as a nonprototype. This is the youngest age at which language experience has been shown to affect phonetic perception.

The perceptual magnet effect thus occurs prior to word learning. What this means is that in the absence of formal language understanding or use—before infants utter or understand their first words—infants' perceptual and perceptual–motor systems strongly conform to the characteristics of the ambient language. We previously believed that word learning caused infants to recognize that phonetic changes that they could hear, such as the change that Japanese infants perceived between /r/ and /l/, did not change the meaning of a word in their language. This discovery was thought to cause the change in phonetic perception. We now know that just the opposite is true. Language input sculpts the brain to create a perceptual system that highlights the contrasts used in the language, while deemphasizing those that do not, and this happens prior to word learning. The change in phonetic perception thus assists word learning, rather than the reverse.

Further tests on adults suggested that the magnet effect distorted perception to highlight sound contrasts in the native-language and that the mechanisms underlying categorical perception and the perceptual magnet effect differ (Iverson & Kuhl, 2000). Studies on the perception of the phonetic units /r/ and /l/ as in the words "rake" and "lake," illustrate this point. The /r–l/ distinction is one notoriously difficult for Japanese speakers and our studies sought to determine how adults from different cultures perceived these two sounds. To conduct the study, we used computer synthesized syllables beginning with /r/ and /l/, spacing them at equal physical intervals in a 2-dimensional acoustic grid (Iverson & Kuhl, 1996; Fig. 6.3 A). American listeners identified each syllable as beginning with either /r/ or /l/, rated its category goodness, and estimated the perceived similarity for all possible pairs of stimuli using a scale from 1 (*very dissimilar*) to 7 (*very similar*). Similarity ratings were scaled using multidimensional scaling (MDS) techniques. The results revealed that perception distorts physical space. The physical (acoustic) differences between pairs of stimuli were equal; however, perceived distance was "warped" (Fig. 6.3 B). The perceptual space around the best /r/ and the best /l/ was greatly reduced, as predicted by the perceptual magnet effect, while the space near the boundary between the two categories was expanded.

This experiment has now been done using Japanese monolingual listeners (Iverson, Kuhl, Yamada, Tohkura, & Stevens, submitted) and the results show a strong contrast in the way the /r–l/ stimuli are perceived by Ameri-

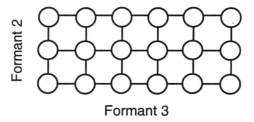

Formant 2

Formant 3

B. Perceptual World: Americans

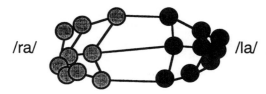

/ra/   /la/

C. Perceptual World: Japanese

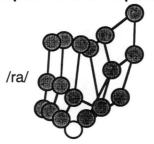

/ra/

FIG. 6.3. Physical (acoustic) versus perceptual distance. Consonant tokens of /r/ and /l/ were generated to be equally distant from one another in acoustic space (A). However, American listeners perceive perceptual space as shrunk near the best instances of /r/ (gray dots) and /l/ (black dots) and stretched at the boundary between the two (B). Japanese listeners' perceptual world differs dramatically; neither magnet effects nor a boundary between the two categories are seen (C) (from Kuhl, 1998).

can and Japanese adults (Fig. 6.3 C). Japanese adults hear almost all the sounds as /r/; there is no /l/ in Japanese. More striking is the complete absence of magnet and boundary effects in the Japanese MDS solution. The results suggested that linguistic experience results in the formation of *perceptual maps* specifying the perceived distances between stimuli. These maps increase internal category cohesion while maximizing the distinction between categories. The critical point for theory is that neither group perceives physical reality, the actual physical differences between sounds. For each language group, experience has altered perception to create a language-specific map of auditory similarities and differences, one that highlights the sound contrasts of the speaker's native language. These mental maps for speech are the front-end of the language mechanism. They filter language in a way that promotes semantic and syntactic analysis.

The theoretical position developed here is that the mental maps for speech are developed early in infancy, prior to the development of word acquisition. Infants are engaged in an active "mapping" process, one that has nothing to do with Skinnerian reinforcement, and also one not described by the selectionist view that innately specified options are either "maintained" or "lost" (Kuhl, 2000a). Our data suggest that infants' performance on native-language contrasts increases significantly between 7 and 11 months, providing evidence that the process does not involve "maintenance" (Kuhl et al., submitted). For example, American infants show significant improvement between 7 and 11 months on discrimination of /r/ and /l/, and Taiwanese infants show the same degree of improvement on /ɕ/ and /tɕʰ/, a contrast not phonemic in English. Perception of foreign contrasts shows a decline but one that is not always statistically significant (Kuhl et al., submitted). The primary process is thus argued to be the construction of mental maps for speech; the change in perception of foreign-language contrasts is a secondary process (Kuhl, 2000a).

On this view, infants' developing maps assist word acquisition. The collapsing of /r/ and /l/ into a single category makes it possible for Japanese infants to perceive their parents' productions of /r/–like and /l/–like sounds as one entity at 10 months, when the process of word acquisition begins. If they did not do so, it would presumably make it more difficult to map sound patterns onto objects and events. The view that phonetic mapping supports the recognition of higher order units is supported by data showing that infants use information about phonetic units to recognize word-like forms. Jusczyk and his colleagues show that by 9 months of age, infants prefer word patterns that are typical of the native language, which requires recognition of native-language phonetic units (Jusczyk, Friederici, Wessels, Svenkerud, & Jusczyk, 1993). Infants have also been shown capable of statistical learning and this requires phonetic-level awareness (Goodsitt, Morgan, & Kuhl, 1993; Saffran, Aslin, & Newport, 1996). Infants' mapping at the phonetic level is thus seen as assisting infants in "chunking" the sound stream into higher order units.

These studies indicate that during the first year of life, infants come to recognize the perceptual properties of their native language. In order to do this, infants must be mentally storing those properties in some form. This occurs in the absence of any formal instruction or reinforcement of the infant's behavior. In this sense, the "learning" that transpires is outside the realm of the historical versions of learning described by psychologists.

A THEORY OF SPEECH DEVELOPMENT

These findings have been incorporated in a 3-step theory of speech development, called the *Native Language Magnet* (NLM) model (Kuhl, 1994, 1998, 2000b). NLM describes infants' initial state as well as changes brought about by experience with language (Fig. 6.4). The model demonstrates how infants' developing native-language speech representations might alter both speech perception and production. The example developed here is for vowels, although the same principles apply to consonant perception.

Phase 1 describes infants' initial abilities. At birth, infants partition the sound stream into gross categories separated by natural auditory boundaries (Fig. 6.4 A). As shown, perceptual boundaries divide a hypothetical

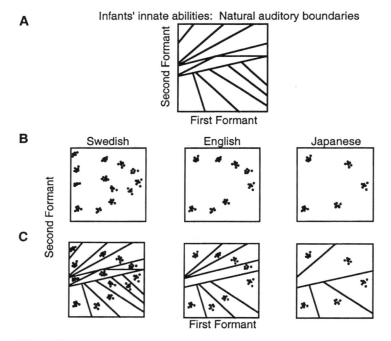

FIG. 6.4. The Native Language Magnet (NLM) model. (A): At birth, infants perceptually partition the acoustic space underlying phonetic distinctions in a language-universal way. They are capable of discriminating all phonetically relevant differences in the world's languages. (B): By 6 months of age, infants reared in different linguistic environments show an effect of language experience. Infants store incoming vowel information in memory in some form. The resulting representations (shown by the dots) are language-specific, and reflect the distributional properties of vowels in the three different languages. (C): After language-specific magnet effects appear, some of the natural boundaries that existed at birth "disappear." Infants now fail to discriminate foreign-language contrasts they once discriminated (from Kuhl, 1998).

vowel space, separating the vowels of all languages. According to NLM, infants' abilities at this stage do not depend on specific language experience. The boundaries initially structure perception in a phonetically relevant way. However, they are not due to a "language module." This notion is buttressed by the fact that these same perceptual boundary phenomena are exhibited in the same places in acoustic space by nonhuman animals (Kuhl, 1991a, 1999).

Phase 2 describes the vowel space at 6 months of age for infants reared in three very different language environments, Swedish, English, and Japanese (Fig. 6.4 B). By 6 months of age, infants show more than the innate boundaries shown in Phase 1. By 6 months, our calculations indicate that infants have heard hundreds of thousands of instances of particular vowels. According to NLM, infants represent this information in memory in some form. The distributional properties of vowels heard by infants being raised in Sweden, America, and Japan differ. As shown in Fig. 6.4 B, their stored representations also differ, reflecting these distributional differences. In each case, linguistic experience has produced stored representations that reflect the vowel system of the ambient language. Language-specific magnet effects, produced by the stored representations, are exhibited by infants at this stage.

Phase 3 shows how magnet effects recursively alter the initial state of speech perception. Magnet effects cause certain perceptual distinctions to be minimized (those near the magnet attractors) while others are maximized (those near the boundaries between two magnets). The consequence is that some of the boundaries that initially divided the space "disappear" as the perceptual space is reconfigured to incorporate a language's particular magnet placement (Fig. 6.4 C). Sensory perception has not changed; higher order memory and representational systems have altered infants' abilities. Magnet effects functionally erase certain boundaries—those relevant to foreign but not native languages. At this stage, a perceptual space once characterized by simple boundaries has been replaced by a warped space dominated by magnets.

Infants at 6 months have no awareness that sound units are used contrastively in language to name things. Yet the infant's perceptual system organizes itself to reflect language-specific phonetic categories. At the next stage in linguistic development, when infants acquire word meanings by relating sounds to objects and events in the world, the language-specific mapping that has already occurred should greatly assist this process.

NLM theory offers an explanation for the transition in speech perception. A developing magnet pulls sounds that were once discriminable toward it, making them less discriminable. Magnet effects should therefore developmentally precede changes in infants' perception of foreignlanguage contrasts; preliminary data indicate that they do (Werker & Polka, 1993).

The magnet effect also helps account for the results of studies on the perception of sounds from a foreign language by adults (Best, 1993; Flege, 1993). For example, NLM theory may help explain Japanese listeners' difficulty with American /r/ and /l/. The magnet effect for the Japanese /r/ category prototype (which is neither American /r/ nor /l/) will attract both /r/ and /l/, making the two sounds difficult for native-speaking Japanese people to discriminate. NLM theory argues that early experience established perceptual "filters" through which language passes. On this view, one's primary language will affect how other languages are perceived.

REINTERPRETING "CRITICAL PERIODS"

The traditional literature on critical periods views them as a strictly timed developmental process, independent of learning and other factors. The critical period thus defines a "window of opportunity" during which environmental stimulation is effective in producing developmental change. Once the window closes, environmental stimulation is no longer effective. Current studies show that the window can be stretched by a variety of factors (Doupe, 1998; Doupe & Kuhl, 1999), but the notion that the critical period is a process governed by maturation remains.

There is an alternative possibility. Later learning may be limited by an *interference* factor. For example, if learning "commits" neural structure in some way (e.g., NLM's argument that learning involves the creation of mental maps for speech), future learning is expected to be affected by this commitment. The mechanisms governing an organism's general ability to learn may not have changed. Rather, initial learning may result in a structure that reflects environmental input and, once committed, the learned structure may interfere with the processing of information that does not conform to the learned pattern. On this account, initial learning can alter future learning independent of a strictly timed period (see Gopnik, Meltzoff, & Kuhl, 1999 for examples in developmental cognition and theory of mind).

The interference view may account for some aspects of second language learning. When acquiring a second language, certain phonetic distinctions are notoriously difficult to master both in speech perception and production. Take the case of the /r–l/ distinction for native speakers of Japanese. Hearing the distinction and production it is very difficult for native speakers of Japanese. According to NLM, this is the case because exposure to Japanese early in life altered the Japanese infant's perceptual system, resulting in magnet effects for the Japanese phoneme /r/, but not for American English /l/ (which is not phonemic in Japanese). Once in place, the magnet effects appropriate for Japanese would not make it easy to process American English. Both American English /r/ and /l/ would be assimilated to

Japanese /r/. Thus, interference effects could make it much more difficult to acquire new phonetic categories later in life.

On this interference account, plasticity would be governed from a statistical standpoint. When additional input does not cause the overall statistical distribution to change substantially, the organism becomes less sensitive to input. Hypothetically, for instance, the infants' representation of the vowel /a/ might not change when the one millionth token of the vowel /a/ is heard. Plasticity might thus be independent of time, but dependent on the amount and varability provided by experience. At some time in the life of the organism one could conceive of a point where new input no longer alters the underlying distribution, and this could, at least in principle, define the end of the "critical period" for learning.

Early in life, interference effects are minimal and new categories can be acquired because input continues to revise the statistical distribution. It is interesting to note in this context that anecdotal evidence suggests that infants exposed to two languages do much better if each parent speaks one of the two languages, rather than both parents speaking both languages. This may be the case because it is easier to map two different sets of phonetic categories (one for each of the two languages) if there was some way to keep them perceptually separate. Males and females produce speech in different frequency ranges, and this could make it easier to maintain separation.

These two factors—a maturationally defined temporal window and initial learning that makes later learning more difficult—could both be operating to produce constraints on learning a second language later in life. If a maturational process induces "readiness" at a particular time, input that misses this timing could reduce learning. At the same time, an "interference" factor might provide an independent mechanism that contributes to the difficulty in readily learning a second language in adulthood.

THE PERCEPTUAL-MOTOR LINK: SPEECH PRODUCTION

Infants not only learn the perceptual properties of their native language, but become proficient speakers of the language. Once learned, our speaking patterns become difficult to alter. Speakers who learn a second language later in life, for example, produce it with an "accent" typical of their primary language. Most speakers of a second language would like to speak like a native speaker, without an accent, but this is difficult to do.

When do we adopt the speech patterns that will mark us as native speakers of a particular language? Developmental studies suggest that by 1 year of age language-specific patterns of speech production appear in infants' spontaneous utterances (de Boysson-Bardies, 1993; Vihman & de Boysson-Bardies, 1994). However, the fundamental capacity to reproduce the sound patterns one hears is in place much earlier. In a recent study, Kuhl and Meltzoff (1996) recorded infant utterances at 12-, 16-, and 20-weeks of age while the infants watched and listened to a video recording of a woman producing a vowel, either /al, /i/, or /u/. Infants watched the video for 5 minutes on each of three consecutive days. Infants' utterances were analyzed both perceptually (phonetic transcription) and instrumentally (computerized spectrographic analysis).

The results showed that there was developmental change in infants' vowel productions between 12- and 20-weeks of age. The areas of vowel space occupied by infants' /a/, /i/, and /u/ vowels become progressively more tightly clustered at each age, and by 20 weeks, a "vowel triangle" typical of that produced in every language of the world, had emerged in infants' own region of the vowel space (Fig. 6.5). This suggested the possibility that infants were listening to language and attempting to vocally imitate the sound patterns they heard (Kuhl & Meltzoff, 1996).

Direct evidence that infants were vocally imitating was also obtained in the study. By 20 weeks, infants were shown to reproduce the vowels they heard. Infants exposed to /a/ were more likely to produce /a/ than when exposed to either /i/ or /u/, similarly, infants exposed to either /i/ or /u/ were more likely to produce the vowel in that condition than when listening to either of the two alternate vowels. The total amount of exposure to a specific vowel in the laboratory was only 15 minutes; yet this was sufficient to influence infants' productions. If 15 minutes of laboratory exposure to a vowel is sufficient to influence infants' vocalizations, then listening to ambient language for weeks would be expected to provide a powerful influence on infants' production of speech. These data suggest that infants' stored representations of speech not only alter infant perception, but alter production as well, serving as auditory patterns that guide motor production. Stored

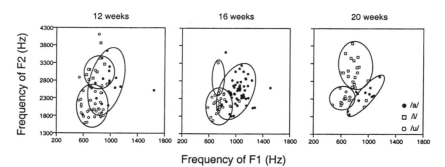

FIG. 6.5. The location of /a/, /i/, and /u/ vowels produced by 12-, 16-, and 20-week-old infants. Infants' vowel productions show progressively tighter clustering in vowel space over the 8-week period and reflect differences between the three vowel categories seen in adults' productions (from Kuhl & Meltzoff, 1996).

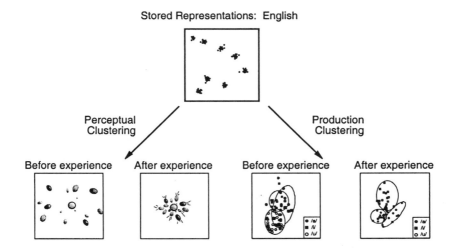

FIG. 6.6. Stored representations of native-language speech affect both speech perception, producing the perceptual clustering evidenced by the magnet effect, as well as speech production, producing the increased clustering seen in infants' vocalizations over time (from Kuhl & Meltzoff, 1997).

representations are thus viewed as the common cause for both the tighter clustering observed in infant vowel production and the tighter clustering observed in infant vowel perception (see Fig. 6.6).

This pattern of learning and self-organization, in which perceptual patterns stored in memory serve as guides for production, is strikingly similar to that seen in other domains involving auditory–perceptual learning, such as birdsong (Doupe, 1998; Doupe & Kuhl, 1999), and in visual–motor learning, such as gestural imitation (Meltzoff & Moore, 1977, 1994). In each of these cases, perceptual experience establishes a representation that guides sensorimotor learning. In the case of infants and speech, perception affects production in the earliest stages of language learning, reinforcing the idea that the speech motor patterns of a specific language are formed very early in life. This would also help explain the fact that speech motor patterns are difficult to alter when we attempt to learn a second language (Kuhl & Meltzoff, 1997).

POLYMODAL SPEECH REPRESENTATION

The link between perception and production can be seen in another experimental situation. Speech perception in adults is strongly affected by the sight of a talker's mouth movements during speech, indicating that our representational codes for speech contain both auditory and visual information. One of the most compelling examples of the polymodal nature of speech is auditory–visual illusions that result when discrepant information is sent to two separate modalities. One such illusion occurs when auditory information for /b/ is combined with visual information for /g/ (Green, Kuhl, Meltzoff, & Stevens, 1991; Kuhl, Tsuzaki, Tohkura, & Meltzoff, 1994; Massaro, 1987; McGurk & MacDonald, 1976). Perceivers report the phenomenal impression of an intermediate articulation (/da/ or /tha/) despite the fact that this information was not delivered to either sense modality. This is a very robust phenomenon and is readily obtained even when the information from the two modalities comes from different speakers, such as when a male voice is combined with a female face (Green et al., 1991). In this case, there is no doubt that the auditory and visual signals do not belong together. Yet the illusion is still unavoidable—our perceptual systems combine the multimodal information (auditory and visual) to give a unified percept.

Language experience affects this auditory–visual illusion. When native speakers watch and listen to incongruent audio–visual speech signals pronounced by a foreign speaker, they show increased auditory–visual effects; greater numbers of illusory responses occur (Kuhl et al., 1994; Sekiyama & Tohkura, 1993). The auditory information in foreign speech does not precisely match the stored representations of native-language speech. When this occurs, visual information may be relied on to a greater extent, reinforcing the idea that speech representations are polymodally mapped.

Young infants also appear to represent speech polymodally. Infants just 18 to 20 weeks old recognize auditory–visual correspondences for speech, akin to what we as adults do when we lipread; in these studies, infants looked longer at a face pronouncing a vowel that matched the vowel sound they heard rather than a mismatched face (Kuhl & Meltzoff, 1982). Young infants demonstrate knowledge about both the auditory and visual information contained in speech, supporting the notion that infants' stored speech representations contain information of both kinds.

NATURE OF LANGUAGE INPUT TO THE CHILD

The studies just reviewed attest to the impact of language input on infants. If language input produces change in both speech perception and production, we need to know a great deal more about it. How much and what kind of speech do infants hear?

Estimates indicate that a typical listening day for a 2-year-old includes 20,000–40,000 words (Chapman et al., 1992). Speech addressed to infants (often called *motherese* or *parentese*) is unique: It has a characteristic prosodic structure which includes a higher pitch, a slower tempo, and exaggerated intonation contours, and it is syntactically and semantically simplified. Research supports the idea that this speaking style is near universal in the speech of caretakers around the world and that infants prefer it (Fernald, 1985; Fernald & Kuhl, 1987). The motherese pattern of speech, with its higher pitch and expanded intonation contours, is attractive to infants, but may not be necessary for infant learning.

In new studies, we have uncovered another modification made by parents when addressing infants that may be much more important to infant learning. We examined natural language input at the phonetic level to infants in the United States, Russia, and Sweden (Kuhl et al., 1997). The study shows that across three very diverse languages, infant-directed speech exhibited a universal alteration of phonetic units when compared to adult-directed speech. Parents addressing their infants produced acoustically more extreme tokens of vowel sounds, resulting in a "stretching" of the acoustic space encompassing the vowel triangle (Fig. 6.7). A stretched vowel triangle not only makes speech more discriminable for infants, it highlights critical spectral parameters that allow speech to be produced by the child. The results suggest that at the phonetic level of language, linguistic input to infants provides exceptionally well-specified information about the units that form the building blocks for words.

A stretched vowel space is not necessary from the standpoint of the infant's capacity to distinguish vowels. The formant frequency changes from adult-directed to infant-directed speech were substantial and would clearly be registered by the infant auditory system. Previous data on infants' capacities to discern subtle differences between vowels indicate that infants are capable of hearing differences a great deal smaller than those produced by mothers in the study (Kuhl, 1991a).

If not required for infant discrimination, what function does a stretched vowel space serve? We hypothesized that stretching the vowel triangle could

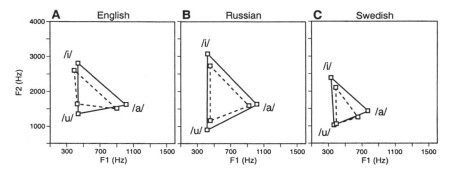

FIG. 6.7. The vowel triangle of maternal speech directed toward infants (solid line) across three diverse languages shows a "stretching" relative to the adult-directed vowel triangle (dashed line), an effect that both makes vowels more discriminable and highlights the abstract features that infants must use to produce speech themselves (from Kuhl, 1998).

benefit infants in three ways. First, it increases the distance between vowels, making them more distinct from one another. In recent studies, language-delayed children showed substantial improvements in measures of speech and language after treatment in a program in which they listened to speech altered by computer to exaggerate phonetic differences (Merzenich et al., 1996; Tallal et al., 1996). Normally developing infants may benefit similarly from the enhanced acoustic differences provided in infant-directed speech.

Second, to achieve the stretching, mothers produce vowels that go beyond those produced in typical adult conversation. From both an acoustic and articulatory perspective, these vowels are "hyperarticulated" (Lindblom, 1990). Hyperarticulated vowels are perceived by adults as "better instances" of vowel categories (Iverson & Kuhl, 1995; Johnson, Flemming, & Wright, 1993), and laboratory tests show that when listening to good instances of phonetic categories, infants show greater phonetic categorization ability. The new motherese study thus shows that hyperarticulated vowels are a part of infants' linguistic experience and raises the possibility that they may play an important role in the development of infants' vowel categories.

Third, expanding the vowel triangle allows mothers to produce a greater variety of instances representing each vowel category without creating acoustic overlap between vowel categories. Greater variety may cause infants to attend to non-frequency-specific spectral dimensions that characterize a vowel category, rather than to any one particular set of frequencies that the mother uses to produce a vowel, and studies indicate that variability assists foreign listeners' speech discrimination (Lively, Logan, & Pisoni, 1993). Converting the formant values to spectral features shows that infant-directed speech maximizes the featural contrast between vowels (Kuhl et al., 1997). This is especially critical for infants because they cannot duplicate the absolute frequencies of adult speech—their vocal tracts are too small (Kent & Murray, 1982). In order to speak, infants must reproduce the appropriate spectral dimensions in their own frequency range (Kuhl & Meltzoff, 1996). Our recent study indicates that maternal language input emphasizes these dimensions.

NEURAL CORRELATES OF SPEECH PROCESSING

Various techniques of neuroscience (PET, MRI, fMRI, and MEG) have been applied to phonetic processing in adults (Näätänen et al., 1997), and infant studies are beginning to appear. High-density event-related potentials (ERPS) have recently been used to study word processing in young children (Mills, Coffey-Corina, & Neville, 1993). These techniques are now being applied to study speech processing in infants in our laboratory (Kuhl, 1998), and others (Cheour-Luhtanen et al., 1995; Dehaene-Lambertz & Dehaene, 1994).

Recent studies suggest that phonetic prototypes provide a particularly good measure of language experience (Näätänen et al., 1997). In new studies using adult Japanese and American subjects, we have shown that the mismatched negativity (MMN) response, an ERP component thought to reflect preattentive auditory processes (Sharma, Kraus, McGee, Carrell, & Nicol, 1993) can be measured using magnetoencephalography (MEG) as a mismatched magnetic field (MMF) (Zhang et al., 2000). Such measures hold promise for providing highly sensitive indicators that will allow us to map the brain's responses to speech over the life span.

CONCLUSIONS

In the first year of life infants learn a great deal about the perceptual characteristics of their native language. Learning subsequently alters the perception and production of speech. According to Kuhl's Native Language Magnet model, perceptual learning early in life results in the formation of stored representations that capture native-language regularities. The theory emphasizes the role of linguistic input. Input does not act like a trigger for innately stored information. Rather, it is mapped in such a way as to "warp" the underlying acoustic space. Stored representations act like *perceptual magnets* for similar patterns of sound, resulting in maps that specify perceived distances between sounds. The map shrinks perceptual distances near a category's most typical instances and stretches perceptual distances between categories. Perceptual maps differ in adults who speak different languages. The magnet effects and the perceptual maps they produce also affect speech production. This helps explain speech development in infants and helps explain why, as adults, we do not hear or produce foreign-language sounds very well. Current work is aimed at examining the brain changes that accompany language learning using the techniques of modern neuroscience.

ACKNOWLEDGMENTS

This chapter was supported by grants to PKK from the National Institutes of Health (HD 37954) and the Human Frontiers Science Program (RG 0159).

REFERENCES

Abramson, A. S., & Lisker, L. (1970). Discriminability along the voicing continuum: Cross-language tests. *Proceedings of the Sixth International Congress of Phonetic Sciences Prague 1967*, pp. 569–573. Prague: Academia.
Best, C. T. (1993). Language-specific changes in non-native speech perception: A window on early phonological development. In B. de Boysson-Bardies, S. de Schonen, P. Jusczyk, P.

McNeilage, & J. Morton (Eds.), *Developmental neurocognition: Speech and face processing in the first year of life* (pp. 289–304). Dordrecht, The Netherlands: Kluwer.

Bonhoeffer, T., & Shatz, C. J. (1998). Neurotrophins and visual system plasticity. In T. J. Carew, R. Menzel, & C. J. Shatz (Eds.), *Mechanistic relationships between development and learning* (pp. 93–112). Cambridge, England: Wiley.

Chapman, R. S., Streim, N. W., Crais, E. R., Salmon, D., Strand, E. A., & Negri, N. A. (1992). Child talk: Assumptions of a developmental process model for early language learning. In R. A. Chapman (Ed.), *Processes in language acquisition and disorders* (pp. 3–19). St. Louis, MO: Mosby Year Book.

Cheour-Luhtanen, M., Alho, K., Kujala, T., Sainio, K., Reinikainen, K., Renlund, M., Aaltonen, O. Eerola, O., & Näätänen, R. (1995). Mismatch negativity indicates vowel discrimination in newborns. *Hearing Research, 82,* 53–58.

Chomsky, N. (1957). A review of B. F. Skinner's *Verbal behavior. Language, 35,* 26–58.

Chomsky, N. (1965). *Aspects of the theory of syntax.* Cambridge, MA: MIT Press.

Chomsky, N. (1981). *Rules and representations.* New York: Columbia University Press.

de Boysson-Bardies, B. (1993). Ontogeny of language-specific syllabic productions. In B. de Boysson-Bardies, S. de Schonen, P. Jusczyk, P. McNeilage, & J. Morton (Eds.), *Developmental neurocognition: Speech and face processing in the first year of life* (pp. 353–363). Dordrecht, The Netherlands: Kluwer.

Dehaene-Larnbertz, G., & Dehaene, S. (1994). Speed and cerebral correlates of syllable discrimination in infants. *Nature, 370,* 292–295.

Doupe, A. (1998). Development and learning in the birdsong system: Are there shared mechanisms? In T. J. Carew, R. Menzel, & C. J. Shatz (Eds.) *Mechanistic relationships between development and learning* (pp. 29–52). Cambridge, England: Wiley.

Doupe, A., & Kuhl, P. K. (1999). Birdsong and speech: Common themes and mechanisms. *Annual Review of Neuroscience, 22,* 567–631.

Eimas, P. D., Miller, J. L., & Jusczyk, P. W. (1987). On infant speech perception and the acquisition of language. In S. Harnad (Ed.), *Categorical perception: The groundwork of cognition* (pp. 161–195). New York: Cambridge University Press.

Faneslow, M., & Rudy, J. (1998). Convergence of experimental and developmental approaches to animal learning and memory processses. In T. J. Carew, R. Menzel, & C. J. Shatz (Eds.), *Mechanistic relationships between development and learning* (pp. 15–28). Cambridge, England: Wiley.

Ferguson, C. A., Menn, L., & Stoel-Gammon, C. (Eds.). (1992). *Phonological development: Models, research, implications.* Timonium, MD: York Press.

Fernald, A. (1985). Four-month-old infants prefer to listen to motherese. *Infant Behavior and Development 8,* 181–195.

Fernald, A., & Kuhl, P. (1987). Acoustic determinants of infant preference for Motherese speech. *Infant Behavior and Development, 10,* 279–293.

Flege, J. E. (1993). Production and perception of a novel, second-language phonetic contrast. *Journal of the Acoustical Society of America, 93,* 1589–1608.

Goodsitt, J. V., Morgan, J. L., & Kuhl, P. K. (1993). Perceptual strategies in prelingual speech segmentation. *Journal of Child Language, 20,* 229–252.

Gopnik, A., & Meltzoff, A. N. (1997). *Words, thoughts, and theories.* Cambridge, MA: MIT Press.

Gopnik, A., Meltzoff, A. N., & Kuhl, P. K. (1999). *The scientist in the crib: Minds, brains, and how children learn.* New York: William Morrow.

Green, K. P., Kuhl, P. K., Meltzoff, A. N., & Stevens E. B. (1991). Integrating speech information across talkers, gender, and sensory modality: Female faces and male voices in the McGurk effect. *Perception & Psychophysics 50,* 524–536.

Greenough, W. T., & Black, J. E. (1992). Induction of brain structure by experience: Substrates for cognitive development. In M. Gunnar & C. Nelson (Eds.), *The Minnesota symposia on child psychology, Vol. 24: Developmental behavioral neuroscience* (pp. 155–200). Hillsdale, NJ: Lawrence Erlbaum Associates.

Iverson, P., & Kuhl, P. K. (1995). Mapping the perceptual magnet effect for speech using signal detection theory and multidimensional scaling. *Journal of the Acoustical Society of America, 97,* 553–562.

Iverson, P., & Kuhl, P. K. (1996). Influences of phonetic identification and category goodness on American listeners' perception of /r/ and /l/. *Journal of the Acoustical Society of America, 99,* 1130–1140.

Iverson, P., & Kuhl, P. K. (2000). Perceptual magnet and phoneme boundary effects in speech perception: Do they arise from a common mechanism? *Perception & Psychophysics, 62,* 874–886.

Iverson, P., Kuhl, P. K., Yamada, R., Tohkura, Y., & Stevens, E. (submitted). *Effects of language experience on phonetic perception: Perception of American English /r/ and /l/.*

Johnson, K., Flemming, E., & Wright, R. (1993). The hyperspace effect: Phonetic targets are hyperarticulated. *Language, 69,* 505–528.

Jusczyk, P. W., Friederici, A. D., Wessels, J. M. I., Svenkerud V. Y., & Jusczyk, A. M. (1993). Infants' sensitivity to the sound patterns of native language words. *Journal of Memory and Language, 32,* 402–420.

Kent, R. D., & Murray, A. D. (1982). Acoustic features of infant vocalic utterances at 3, 6, and 9 months. *Journal of the Acoustical Society of America, 72,* 353–365.

Kuhl, P. K. (1991a). Perception, cognition, and the ontogenetic and phylogenetic emergence of human speech. In S. E. Brauth, W. S. Hall, & R. J. Dooling (Eds.), *Plasticity of development* (pp. 73–106). Cambridge, MA: MIT Press.

Kuhl, P. K. (1991b). Human adults and human infants show a "perceptual magnet effect" for the prototypes of speech categories, monkeys do not. *Perception & Psychophysics, 50,* 93–107.

Kuhl, P. K. (1992). Infants perception and representation of speech: Development of a new theory. In J. J. Ohala, T. M. Nearey, B. L. Derwing, M. M. Hodge, & G. E. Wiebe (Eds.), *Proceedings of the International Conference on Spoken Language Processing* (pp. 449–456). Edmonton, Alberta: University of Alberta.

Kuhl, P. K. (1994). Learning and representation in speech and language. *Current Opinion in Neurobiology, 4,* 812–822.

Kuhl, P. K. (1998). The development of speech and language. In T. J. Carew, R. Menzel, & C. J. Shatz (Eds.), *Mechanistic relationships between development and learning* (pp. 53–73). Cambridge, England: Wiley.

Kuhl, P. K. (1999). Speech, language, and the brain: Innate preparation for learning. In M. D. Hauser & M. Konishi (Eds.), *The design of animal communication* (pp. 419–450). Cambridge, MA: MIT Press.

Kuhl, P. K. (2000a). A new view of language acquisition. *Proceedings of the National Academy of Sciences.* In press.

Kuhl, P. K. (2000b). Language, mind, and brain: Experience alters perception. In M. S. Gazzaniga (Ed.), *The new cognitive neurosciences* (pp. 99–115). Cambridge, MA: MIT Press.

Kuhl, P. K., Andruski, J. E., Chistovich, I. A., Chistovich, L. A., Kozhevnikova, E. V., Ryskina, V. L., Stolyarova, E. I., Sundberg, U., & Lacerda, F. (1997). Cross-language analysis of phonetic units in language addressed to infants. *Science, 277,* 684–686.

Kuhl, P. K., & Meltzoff, A. N. (1982). The bimodal perception of speech in infancy. *Science, 218,* 1138–1141.

Kuhl, P. K., & Meltzoff, A. N. (1997). Evolution, nativism, and learning in the development of language and speech. In M. Gopnik (Ed.), *The inheritance and innateness of grammars* (pp. 7–44). New York: Oxford University Press.

Kuhl, P. K., & Meltzoff, A. N. (1996). Infant vocalizations in response to speech: Vocal imitation and developmental change. *Journal of the Acoustical Society of America, 100,* 2425–2438.

Kuhl, P. K., Tsao F. -M. Hayashi, A., Stevens, E., Liu, H. -M., Deguchi, T., Kiritani, S., Tseng, C., & Iverson, P. (submitted). *Mechanisms underlying developmental change in infants' perception of speech.*

Kuhl, P. K., Tsuzaki, M., Tohkura, Y., & Meltzoff, A. N. (1994). Human processing of auditory-visual information in speech perception: Potential for multimodal human-machine interfaces. *Proceedings of the International Conference on Spoken Language Processing* (pp. 539–542). Tokyo: Acoustical Society of Japan.

Kuhl, P. K., Williams, K. A., Lacerda, F., Stevens, K. N., & Lindblom, B. (1992). Linguistic experience alters phonetic perception in infants by 6 months of age. *Science, 255*, 606–608.

Lindblom, B. (1990). Explaining phonetic variation: A sketch of the H&H theory. In W. J. Hardcastle & A. Marchal (Eds.), *Speech production and speech modeling* (pp. 403–439). Dordrecht, The Netherlands: Kluwer.

Lively, S. E., Logan, J. S., & Pisoni, D. B. (1993). Training Japanese listeners to identify English /r/ and /l/: H. The role of phonetic environment and talker variability in learning new perceptual categories. *Journal of the Acoustical Society of America, 94*, 1242–1255.

Marler, P. (1974). Constraints on learning: Development of bird song. In W. F. Norman (Ed.), *Ethnology and psychiatry* (pp. 69–83). Toronto: University of Toronto Press.

Massaro, D. W. (1987). *Speech perception by ear and eye: A paradigm for psychological inquiry.* Hillsdale, NJ: Lawrence Erlbaum Associates.

McGurk, H., & MacDonald, J. (1976). Hearing lips and seeing voices. *Nature, 264*, 746–748.

Meltzoff, A. N., & Moore, M. K. (1977). Imitation of facial and manual gestures by human neonates. *Science, 198*, 75–78.

Meltzoff, A. N., & Moore, M. K. (1994). Imitation, memory and the representation of persons. *Infant Behavior and Development, 17*, 83–99.

Merzenich, M. M., Jenkins, W. M., Johnston, P., Schreiner, C., Miller, S. L., & Tallal, P. (1996). Temporal processing deficits of language-learning impaired children ameliorated by training. *Science, 271*, 77–81.

Miller, J. L. (1994). On the internal structure of phonetic categories: A progress report. *Cognition, 50*, 271–285.

Mills, D. L., Coffey-Corina, S. A., & Neville, H. J. (1993). Language acquisition and cerebral specialization in 20-month-old infants. *Journal of Cognitive Neuroscience, 5*, 317–334.

Näätänen, R., Lehtokoski, A., Lennes, M., Cheour, M., Huotilainen, M., Iivonen, A., Vainio, M., Alku, P., Ilmoniemi, R. J., Luuk, A., Allik, J., Sinkkonen, J., & Alho, K.. (1997). Language-specific phoneme representations revealed by electric and magnetic brain responses. *Nature, 385*, 432–434.

Piaget, J. (1954). *The construction of reality in the child.* New York: Basic Books.

Saffran, J. R., Aslin, R. N., & Newport, E. L. (1996). Statistical learning by 8-month-old infants. *Science, 274*, 1926–1928.

Sekiyama, K., & Tohkura, Y. (1993). Inter-language differences in the influence of visual cues in speech perception. *Journal of Phonetics, 21*, 427–444.

Sharma, A., Kraus, N., McGee, T., Carrell, T., & Nicol, T. (1993). Acoustic versus phonetic representations of speech as reflected by the mismatch negativity event-related potential. *Electroencephalography and Clinical Neurophysiology, 88*, 64–71.

Skinner, B. F. (1957). *Verbal behavior.* New York: Appleton-Century-Crofts.

Strange, W. (Ed.). (1995). *Speech perception and linguistic experience: Issues in cross-language research.* Timonium, MD: York.

Sussman, J. E., & Lauckner-Morano, V. J. (1995). Further tests of the "perceptual magnet effect" in the perception of [i]: Identification and change/no-change discrimination. *Journal of the Acoustical Society of America, 97*, 539–552.

Tallal, R., Miller, S. L., Bedi, G., Byma, G., Wang, X., Nagarajan, S. S., Schreiner, C., Jenkins, W. M., & Merzenich, M. M. (1996). Language comprehension in language-learning impaired children improved with acoustically modified speech. *Science, 271*, 81–84.

Vihman, M. M., & de Boysson-Bardies, B. (1994). The nature and origins of ambient language influence on infant vocal production and early words. *Phonetica, 51*, 159–169.

Vygotsky, L. S. (1979). Interaction between learning and development. In M. Cole, V. John-Steiner, S. Scribner, & E. Souberman (Eds.), Mind in society: The development of higher psychological processes (pp. 79–91). Cambridge, MA: Harvard University Press.

Werker, J. F., & Tees, R. C. (1984). Cross-language speech perception: Evidence for perceptual reorganization during the first year of life. *Infant Behavior and Development, 7*, 49–63.

Werker, J. F., & Polka, L. (1993). The ontogeny and developmental significance of language-specific phonetic perception. In B. de Boysson-Bardies, S. de Schonen, R. Jusczyk, P. McNeilage, & J. Morton (Eds.), *Developmental neurocognition: Speech and face processing in the first year of life* (pp. 275–288). Dordrecht, The Netherlands: Kluwer.

Willerman, R., & Kuhl, P. K. (1996). Cross-language speech perception: Swedish, English, and Spanish speakers' perception of front rounded vowels. *Proceedings of the 1996 International Conference on Spoken Language Processing, 1*, 442–445.

Zhang, Y., Kuhl, P. K., Imada, T., Naito, S., Kotani, M., Stevens, E. B., Tohkura, Y. (2000, July). *Does the Japanese subject's brain show different neuromagnetic responses to the syllables /la/ and /ra/?* Paper presented at the XXVII International Congress of Psychology, Stockholm, Sweden.

7

Phonetic Variability in Baby Talk and Development of Vowel Categories

Barbara L. Davis
The University of Texas at Austin

Björn Lindblom
Stockholm University, Sweden

It is generally acknowledged that speech addressed to infants (baby talk) is modified in a variety of ways (Ferguson, 1977) which appear to facilitate acquisition and structure the input for the infant. It is also widely recognized, however, that speech produced under natural, rather than laboratory, conditions is complex and contains extensive reductions and coarticulations (Lindblom, Brownlee, Davis, & Moon, 1992; Perkell & Klatt, 1986). Are the acoustic properties of baby talk (BT) different from those of spontaneous adult speech? If not, the infant's learning of specific sound categories would seem to pose a significant research problem.

Kuhl (1991, 1993, 1994) has suggested that the infant may represent and structure perceptual information in terms of prototypes. According to Kuhl's *prototype hypothesis*, formation of perceptual categories is based on "best" instances of a particular category, which contain more of the features essential to membership in that category. New incoming stimuli are then categorized with reference to their degree of resemblance to the prototypical instances of the category. Studies by Grieser and Kuhl (1989) and Kuhl (1991) have evaluated the "prototype" effect in speech perception abilities of 6-month-old infants. Their results indicate that infants do indeed seem to assimilate speech stimuli based on their degree of resemblance to prototypical exemplars. Hence their behavior would appear to support the prototype hypothesis.

Kuhl's initial experiment using the vowels /i/ and /I/ first demonstrated equivalence classification. Using synthetic vowel tokens, infants were trained to indicate discrimination of single good exemplars of the two vowel categories by producing a head turn response to the first category but not the second. Subjects were then tested on novel exemplars from each category. Infants sorted novel exemplars 90% of the time on the first trial, no matter how prototypical the variant of the category happened to be, showing attention to critical differences between categories as well as disregard for differences among stimuli belonging to a single category. Subsequently, another group of infants were trained to discriminate instances of synthetic speech of a good prototypical /i/ vowel (average reference formant values for adult male speakers; Peterson & Barney, 1952). A second group of infants was trained on a "poor" /i/ that differed markedly from the Peterson and Barney /i/ values. The first group of infants, trained with prototypical exemplars, generalized significantly more novel exemplars than did the second group trained with poor vowel values.

In a companion experiment, adult listeners were asked to judge synthetic variants of the same /i/ stimuli with respect to how well they represented the /i/ category. Stimuli near the good /i/ received the highest ratings, whereas ratings of vowel goodness tended to decrease with increase in distance from the good /i/. The opposite result pertained with the poor /i/ values; stimuli surrounding the poor /i/ received low ratings, with ratings of goodness increasing as the stimuli were further from the poor values and correspondingly closer to the prototypical values. Subsequent correlation analysis showed a high correlation between infant generalization to novel exemplars and adult judgments of goodness, both changing systematically as a function of distance and direction from the Peterson and Barney reference stimulus.

According to Kuhl, these results suggest that young infants organize perceptual vowel representations around prototypical members of a category. She proposed two potential explanatory hypotheses for the questions raised by her data. The first explanation suggests that vowel goodness is inherently defined by the auditory perceptual system, a result in analogy with results found in the visual perceptual system, in which infants and adults prefer the same focal colors regardless of culture. The second hypothesis suggests that these effects are due to experience in listening to a specific language. Effects of linguistic experience have been shown in 10 to 12-month-old infants (Best, McRoberts, & Sithole, 1988; Werker & Polka, 1993; Werker & Tees, 1984) as well as in impaired populations (Mills, 1983; Stoel-Gammon, 1988). If Kuhl's findings on the prototype effect were due to linguistic experience, the period during which infants use such experience to organize or establish perceptual categories would occur much earlier than has been demonstrated previously. Recent work (Kuhl, Williams,

Lacerda, Stevens, & Lindblom, 1992) provides data favoring such an experience-based scenario.

To examine the balance between innate and perceptual factors as determinants of infant prototypes, it appears natural to ask: What is the nature of the speech stimuli typically directed to 6-month-olds? How much is known about the acoustic phonetic properties of BT to such infants? Is BT structured acoustically so as to facilitate prototype formation?

These questions have relevance not only in the context of infant speech perception. They are also related to more general research problems. For instance, because BT has been characterized as a listener-oriented speech style (Ferguson, 1977), acoustic characteristics might shed light on the invariance issue (Perkell & Klatt, 1986), the classical topic of speech research that consists of defining physical correlates of vowels, consonants, and other linguistic units in such a way that they remain constant and independent of context.

Given the background of the abovementioned questions, the goal of this study was to investigate whether prototypical information, as defined by Kuhl, is present in BT speech addressed to a 6-month-old infant. A prototypical instance of the vowel /i/ is defined operationally by Kuhl as having the average formant frequencies of the vowel /i/ for adult male speakers (Peterson & Barney, 1952). Looking closely at the acoustic characteristics of BT should allow initial evaluation of Kuhl's two hypotheses.

Multiple studies of BT have specified suprasegmental, segmental, semantic, and syntactic characteristics of this speech mode as being special and uniquely tailored to the needs of the infant learner (Ferguson, 1977; Newport, 1975). Studies have shown that infants prefer to listen to infant-directed speech (Fernald, 1985), and that communicative intent is signaled more clearly in the BT register (Fernald, 1989). For several languages, including Swedish (Sundberg, 1993), it has been shown that pitch contours tend to show much wider excursions in BT than in adult-directed conversation.

BT speech is connected, spontaneous speech. It is very different from the types of speech signals, often synthetic and highly controlled, which are used to demonstrate infant abilities in early perception studies. Phonetic studies of adult-oriented connected speech frequently show extensive reductions and coarticulations. Studying adult perception, Pickett and Pollack (1963), and Pollack and Pickett (1964), found that fragments of word tokens, from which surrounding context had been removed, were recognized at only about 50% accuracy, even though they could be easily identified in the original linguistic context. This type of finding supports the proposal that, in conversational situations, adult listeners regularly compensate for the incompleteness of the acoustic signal by use of contextual information. Accordingly, this study investigates the phonetic properties of BT to assess the presence of these same properties of reduction and coarticulation. It is assumed that, during the first year of life, infants do not have the same access to "linguistic context"[1] as do adult listeners and would be expected to rely on the quality of the signal more heavily in building perceptual categories. Certainly that is strongly implied by the experiential hypothesis Kuhl proposes for speech sound prototypes.

Although there are many laboratory studies of infant perception abilities, fewer studies have looked specifically at the acoustic phonetics of BT. How do infants go about establishing the proposed prototype mechanisms postulated by Kuhl and demonstrated using synthetic speech in a laboratory setting? Several studies have suggested that phonetic segments are better acoustically represented in infant-directed speech than in adult-directed speech. Bernstein-Ratner (1982, 1984) looked at vowel clarification in speech to infants in preverbal (no meaningful words) and at the holophrastic stage (first meaningful word use), and at the 2.5+ MLU (early multiword utterance) point. She showed that phonetic clarification of vowels is present in BT, when infants begin to use meaningful words, but may not be so pronounced in periods before or after that time. Comparing the preverbal mother–infant dyads with the holophrastic mother–infant dyads, Bernstein-Ratner also noted an emerging pattern of content word clarification as measured by wider dispersion and decreased overlap of formant values. In the 2.5+ MLU group, however, clarification for function words was far more pronounced.

Malsheen (1980) examined VOT distinctions in voiced and voiceless stop consonants in the speech of six mothers in infant-directed and adult-directed speech. Three groups of two subjects were included; two infants in the preverbal stage, two infants in the stage of first word use, and two infants producing multisyllabic utterances. Prevocalic stops in stressed and unstressed word positions and in function and content words were analyzed. Malsheen found VOT values significantly more likely to overlap in adult-directed than infant-directed conversation. Speech addressed to infants learning first words showed the most clear VOT distinction for the two categories, primarily by increase in the mean VOT of voiceless stops. Malsheen concluded that, on all indices evaluated, these adult speakers were presenting their language learning infants with an "idealized corpus of voiced and voiceless segments" (p. 184).

---

[1]We should note that "context" is often used in two senses. In Pollack and Pickett's studies, the stimuli were produced by removing "signal context," that is the surrounding portions of the signal. Most probably there is another type of context that came into play in their experiment, namely context used with reference to the signal-independent information (lexical, grammatical, and other knowledge) that adult listeners normally bring to bear in processing the incoming speech. An example would be the two interpretations of "less'n three," which depending on both "signal context" and stored linguistic knowledge would be heard as either "less than three" or "lesson three."

Bernstein-Ratner (1984) also found vowel duration significantly affected in infant-directed speech in eight mother–infant dyads. Vowels before voiced consonants doubled in duration and final consonants were frequently deleted or glottalized. Furthermore, in a separate study of durational cues marking clause boundaries in infant-directed speech, Bernstein-Ratner (1984) found evidence of developmentally related adaptations. F_0 contours, preboundary vowel lengthening, and pauses were examined in infants on the verge of expressive language, infants using one-word utterances and infants combining words. In infants on the verge of expressive language use, statistically significant prepausal vowel lengthening was noted. In the two developmentally more mature groups, differences in vowel lengthening were observable but not significant.

Two other studies of phonetic modifications in infant-directed speech report results that differ from the foregoing trends. Baran, Loffler, and Daniloff (1977) studied VOT for prevocalic segments in the speech of three mother–infant dyads. The infants studied were in the period of development preceding meaningful word use. Baran et al. found that mothers did not enhance VOT contrast for voiced and voiceless stops more when talking to their infants than when talking to adult listeners. However, they added that stage of language acquisition might be a critical factor affecting phonetic characteristics of mother–infant speech.

Shockey and Bond (1980) looked for several optional phonological reduction rules operating in conversational speech in the infant-directed speech of eight mother–infant dyads. The children in their study were 2 to 4 years old, much older than the population studied by Bernstein-Ratner and Malsheen. Child-directed speech was found to be "less intelligible" (i.e., to contain more instances of phonological reduction rules). They speculated that the function of the phonological reductions was to establish a sense of intimacy in communication with the child. Again, because Shockey and Bond's subjects were much older, their study tends to converge with that of Baran et al. in suggesting that phonological modifications may be tuned to developmental stage. Bernstein-Ratner (1984) replicated the Shockey and Bond study with younger infants in the one- to two-word stage. Phonological reduction rules, with the exception of palatalization, were found to occur less frequently in infant-directed speech than in adult-directed conversation. In addition, in Bernstein-Ratner's sample, mothers frequently alternated between reduced and nonreduced forms. Alternations were proposed as serving the function of modeling for infants the potential appropriate occurrence of reduced and nonreduced forms in conversation.

The few studies available suggest phonetic fine tuning in BT. Conflicting results with respect to VOT overlap and use of phonological reduction rules could potentially be accounted for in terms of developmental level. Subjects in these studies are, however, older than those in Kuhl's prototype experiments.

METHOD

In order to learn more about the acoustic phonetics of BT and to search for possible measurable prototype correlates, a natural sample of BT speech addressed to a 6-month-old infant was recorded. One English-speaking mother was audiotaped with her 6-month-old infant in a 1-hour free-play situation. She was not informed about the purpose of the experiment, but was simply asked to play naturally with her baby. No other instructions were given. Subsequently, she was also recorded in conversation with another adult (henceforth AA speech). For both samples, the tokens analyzed were those investigated by Kuhl, viz the English tense vowel /i/ and the lax /ɪ/. All occurrences of words whose citation forms contained /i/ and /ɪ/ were analyzed, both stressed and unstressed. Third, a recording was made of the same female speaker repeating the words /hid/ and /hɪd/ in citation-form style, 20 times each. In conformity with Kuhl's use of average Peterson and Barney formant measurements, prototypical values for this speaker's /i/ and /ɪ/ were considered to be her average formant patterns as spoken in citation-form /hVd/ words. In order to allow compatibility of the present data with Kuhl's, all formant values were converted to mel units for the BT as well as the AA and the citation speech samples. The following formula (Fant, 1968) was used for the conversion:

$$\text{Mel} = 1000/\log 2 \, \log \, (1 + f/1000) \tag{1}$$

In performing the acoustic analyses, problems were encountered associated with voice quality changes, the large range of F_0, variability in the signal, and the non-laboratory conditions under which the recordings had been made. Data analysis procedures were therefore carefully monitored to assure accurate estimation of formant values across speaking styles.

The relevant portions of the recordings were fed into a VaxStation GPX/II at a 10 kHz sampling rate, after anti-aliasing low-pass filtering at 4 kHz. After digitization the signals were examined with a waveform editor. Individual files were created for each vowel to be analyzed. In addition to the vowel segment itself, each waveform chunk included short fragments of the preceding and following signal context, usually the signal information corresponding to the immediately adjacent consonants. As a general rule, vowel formant patterns were sampled at four time points taken within an interval beginning at least 40 msec into the vowel and ending at least 40 msec before the boundary of the following consonant. When a diphthong pronunciation was encountered, observations were made near the nucleus of the segment. An estimate of the F_2 value was also made at the beginning of every vowel, that is normally at the CV boundary. Information on vowel duration and the relative *rms*-value in dB were also collected for every vowel token.

All measurements were made using KLAME, a software package for acoustic analyses developed by Jerry Lame, and programs written by Dennis Klatt (the MIT SpeechVax programs). KLAME was used extensively to produce spectrogram displays on the computer screen. As is well known, the identification of formants is reasonably easy from spectrograms of male low-pitched speech analyzed with a 300 Hz filter. At high F_0:s however, harmonics rather than formants tend to dominate the spectrographic picture. Formant frequencies become more difficult to measure, unless the width of the analyzing filter is made sufficiently broad. KLAME offers the user the option of adapting the filter width to the F_0 of the sample under analysis. That is done by adjusting the window length of the Fourier analysis. In addition, it also allows modifying the upper and lower limits of the dynamic range of the display so that weak spectral energy may be adequately portrayed. The majority of the formant frequency estimations were made using KLAME and by locating formant frequencies on the KLAME spectrograms at the center frequencies of the formant bands.

In the case of low-pitched samples, spectrogram estimations tended to differ very little from the results of using LPC and short-term spectral information derived from spectral averaging based on a 300 Hz bandwidth. However, when F_0 became high (> 300 Hz), when the vowel was heavily nasalized, or when it exhibited irregular voice quality characteristics (e.g., aspiration), short-term spectral analyses tended to provide the most reliable information. Three types of computations were routinely included on all spectral displays. First, harmonic spectra which were 512-point Discrete Fourier Transforms (DFT's) based on a Hamming window of 25.6 msec duration. In addition, two different spectral curves were superimposed on the DFT's: One was based on an LPC analysis and the second on an algorithm generating broad-band envelopes and picking the frequencies of major spectral peaks.

The present BT recording conforms with BT descriptions presented in the literature (Fernald, 1984). It is lively and engaging. Prosodically it is extremely varied, showing a large range of fundamental frequency variation and a high frequency of occurrence of very high F_0 values (see Fig. 7.1).

As often reported in the literature, high fundamental frequencies make accurate formant frequency estimations difficult. In such cases, an LPC method has to be monitored closely, as it will tend to assign formant peaks to individual partials. Spectral averaging using a 300 Hz filter behaves similarly, especially when F_0 gets significantly larger than 300 Hz. The procedure adopted for such cases was to inspect the harmonic spectra of the DFT displays. In particular, the configuration of harmonics within a formant was examined either for coincidence between formant frequency and a given harmonic ($F_n = nF_0$—which would be indicated by the presence of a single very strong harmonic), or for evidence of the peak being located half-way between two harmonics $[F_n = F_0(2n + 1)/2]$—as indicated by two equally strong harmonics). If neither of these clear-cut patterns was identified, the formant frequency was calculated by interpolating between the two in accordance with the relative amplitudes of the most prominent harmonics. As a result, this procedure implied a visual estimate of a weighted average of harmonic amplitudes as proposed by Potter and Steinberg (1950). To give an example, if a peak occurred between the third and the fourth harmonic and the fourth harmonic seemed to be stronger than the third, the frequency would be calculated say according to $Fn = kF_0$, where k would be between 3.5 and 4.

The problem of making formant measures at high F_0's has been addressed by several investigators. Atal and Schroeder (1974) synthesized signals consisting of a single formant at different fundamental frequencies and analyzed them by the linear prediction method (LPC). At F_0's of 100, 200, and 400 Hz, maximum errors were 11 (11%), 30 (15%), and 67 Hz (17%). Monsen and Engebretson (1983) used synthesized vowels in comparing formant frequency estimations by experienced spectrogram readers and by linear prediction analysis. They found that, for fundamental frequencies below 300 Hz, the two methods were accurate to within +/− 60 Hz for F_1 and F_2, but that accuracy decreased drastically as fundamental frequencies exceeded 300 Hz.

The probable magnitude of the present measurement errors can be estimated as follows. In addressing this issue earlier (Lindblom, 1991/1961), F_0-related errors were found to pattern in a fairly lawful manner. Rarely did they exceed $F_0/4$. The reason can be linked to the way in which harmonics and formant peaks interact. For instance, in cases where the formant frequency F_n coincides with a harmonic, that harmonic is usually strongly amplified and rises above its neighbors. Selecting the "strongest harmonic" should in such cases give a good formant frequency estimate. Another fairly easily identified situation occurs when $F_n = F_0(2n + 1)/2$, that is when the formant falls halfway between two harmonics. Ideally, this situation results in two harmonics of more or less equal amplitude. Locating the formant halfway between those harmonics would then be the best strategy. All other cases of formant/harmonic interactions fall in between those extremes. Mistaking a "strongest harmonic" for a "halfway" case, or the converse, would give an error of $F_0/2$, but because these configurations are relatively well defined, maximum errors are closer to half of that value.

Figure 7.1 compares the formant frequency measurements with the F_0 values at the moment of the formant sample. Data for F_1 in /i/ and /I/ are included. The lines represent the frequencies that would be expected, if estimates had been made according to a strongest harmonic strategy, that is $Fn = F_0$, $F_n = 2F_0$, or $F_n = 3F_0$, and so forth. Note the remarkably large ranges of both F_0 and F_n. We should also note how subsets of the F_1 data tend to ei-

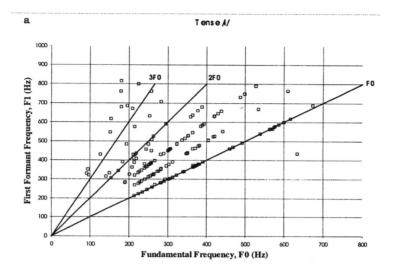

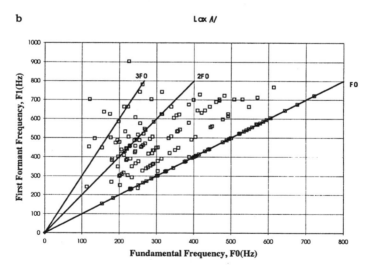

FIG. 7.1. Formant frequency measurements plotted against fundamental frequency values for corresponding time samples. Data for F_1 and F_2 of /i/ and /I/ are shown. The lines represent $F_n = F_0$, $F_n = 2F_0$, or $F_n = 3F_0$ etc., that is the cases where the formant frequency would coincide with the frequency of the harmonic. Points falling on those lines illustrate the "strongest harmonic strategy" of formant frequency estimation.

ther coincide with the corresponding F_0 value—in other words, they lie on the line—or they form a linear cluster that falls in between two lines which corresponds to the interpolation strategy just described.

Figure 7.1 suggests the general observation that the formant judgments at high F_0's were not exclusively determined by the strongest harmonic component, but that interpolation was frequently resorted to.

Relevant to the evaluation of the F_2 estimates is the fact that spectra with high F_0 very often failed to resolve the F_2 and F_3 peaks individually. Accordingly, they exhibited only a single maximum. In those cases, F_2 was measured at the frequency of that maximum. Accordingly, the F_2 values reported here should strictly speaking be seen as estimates of an upper formant complex resulting from a merger of higher formants including F_2 and F_3, the so-called F_2-prime, or F_2' measure explored by Carlson, Granström, and Fant (1970).

RESULTS

Four Questions

Two definitions of *prototype* will be applied in the presentation of the results. First, we take prototype to mean average formant pattern observed in citation-style /hVd/ words, which corresponds to Kuhl's acoustic definition. If such prototypes occur in BT, they should be *directly observable* at the level of the acoustic signal. Thus we begin by asking: (1) *"Are there /i/ and /ɪ/ 'prototypes' in this sample of BT speech addressed to a 6-month-old infant?"* This question will be considered for the total set of measurements and for certain subsets of the data, namely for the syllables most likely to carry strong stress, for vowels with long durations and for nonnasal environments. Narrowing the search in that way, we restate (1) as: (2) *"Are there attributes in the signal context that 'ear-mark' certain BT tokens as prototypical for the infant?"*

Then we explore a second definition according to which prototypical values emerge only after vowel formant patterns have been related to other signal attributes in the vowel and in its context, for example, the formant patterns of the adjacent segments and the duration of the vowel. On this view, prototype is seen as a signal-based, but *derived phenomenon*. The question becomes: (3) *"Are prototypes derivable from signal dynamics, that is, from vowel information used in conjunction with other properties present in the vowel's immediate signal context?"*

In the first case, prototypes are simply "selected" from the "raw" signal. In the second case, they are products of contextual normalization, that is, an interaction among signal properties that presupposes a certain amount of cognitive processing. Finally, we compare the BT and the AA measurements looking for evidence of phonetic adaptation. For instance: (4) *"Does BT show less variability than AA?"*

Overall BT Characteristics

The first question takes Kuhl's hypothesis literally. It leads us to examine the BT speech sample for appearance of prototypical acoustic values. Figures 7.2 and 7.3 show the results for the /i/ and /ɪ/ vowels. All the vowel tokens for the BT sample are displayed in F_1–F_2 plots with axes calibrated in mel units. For each vowel, the speaker's mean /hVd/ value for the 20 citation-form tokens is represented with a small open circle. This is the prototypical F-pattern for this female speaker. A circle is drawn with a radius of 120 mel from the /hVd/ value. Values 120 mel from the center vowel values were taken by Kuhl as *poor* values in training infants using the /i/ vowel and were considered poor exemplars of /i/ by adult listeners in her study. These figures demonstrate that there are indeed tokens within the 120-mel ring, but also that a great number are widely scattered outside that ring in both

Mother Speech Tense

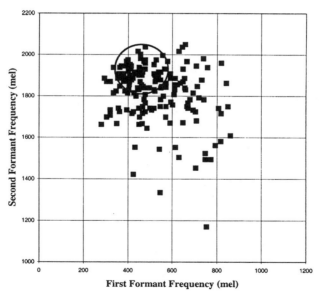

FIG. 7.2. Formant frequency measurements for the vowel /i/ displayed in a $F1$–$F2$ diagram with axes calibrated in mel units. A small open circle represents prototypical F-pattern, that is the speaker's mean $F1$ and $F2$ values for 20 citation-form /hVd/ tokens. A circle is drawn with a radius of 120 mel from this reference /hVd/ value.

Mother Speech Lax

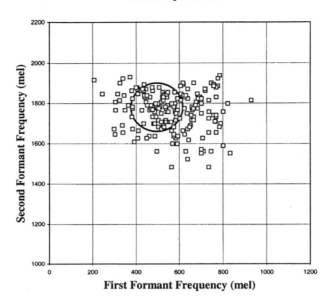

FIG. 7.3. *F*1–*F*2 diagram for the BT /I/ tokens prepared in analogy with Fig. 7.2.

the F_1 and F_2 dimensions. For /I/, points are more tightly clustered in F_2 than F_1.

The use of the 120-mel criterion for an outer bound of prototypical values is a broad interpretation of prototypes. It allows for a very large amount of acoustic variability to be considered prototypical. From the viewpoint of Kuhl's adult listener judgments, it is clearly too large. Nevertheless, a large number of cases do not meet the criterion. And as we make that criterion more and more severe, narrowing the circle radius to 90, 60 and 30 mel units, it is evident that an overwhelming majority of data points are going to be nonprototypical. We conclude that, if definition 1 prototypes are present at all in this sample, they form very small subsets of the observations.

Effect of Nasal Context

It is well known that vowels next to nasal consonants show assimilatory nasalization which adds components to the spectrum of an oral vowel. In the region of the vowel's first formant, an extra formant–antiformant pair typically appears (Fujimura, 1962; Kent & Read, 1992) that complicates the determination of F_1. Conceivably, the effects of nasal assimilation may have contributed to increasing the ranges of variation of the present measurements.

TABLE 7.1
Context Effects Nasal and Nonnasal Environments

	/i/			
	F_1		F_2	
	+N	-N	+N	-N
Mean	508	403	2459	2607
s.d	156	110	39	242
n	66	104	66	104
F	105		-148	

	/i/			
	F_1		F_2	
	+N	-N	+N	-N
Mean	476	486	2402	2400
s.d.				
n	43	145	43	145
F	-10		2	

To address this issue, the vowel tokens were divided into two groups, those occurring where either the preceding or following consonant was a nasal (or both), and those occurring in nonnasal environments. Table 7.1 displays mean formant data and standard deviations for these categories. Overall, the analysis indicates that standard deviations are high in all cases (> 100 Hz) and do not change dramatically when tokens in nasal contexts are removed.

The F_1 values for /i/ is higher in the nasal than in the nonnasal context. This is the only difference that reaches significance. In subsets of words and when the vowel is followed by a nasal, the effects are clearer. For instance, the corpus contains 37 instances of word forms ending in -ing in which F_1 is displaced up by 150 Hz relative to the corresponding nonnasal environments. These trends are fully compatible with acoustic theories of vowel nasalization (House & Stevens, 1956).

Vowel Duration Effects

One strategy of ear-marking good prototypical tokens for the infant might be to make the duration of the vowel longer. The assumption behind that expectation would be that, in prolonging a vowel, the speaker not only high-

TABLE 7.2
Duration—Mean F_2 Relationships

		i	I
HVd	F_2	2781	2399
Shortest Duration	F_2:	2442	2374
Mid Duration	F_2:	2506	2415
Longest Duration	F_2:	2690	2413

lights the vowel, but provides herself with more time to hit the prototypical target and to minimize possible "formant undershoot" effects arising from shorter duration (Lindblom, 1963; Moon & Lindblom, 1994). To investigate this question, the relationship between duration and F_2 values was examined. Durations for each vowel were rank ordered from *shortest* to *longest*. The resulting ordered values were divided arbitrarily into three groups with an equal number of tokens in each. Mean F_2 values for each group were calculated and compared with the speaker's /hVd/ mean values. Table 7.2 displays summary statistics for each vowel type.

Mean values for F_2 for /I/ are very tightly clustered around the mean prototypical F_2 value (at 2399 Hz) for this speaker with the mid and longest duration groups being slightly closer. For /i/, mean values for the longest duration tokens are closest to this speaker's prototypical /hVd/ value (at 2781 Hz), the shortest duration tokens are farthest from the prototypical value. For /i/, longer duration *does* seem to produce more prototypical values in this speaker. For /I/, an effect of duration is not so clearly apparent, inasmuch as all three group averages are close to the prototype value to begin with. This observation is also reflected by regression analyses for vowel duration and F_2 which resulted in an r-score of .39 for /i/ and .00 for /I/.

Dynamic Context Effects

In a CVC sequence, the role of duration as a determinant of vowel formant undershoot is closely linked to the extent of the formant transition from the initial consonant to the vowel and from the vowel to the following consonant. In the vowel reduction literature (Lindblom, 1963; Moon & Lindblom, 1994), it has been customary to quantify the similarity between transition onset and the intended formant position in the vowel in terms of the so-called "locus-target" distance. If the transition is extensive, the effect of

Mother Speech Tense

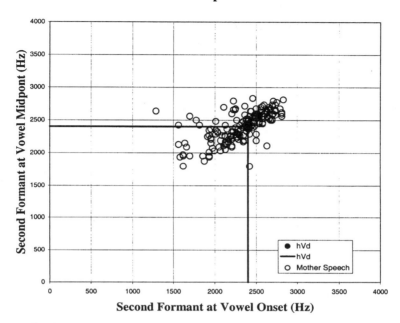

FIG. 7.4. BT speech tense vowels in /hVd/ context. The *x* axis shows vowel on-set values, and the *y* axis shows vowel midpoint measurements. Dotted lines connected to the open circle in each figure indicate /hVd/ citation values for the speaker.

shortening the vowel is expected to be more marked than in a sequence in which onset and vowel midpoint frequencies differ minimally.[2] In other words, with a large "locus-target" distance, there is a greater probability that the formant in question will reflect contextual assimilation and reduction.

From the vantage point of this model of formant undershoot, vowel formant variations are seen as a function of both durational factors and consonant context. An additional analysis was therefore done to examine whether the present vowels showed effects of coarticulation with surrounding consonants.

F_2 was measured for both vowels at the vowel midpoint and at the vowel onset which was defined as the CV-boundary. Results are presented in Figs. 7.4 and 7.5 in which F_2 at the vowel midpoint (*y*-axis) is plotted against the F_2 at the vowel onset (*x*-axis). The format of the diagram is similar to that for

---

[2]Words like *wheel, chewed, sauce,* etc. show extensive F2 transitions and thus have large "locus"–"target" distances, whereas the F2 transitions in *dad* and *wool* have limited frequency spans.

Mother Speech Lax

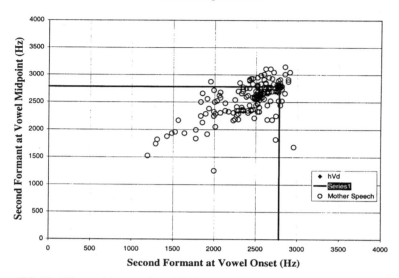

FIG. 7.5. BT speech lax vowels in /hVd/ context. The x axis shows vowel onset
values, and the y axis shows vowel midpoint measurements. Dotted lines connected to the open circle in each figure indicate /hVd/ citation values for the
speaker.

"locus equations" (Sussman, McCaffrey, & Matthews, 1991), except that in
the present case the interest is in predicting the vowel attributes from the
consonant rather than the other way around. Dotted lines connected to the
open circle in each figure indicate /hVd/ citation values for the speaker.
Data points fit a generally linear trend (tense vowel, $r = .64$; lax vowel, $r =
.66$). We conclude that there is apparently a great deal of consonant–vowel
coarticulation in the present data and that, if the vowel onset is known, the
value at the vowel midpoint can be estimated with reasonable accuracy.

Multiple regression analyses were also performed using F_2 midpoint as
the dependent variable and with vowel duration and vowel onset as the independent variables. As predicted by the duration and context dependent
undershoot model, there was improvement in predicting F_2 midpoints. The
r-scores improved especially in vowels preceded by alveolar consonants
for which the locus–target distances were in general the largest (tense
vowel, $r = .84$; lax vowel, $r = .83$).

We conclude that the F_2 variance of this BT sample is not unlike other
types of speech in exhibiting contextual assimilation and in reflecting the
dynamic coarticulatory interplay between consonant and vowel gestures.
Accordingly, vowel formant variability appears to be determined by durational and contextual factors to a large extent.

Morpheme Type Effects

Another possible dimension that might highlight prototypical values for the infant is stress and prosodic salience. Because it has long been recognized that the auditory analysis of prosodic phenomena and their transcription are difficult tasks that depend strongly on, among other things, the native language of the transcriber and the framework that she has been trained in (Lieberman, 1965). As an alternative to making subjective perceptual judgments of the relative stress among syllables, we adopted a classification method that would *reflect* their *prominence in an indirect manner*. The reasoning behind the choice was based on the observation that "content words" are more likely to exhibit a prominent syllable in connected speech than are "function words." Content words contain semantic morphemes classified as nouns, verbs, adjectives, and adverbs. Function words are essentially free grammatical morphemes such as pronouns, articles, prepositions. Accordingly, t tests were performed for both /i/ and /ɪ/. They indicated nonsignificant differences between grammatical and semantic morphemes. The single exception was F_2 for /i/, which showed a barely significant difference between the two morpheme types. For each vowel, morpheme types were further subdivided into those carrying lexical stress and those without lexical stress. None of these comparisons showed a significant difference.

Adaptation Effects

The variability in this corpus appears to be the sort of variability usually encountered in acoustic analyses of connected speech (Lindblom et al., 1992). None of the variables examined revealed a clear acoustic prototype. The question then arises whether this BT sample, which clearly sounds like talk to a baby, differs from an adult-directed speech style in the formant values for /i/ and /ɪ/. Specifically, does this speaker show acoustic adaptation in BT compared with her adult-directed speech? Before we can address those questions, there is a methodological issue to address; whether there are differences in the distribution of consonant contexts that might give rise to effects of contextual assimilation and might effect the two styles differently.

Both vowels were analyzed with respect to place of articulation of the preceding and following consonants for both speech styles (BT and AA). Pairwise comparisons were made of percentage of occurrence of place use in initial and final contexts. They showed a high correlation between the two styles for both vowels (r for /i/: .73; for /ɪ/: .81) indicating that the two styles were statistically comparable in their use of place and that, accordingly, no style-dependent contextual bias is likely to have influenced formant values differentially.

Figures 7.6 and 7.7 display results from a comparison of BT speech and adult-directed speech for /i/ and /ɪ/. Both figures are arrayed in F_1–F_2 space and values are in mel. BT speech values are represented by dark circles, adult-directed speech values by open circles. For /i/ BT values are quite diffuse, ranging from 200–800 mel in F_1, from 1100–2200 mel in F_2. AA values are also quite diffuse, with approximately the same range of values for both speech styles. BT values for /ɪ/ are somewhat more compact. In contrast, AA /i/ values are more diffuse in F_1 than F_2. A t test for significance confirms the visual impression of these figures. For /i/, a t test for difference in F_1 and F_2 between the AA and BT samples was not significant for either formant value. For /ɪ/, the t test results were significant for both F_1 and F_2 between the two speech styles. Mean formant values displayed in Table 7.3 show certain regular trends.

In every instance, values for AA speech are lower than BT speech. The /ɪ/ differences are significant, /i/ differences are not. It appears reasonable to assume that the F_1 differences derive mostly from the higher F_0's associated with the BT style. If the F_2 differences are seen as reflecting the effect of consonant context which tends to lower formant values, there would be some basis for saying that, showing a somewhat more restricted F_2 range, BT presents some evidence of formant adaptation.

Adult-Adult with Mother Speech Lax

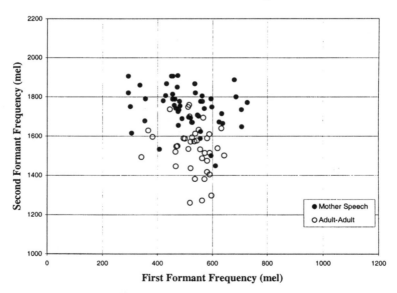

FIG. 7.6. BT and AA speech for lax /ɪ/. $F1$–$F2$ diagrams calibrated in mel units for /ɪ/ (Fig. 7.6) and /i/ (Fig. 7.7). Comparisons of BT (dark circles) with AA (open circles) are shown.

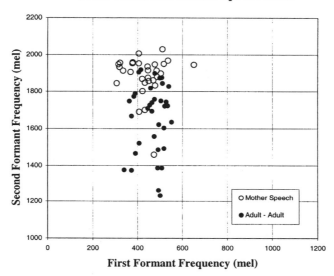

FIG. 7.7. BT and AA speech for tense /I/. *F*1–*F*2 diagrams calibrated in mel units for /I/ (Fig. 7.6) and /i/ (Fig. 7.7). Comparisons of BT (dark circles) with AA (open circles) are shown.

Summary of Findings

The four questions raised at the beginning of the results section were answered as follows:

- "Are there /i/ and /ɪ/ prototypes in this sample of BT speech addressed to a 6-month old infant?" Taking the prototype of a vowel to be defined as the mean average formant pattern identical with that observed in a citation-style /hVd/ word, our conclusion was that, if they exist at all, they form an extremely small subsets of the observations.

TABLE 7.3
Adaptation MS/AA

	/i/		/ɪ/	
	AA	MS	AA	MS
F_1	453	521	529	563*
F_2	1655	1820	1537	1755*

- "Are there attributes in the signal context that ear-mark certain BT tokens as prototypical for the infant?" We looked at *nasalization, vowel duration*, and *prominence* effects indirectly estimated in terms of morpheme type. We concluded that, although nasalization effects were strongly masked by overall variability, they were discernible particularly in vowels preceding nasal segments. With respect to vowel duration, it was found that, for /i/, longer duration *did* seem to produce more prototypical values in this speaker, whereas, for /ɪ/, an effect of duration was not apparent. As for morpheme type, we observed that F_2 for /i/ showed a barely significant difference between grammatical and semantic morpheme categories.
- "Are prototypes derivable from signal dynamics, that is, from vowel information used in conjunction with other properties present in the vowel's immediate signal context? We concluded that this BT sample is not unlike other types of speech in exhibiting contextual assimilation and that the observed F_2 variability is systematic and can, to a large extent, be explained in terms of durational and contextual factors.
- "Does BT show less variability than AA?" Although the effect was not strong, some evidence of formant adaptation was evident.

The key characteristic of the /i/ and /ɪ/ vowels of this BT sample is the extensive variability of their formant patterns. At the same time, there *are* certain patterns of covariation between those formant patterns and other signal attributes, some stronger such as the combined effect of consonant context and duration, others present in more subtle ways such as nasalization.

DISCUSSION

Facts or Artifacts?

The present results offer minimal support for the suggestion that vowel prototypes be identified as absolute and invariant formant values, directly, or indirectly, observable in BT speech. In view of the fact that, in a series of papers, Kuhl has presented a strong case for believing that speech perception by infants as young as 6 months old is organized in terms of prototypes, it seems natural to begin the discussion of the present findings by examining the quality of the observations. An obvious question is: In view of the massive variability, can the measurements be trusted? Is the variability genuine or spurious? Are the present formant data representative of American English BT in general? Are the present large formant variations typical of BT?

Comparing the present sample of BT with descriptions of Motherese by others for English (Fernald, 1985, 1993; Fernald & Simon, 1984; Snow, 1972, 1977; Stern, Spieker, Barnett, & MacKain, 1983), and for other languages

(Fernald, Taeschner, Dunn, Papousek, Boysson-Bardies, & Fukui, 1989), we are struck by the many similarities. Prosodically, BT is reported to show, among other things, higher average F_0, wider F_0 range, redundant repetition and longer pauses. The present sample is compatible with those reports in exhibiting all of those characteristics. It accordingly appears justified to assume that, with respect to prosody, the present BT is in no way anomalous.

What about segmental aspects? We note that the present recording took place under naturalistic conditions. The speaker appeared oblivious of being recorded and adopted a very lively, spontaneous style and sounded very much like "talking to a young baby." Spontaneous speech is of course very different from citation forms produced under laboratory conditions. As already pointed out, numerous factors in spontaneous speech (e.g., high F_0) make accurate formant frequency measurements rather difficult. Acoustic phonetics still lacks established procedures for estimating formant frequencies in sounds with high F_0 values. As discussed earlier, one of the difficulties is that a high F_0 reduces the definition of the spectral envelope and, hence, of the formant peaks. It might therefore be suggested that, if more accurate formant estimations had been obtained, it would in fact have been possible to establish prototypical formant patterns (in the sense of mean absolute formant frequency patterns identical with the formant patterns observed in citation-style /hVd/ words).

After carefully and repeatedly working through the present database, we feel confident that the extensive formant variability reported here is not, to any significant degree, caused by spurious measurement errors. To be sure, there are such errors, but they do not dominate other sources of variation. This conclusion is based on two main lines of argument. First, there are strong a priori reasons not to expect absolute "prototypical formant values" to be present in BT, or any other speaking style for that matter (see pp. 145–146). Second, it has been shown that the observed formant variations are definitely systematic in nature (pp. 148–150).

Making Sense of BT Variability: A Preview

Having concluded that the varibility of this BT sample cannot be dismissed as artefactual, we are faced with the task of trying to make sense of it. Such a goal is an ambitious one that amounts to tackling key issues, not only of BT, but of speech research in general. Thus it cannot realistically be reached in one step, but, nonetheless, we shall here make a preliminary approach to it. The discussion is structured in seven steps.

We begin by relating our findings on observations on speaking styles and to the account of phonetic variation proposed by the proposed H&H theory (Lindblom, 1990). Those two steps will lead us to conclude that we should not expect prototypes (in the sense of absolute and constant formant patterns) in any speaking style. From this theoretical vantage point, they cannot be expected to be directly observable, nor embedded along with other linguistically irrelevant attributes under the signal surface (cf. Lindblom et al., 1992). In these sections we also establish that phonetic variations in BT cannot plausibly be explained by invoking H&H theory because its account of variability attributes a role to "signal-independent knowledge," a type of information that, in all probability, remains to be developed by 6-month-old listeners (pp. 138–139).

The next three steps consider how the phonetic aspects of such knowledge might get established in acquisition. Here experiments on speech perception in animals offer important clues. In particular, they suggest that, if phonetic memory is assumed to develop by a process of "exemplar-based learning" (Estes, 1994), a mechanism becomes available that will handle any stimulus variability as long as it is lawful and systematic (p. 154). Such a mechanism appears plausible and parsimonious in that it implements context-sensitive processing in a direct and implicit manner—that is, it does not necessitate attributing to the infant the ability to correct for context effects by explicit cognitive computation (pp. 138–139).

The sixth step resumes discussion of the present results. The F_0-dependence of F_1 and the prediction of F_2 values from contextual information are highlighted. The commentary on these analyses also bring in findings by other investigations that help explain why variability of the observed kind should be expected rather than suspected. They amplify the previous conclusions in indicating that, although considerable, the formant variability of the present BT is systematic.

By way of final conclusion, we shall propose an attempt at resolving the paradox out of which the present investigation originates. Albeit at first they appear incompatible, prototypes in infant speech perception and the variability of BT speech can indeed be reconciled. If prototype is defined, not as a single *point* in phonetic space, but as a *function* established exclusively by experience and tuned, during the course of acquisition, to express the lawful covariation between the aspect of the signal that undergoes modulation (in this study: vowel formant pattern) and the factors that induce that modulation (the several dimensions of vowel context).

Consequently, it seems possible to make some preliminary sense of phonetic BT variability provided that the ideas of "signal-driven phonetic memory" and "precompilation of context effects" are introduced and the notion of prototype is reinterpreted.

Prototypes and the Variety of Speech Functions

Human speech serves a number of functions. Being intelligible is often one of the most important ones, but it is not the only condition that is met by normal speech. For instance, when a mother speaks to her baby, she does so with many implicit goals in mind: for instance, to establish and maintain contact with her child (in Jakobson's terminology so-called *phatic* communication) and to keep the baby happy and motivated (the *emotive* function (Jakobson, 1960)). In many situations, those aspects become more important than optimizing the speech signal with respect to intelligibility.

Fónagy (1983) offers important insights on the topic of speaking styles. In *La vive voix*, he presents results of X-ray analyses of Hungarian vowels produced by an actress in different tones of voice. An /e/ in a sadly spoken phrase is seen to exhibit a larger constriction opening than the corresponding angry variant. As a result of such emotional transforms, a vowel which is psychologically and linguistically an /e:/ is found to be physically more like an [I:] when articulated with "tension," as in an angry utterance. And, conversely, an intended /i/ is produced phonetically more like an [e] when a relaxed style is used as, for instance, when expressing "indifference." The point is that normal utterances contain a number of cues that contribute to give the listener the impression of "anger," "sadness," "indifference," and so forth. Listeners perceive those cues and use them in processing the speech signal. Thus, in talking to her child, a French mother may say: "*Mais si voyons!*" In a neutral pronunciation, this utterance would be rendered as: [msivwajõ]. However, in baby talk, it is more likely to come out as: *meu su voyons!* [moesyvwajõ] with strong lip rounding, a cross-culturally common sign of affection. To another adult, the utterance is likely to be heard as intended but also as produced in an affectionate tone of voice. The work of Fónagy suggests that listeners are able, as it were, to "undo" the various style-dependent transforms that utterances undergo and recover its linguistic contents despite sometimes radical departures from their neutral or prototypical phonetic form.

Clearly, such observations raise a number of questions about the nature of phonetic prototypes. If stylistic transforms are capable of modifying speech patterns that drastically, the prospects seem extremely remote of finding absolute and constant formant patterns under the surface of other noisy and linguistically irrelevant attributes also carried by that signal. We realize that for a priori reasons we should not expect prototypes so defined to be present in BT or other speaking styles.

Prototypes and H&H Theory

How should the problem of accounting for the variability of speech directed to children be approached? The following brief summary of a recently proposed theory should provide a useful perspective on that question. This is a theory that can be said to offer a "*presupposition*" account of (intraspeaker) phonetic variation—for short, the *H(yper)&H(ypo)* theory (Lindblom, 1990; Lindblom et al., 1992).

In linguistics, the term *presupposition* is normally used with reference to how producers of text and speakers handle old and new information. The choice of the grammatical and lexical form of a sentence depends in a significant way on the assumptions that the speaker makes about what the listener knows or does not know. In saying, for instance, "he put it there," rather than "the carpenter put the hammer on the table," the speaker makes the tacit assumption, the *presupposition*, that since the listener already knows what the current topic is, and that, therefore (s)he does not need to use the forms "carpenter" and "hammer" again.

H&H theory views the phonetics of speech production as highly analogous to the generation of lexical and grammatical forms. It is derived from experimental evidence indicating that speech intelligibility depends partly on the quality and contents of the signal, partly on the extent to which the signal engages short- and long-term phonetic, lexical, grammatical, and other knowledge stored in the native listener's brain (Pickett & Pollack, 1963; Pollack & Pickett, 1964). The amount of such signal-independent information fluctuates between and within utterances during processing. As a consequence, the probability, or predictability, of a given phonetic unit does not stay constant, but tends to vary from one situation to the next. That is illustrated by comparing expressions such as *(a) The next word is __* with *(b) A bird in the hand is worth two in the __*.

Evidently, the formation of the speech percept is not the responsibility of the signal alone. Therefore it need not contain *all* the information, only an amount sufficient for the percept to emerge in interaction with the stored knowledge. Logically, the minimal task of the speaker is to ensure that linguistic units have enough discriminatory power for correct lexical identification. Of particular significance in this context is to note that, in principle, these units need not necessarily be instantiated in the signal in their invariant, *prototypical* form.

The reasoning may be further clarified by the following scenario. For an idealized case, the theory assumes that the speaker makes a running estimate of the listener's need for explicit signal information on a moment-to-moment basis and then adapts the production of the utterance elements (words, syllables, or phonemes) to those needs. This occurs along a continuum with more forcefully articulated "hyper"-forms at one end and less energetic "hypo"-forms at the other.

To provide a hypothetical example, let us consider a talk on voice production in which the lecturer describes the *adduction* and *abduction* of the vocal folds. When these terms are first introduced, there is a clear risk that the listener will confuse them, because, especially in casual pronunciation and class-room acoustics, they sound very similar. The lecturer may intuitively know that and may therefore initially adopt a more overarticulated pronunciation (*hyperspeech*), or, (s)he may maintain a casual style (*hypo-*

speech) which is likely to generate misunderstandings and give rise to requests for clarification. In both cases, forms that highlight the relevant contrast will eventually be produced, for instance AD-Duction versus AB-Duction (with clear segmentation into syllables and with stress on the first rather than the second syllable).

As the performance goes from hypo to hyper, the duration and the amplitude of articulatory gestures tend to increase, whereas their temporal overlap tends to decrease. As a result, the context-dependence of articulatory and acoustic patterns is minimal in hyper-speech and maximal in hypo-speech. Further consequences are that coarticulation and reduction are typical of the hypo-mode and that the vowels and consonants of hyper-speech are closer to their target values in hyper-speech. The exact point on the *hyper–hypo* continuum at which a given phonetic form is produced is determined by the speaker's assumptions about the informational needs of the listener and by his own tacit demand for articulatory simplification. It is in this sense that H&H theory can be said to give a "*presupposition*" *account* of *phonetic variation*.

Accordingly, H&H claims that, for principled rather than empirical reasons, the search for absolute and constant formant patterns will be in vain, and that speech signals do not encode vowel prototypes as absolute and invariant formant patterns (cf. question (1) earlier) embedded in noise and other linguistically irrelevant signal attributes. It thus reinforces the conclusions reached in the previous discussion of stylistic transforms.

On the Development of Phonetic Memory: Exemplar-Based Learning

In the H&H explanation of phonetic variation, the task of the signal is essentially to supply "missing information." The remaining factors underlying the formation of speech percepts are assumed to originate from short-term and long-term knowledge stored in the listener's memory (*signal-independent information*). Because it goes without saying that such knowledge is largely still to be developed by infants, phonetic variation in BT directed to a 6-month-old child cannot be successfully accounted for by invoking H&H theory. Again we must ask, how should finding a plausible account be approached?

In proposing an answer, we first review some experimental results on speech perception by animals reported by Kluender, Diehl, and Killeen (1987). In this study, Japanese quail were trained to peck in response to /dVs/-syllables, but to avoid pecking when hearing the corresponding /bVs/- or /gVs/-sequences. This task was successfully mastered by the birds for a stimulus set in which the vowels were: /i/, /u/, /æ/, and /a/.

In a second experiment, the same quail were presented with new stimuli containing the same consonants but different vowels: /ɪ ʊ eɪ oʊ ɔɪ ʼ /. The birds were able to generalize their responses to the new stimuli indicating that the syllables presented to the quail were sufficiently rich acoustically to support correct categorization. Consequently, at least for isolated, clearly spoken syllables, phonetic categories appear to be definable acoustically.

We cannot know how the stimuli were represented in the quails' brains, or what acoustic and auditory parameters were used. However, we *can* find some indirect clues in some acoustic measurements published in the literature, for instance, by Öhman (1966), who examined speech samples not unlike the stimuli of the quail study. Symmetrical and asymmetrical V_1CV_2 sequences were used. They contained all possible combinations of /b d g/ and /y ö a o u/ and were spoken by a single Swedish speaker. Figure 7.8 summarizes the results. At the top, a stylized spectrogram to define the measurements which were taken from Öhman's Table IV and which include the onset of the F_2 transition at the CV_2-boundary (plotted along the x axis in the 3-dimensional diagram), the F_3 transition onset at the CV_2-boundary (y axis), and the F_2 value at the V_2-steady-state (z axis). When the individual measurements[3] from all the test words are enclosed by smooth lines, three cloud-like configurations are obtained. Their elongated shapes reflect vowel–consonant coarticulation effects: In other words, they indicate that formant values at the CV-boundary depend on the identity of the preceding and following vowels.

The principal interest of redescribing the Öhman observations in this manner derives from the fact that the three configurations show no overlap. In this 3-dimensional formant space, they are clearly separated. That result gives us a clue to understanding the results of the quail experiments. During the first experiment, the birds learned to distinguish between syllables with or without /d/. Suppose that this was possible first of all because the auditory parameters of each stimulus were stored in memory in relatively unprocessed and analog form and second, because for each of the three syllable types (those with /b/, with /d/, and with /g/), something neurally equivalent to the discrete, multidimensional "clouds" of Fig. 7.8 was eventually established in the networks of the quail brain[4]. If the syllables containing /b/, /d/, and /g/ can be separated on the acoustic level, they presumably remain distinct also at a neural level. Furthermore, a choice be-

---

[3]A total of 125 data points per consonant were included in this analysis (5 repetitions of 25 $V_1\_V_2$ sequences for each consonant).

[4]If we make the reasonable assumption that perceptual processing has access to *at least* the three dimensions used in the present analyses, it is clear that, in principle, the information available in the acoustic signal is sufficient to disambiguate the place of the consonants. Admittedly, the three dimensions selected here do not by any means exhaust the signal attributes that might carry place information, one obvious omission being the spectral dynamics of the stop releases (Stevens 1968). But adding such dimensions to the consonant space would no doubt only further increase the separation of the three "clouds." Rather than decrease their distinctiveness, it would enhance it.

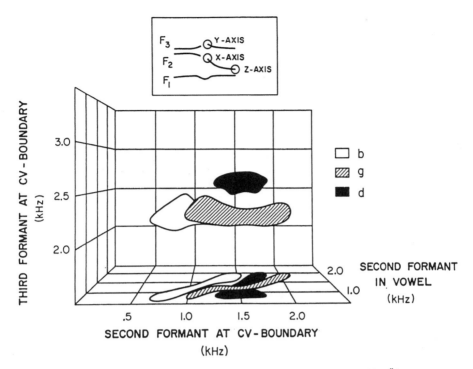

FIG. 7.8. A replotting of formant frequency data originally published by Öhman (1966) for Swedish VCV sequences. The insert at the top center indicate the selected measurements.

tween pecking, or refraining from pecking, gradually gets associated with each cloud. When the new stimuli of the second experiment are presented, the birds can relate the auditory parameters of those stimuli to the stored information on the previous set. A new stimulus falling inside the "/d/-cloud" leads to a pecking response, one that ends up outside it inhibits pecking.

Three points deserve to be highlighted: In the quail stimuli and in the sequences used by Öhman, it would be very difficult to find invariant physical attributes characteristic of each separate consonant category. In view of the account given, there is no longer any need to define such measures. It is the position of H&H theory that there cannot be any such absolute numerical measurements corresponding to the three place categories because that is not the way that speech is organized. The quest for invariance is theoretically misguided.

In the hypothetical phonetic memory that we visualized in terms of 3-D clouds and speculatively attributed to the quail, more and more stimulus information is accumulated during the course of experimental exposure. In the model the memory is assumed to be constructed by *storing* (selected aspects of) *individual stimulus exemplars*. This accumulation leads to an acquisition of phonetic (acoustic–auditory) "knowledge" embodied in the neural networks of the brain. We should note that this is knowledge built from speech signals, but once in the memory it is can no longer be found in individual stimulus instances of a given category. It exemplifies what we have called "signal-independent information."

This way of looking at the creation of memory structures has a fairly long tradition in experimental psychology. For an overview of *exemplar-based learning* see especially Estes (1994). For applications to speech development see Jusczyk (1994) and Lacerda (1995, forthcoming).

Implicit and Explicit Context-Sensitive Rules

The third point worth noting is that the cloud model can be seen as a way of implementing "*context-sensitive rules*" in perceptual processing, and that this implementation of context is totally *implicit*. To clarify that claim, we offer an example of an *explicit* perceptual context-sensitive rule for handling a typical case of consonant-vowel coarticulation.

Consider a language in which a consonant becomes [+palatal] when it precedes a vowel classified as [+palatal]. To capture this fact phonologists usually adopt the rule notation of (2):

$$C \rightarrow [\text{+palatal}] /\_ [\text{+vowel, +palatal}] \qquad (2)$$

Next assume that speech perception involves recovering the prototypical values of phonetic segments from a signal that shows the effects of coarticulation. Describing perceptual processing one might attempt to state (2) in reverse and one would thus obtain:

$$[C, \text{+palatal}] /\_ [V, \text{+palatal}] \rightarrow C \qquad (3)$$

The process specified in (3) is an explicit "computation" which is performed on the sample under analysis, namely [C, +palatal], and its adjacent context, that is /_ [V, +palatal]. With those two pieces of input information, the context-free C is produced as an output.

The rules in (2) and (3) were presented as examples of phonological (language-specific) coarticulation in order to introduce the familiar, and explicit, rule notation that phonologists use. However, the argument is identical if we think of (2) and (3) as describing phonetic phenomena. For instance, we can let "[C, +palatal]" represent a formant pattern sampled at a CV boundary, and "[V, +palatal]" a formant pattern measured in the vowel following the C. Applying (3) at those two points, we can derive the identity of the abstract C category. That is essentially the procedure proposed in discussions of the perceptual implications of so-called "locus equations" (Sussman, Fructer, Hilbert, & Sirosh, 1999; Sussman et al., 1991).

Next we return to the cloud model of phonetic memeory in which each consonant category is represented by a set of syllable patterns whose auditory representations include, at the very least we assume, information on the formant patterns at the CV boundary and in the vowel. Again we note that, the presence of coarticulation implies that, at the CV boundary, formant patterns do not stay constant for each place of articulation but show vowel-dependent variation. The cloud model handles that fact by *storing the information **undergoing** the variation* (in this particular case: F_2 and F_3 variations at the CV boundary) *along with the information **causing** the variation* (F_2 in the vowel). Once the clouds have been established in memory, the recognition of a new instance of a given category becomes a matter of "*pattern matching*" and "*similarity*," that is measuring its "*auditory distance*" to the already stored exemplars, in cloud space systematically arranged in discrete, but categorically coherent sets. There is no need for explicit computation, the "context-sensitive rules" being already embodied in the clouds. Recognition is in a sense *direct* (Fowler, 1986, 1994) and based on instantaneous "*resonance*" between stimulus and memory items (Shepard, 1984) and on handling context effects by "*precompilation*" rather than by means of explicit rules (Klatt 1979, 1989)[5].

Speech Development and Explicit Versus Implicit Context-Sensitive Rules

The point of the preceding considerations is that, on grounds of descriptive simplicity, the implicit model should be our preferred choice. It is signal-driven and thus more parsimonious than explicit processing which presupposes the participation of cognitive structures already in place (see note 6). Phonetic learning is controlled mainly by experience and by the properties of the heard speech.

Such a mechanism has considerable plausibility as a component of a speech development model, for it helps us understand how perceptual prototypes can be established in speech development *despite* extensive variability in the input speech and *in spite of* the fact that, at six months, cognitive abilities are still presumably rudimentary.[6]

---

[5]Quantitative definitions of these notions, necessary in a formal implementation of the model sketched here, are future research tasks.

[6]If we assume that cognitive structures are already in place and that they even possess a certain sophistication in the young child, several additional questions must be faced. How did those structures get there? How did those abilities get established? Postulating a priori capabilities to explain infant behavior, may not necessarily turn out to be wrong, but raises additional questions. Clearly it is nonparsimonious and hence methodologically less desirable.

The Systematic Nature of Phonetic Variability

Figure 7.1 shows that both F_1 and F_0 vary over ranges that are large compared with those observed for laboratory conditions. The reason why F_0 behaves in this way was briefly touched upon earlier (see p. 141): It appears to be a typical characteristic of spontaneous lively conversation, especially BT (Fernald, 1993).

Why does F_1 cover such a broad range? A further examination of the F_1 values of both /i/ and /ɪ/ indicates that there is a clear tendency toward covariation. For /i/, 90% of the F_1 values fall inside the ($2F_0$–F_0) interval. The corresponding number for /ɪ/ is 85%. As mentioned earlier, there is a tendency for vowel tokens followed by a nasal to have a higher F_1. When those cases are disregarded, 96% and 89% of /i/ and /ɪ/ respectively fall between F_0 and $2F_0$. If straight lines are fitted to all tokens not followed by a nasal consonant, for both /i/ and /ɪ/, F_1 is given by $F_1 = m\, F_0$. For /i/, m = 1.198 with a standard error of 0.035. For /ɪ/, m = 1.292 with a standard error of 0.037. Why should there be such a relationship?

In female laboratory speech (Peterson & Barney, 1952), F_1 and F_0 are relatively close in /i/. It is known that when F_0 increases in frequency, under certain conditions there is a tendency for F_1 shift up with it. An example is loud speech (Schulman, 1989). Based on his psychoacoustic experimentation, Hartmut Traunmüller (1981) of Stockholm University has designed a tape demonstration in which both F_0 and F_1 of a naturally spoken female /i/ are modified by means of a computer program based on the technique of LPC-synthesis. When F_1 alone is shifted up in frequency,[7] listeners hear a sequence that begins with /i/ and ends with /æ/, but when F_1 and F_0 are varied together,[8] the /i/ quality is not changed appreciably. That is a bit remarkable in view of the fact that F_1 reaches as high as 838 Hz, whereas the average female /i/ is 310 Hz according to Peterson and Barney (1952). What listeners typically report is that, for the case of F_1–F_0 covarying, the vocal effort of the speaker appears to increase. Presumably, listeners report hearing a relatively fixed /i/ quality because the stimuli of the second series match their experience of normal and loud /i/ sounds. In other words, the reason why they "cope with" the F_1 variations of the second set of /i/ variants is because they do not expect a constant F_1. They expect F_1 and F_0 to covary along the dimension of loudness, as under everyday conditions.

It appears reasonable that F_0 should be largely determined by prosodic and stylistic factors. F_1, on the other hand, ought to serve primarily as a de-

---

[7]In equal Bark steps and with F0 and other formants left unchanged.

[8]In lockstep fashion and in a way that maintains a constant Bark distance between F1 and F0. First series: F0 constant at 161 Hz, while F1 varies from 250, 347, 453, 569, 697, and to 838 Hz. Second series: F1 varies as in the first series. So does F0 but lags one step behind: 161, 250, 347, 453, 569, and 697 Hz.

terminant of segmental information, such as the phonetic vowel quality. Why doesn't F_1 stay constant in vowels varying in loudness? Returning to Fig. 7.1, we must ask: Why don't the F_1 values of the two vowels show very narrow distributions with points clustering tightly around their prototypical values and forming basically horizontal lines?

Keeping F_1 of an /i/ constant, but giving F_0 freedom to vary, has some interesting consequences according to acoustic theory (Fant, 1960). In the upper end of the F_0 range, say from $F_0 > 400-500$ Hz, the first harmonic would be higher than the reference value for a female /i/ (as we recall, it is 310 Hz (Peterson & Barney, 1952)). The spectrum of a vowel with $F_1 = 310$ Hz and $F_0 = 600$ Hz would totally lack energy in the region of F_1. Its first harmonic would be the fundamental frequency at 600 Hz. Since a vowel's intensity is largely determined by the energy in the F_1 region (Fant, 1960), the sound in question would be considerably weakened in amplitude as compared with the case of $F_1 = F_0$.[9] To produce vowels of constant output power, it would be necessary to make F_0 and F_1 values more equal either by lowering F_0, or by raising F_1. Because a speaker's F_0 variations are intimately linked to prosodic and stylistic factors, the necessary change occurs in F_1.

An illustration of these relationships comes from research on singing. Sundberg (1987) has shown that, at high pitches, sopranos change their vowel articulation so as to "track" the high first harmonic with the first formant. When they do so, the power of the radiated sound is more constant. Intuitively, singers seem to know how to do that. Do speakers of BT behave similarly? We believe so as shown by the following considerations.

Mothers and caretakers speaking BT, vary their F_0 a great deal. This is true partly because these speakers also vary their vocal effort. What would happen if, in producing an /i/, BT speakers were to maintain their F_1 values at frequencies typical of normal voice effort, (say at the population average of 310 Hz)? The preceding remarks on F_1-F_0 interaction and output sound intensity indicate that keeping F_1 of /i/ and /ɪ/ constant at prototypical values would totally defeat the purpose of speaking in a loud voice. Keeping F_1 constant while trying to say a loud /i/, would involve increasing phonation amplitude while maintaining the relatively small mouth opening unchanged. What speakers do instead in /i/ and /ɪ/ tokens with high F_0, is to raise the first formant to maintain the level of the output. As the preceding remarks indicate, they are in fact "forced" to do so by acoustic theory. Furthermore, to judge the intended vowel correctly, listeners must process the

---

[9]Unless otherwise stated, these remarks focus on the intensity variations associated with changes in formant values and fundamental frequency. They assume that phonation (voice source) amplitude remains constant in all cases. In lockstep fashion and in a way that maintains a constant Bark distance between F1 and F0. First series: F0 constant at 161 Hz, while F1 varies from 250, 347, 453, 569, 697, and to 838 Hz. Second series: F1 varies as in the first series. So does F0, but lags one step behind: 161, 250, 347, 453, 569, and 697 Hz.

formant pattern in accordance with F_0 cues and other contextual signal information. The Traunmüller demonstration shows that they can indeed do so.

F_2 was found to span the range between 1750 and 2800 Hz in /i/. In /ɪ/ it extended from 1400 up to 3150 Hz. A large portion of this variation was found
to be linked to durational and contextual factors (see pp. 147–150), but as
pointed out in the Methods section, that may not be the only source. Recall
that, at high F_0:s, the F_2 and F_3 peaks were not resolved individually. Only a
single maximum was evident. In those cases, F_2 had to be measured at the
frequency of that maximum, and represents a merger of F_2 and F_3 (F_2-prime),
rather than at the frequency of F_2 per se, which would be identified primarily at low F_0:s. Consequently, the F_2 variance reflects context and dura-
tion-dependence but, to some extent, also the inconsistent way in which F_2
was estimated.

New results on the topic of predicting vowel formant variability are pres-
ently available. Brownlee (1997) undertook an investigation of how stress
influences vowel reduction (= formant undershoot). Analyses were made of
vowels occurring in spontaneous informal conversation as well as in controlled laboratory speech. The lab speech conditions involved reading sentences in which the degree of prominence on the test items was systematically manipulated so as to cover a range from *emphatic stress, focus,
nonfocus,* and *neutral stress.* For comparison, the test items were also spoken as isolated words (citation forms). To maximize the probability of dura-
tion-dependent formant undershoot, the selected test sequences were [wil],
[wɪl], [wl], and [weɪl] (with front vowels occurring between labio-velar consonants so as to provide large locus-target distances). In the lab speech as
well as the informal conversations, all the vowels of all the subjects (three
native American speakers) exhibited the large formant variations expected
according to the duration- and context-dependent undershoot model
(Moon & Lindblom, 1994) with the total range of F_2 was often in excess of
1000 Hz. To account for her results, Brownlee (1997) presented a revised
version of the undershoot model which predicts vowel formant frequencies
by means of three (rather than two) factors: (i) the locus-target distance;
(ii) the duration of the transition from the initial consonant to the vowel;
(iii) the velocity of that transition.

Two circumstances make Brownlee's description of her results particularly compelling and convincing. The quantitative predictions of the model
are excellent[10] both for the read sentences and the spontaneous speech.
Second, the revision was developed on the basis of independent theoretical
grounds. It consisted in adding formant velocity as a biomechanically motivated index of "articulatory effort," a choice suggested by the theoretical
and experimental work of Nelson (1983) and Nelson, Perkell, and Westbury

---

[10]Predicted F_2 regressed on observed F_2 gave r^2-scores > .9 for the vowels spoken by the two
male speakers and > .79 for the female speaker.

(1984). Accordingly, the thorny problem of subjectively assessing degree of stress, is here replaced by measuring an acoustic correlate of production "effort." An interesting consequence of this move is that, in offering an operational definition of stress (effort), her model becomes capable of handling stress as a continuously varying parameter and can be applied very generally across all styles and speaking conditions.

Brownlee's findings make several important points. First, her work opens an avenue for continued work on speaking styles and spontaneous speech in defining the biomechanical space within which stylistically determined phonetic variations are constrained to take place. Second our own findings on vowel duration and dynamic context effects (see pp. 147–150) are paralleled and reinforced by her analyses. Third, in describing acoustic data that pattern in an orderly way, her results add credibility to one of our own main points about speech signal variability: It is systematic. Recall that this systematicity is the key to our proposed explanation of how phonetic prototypes get established in acquisition: We have suggested that a phonetic memory developed by a process of "exemplar-based learning" is a mechanism that is capable of handling any stimulus variability as long as it is lawful and systematic.

CONCLUSION: RESOLVING THE PARADOX AND REDIFINING "PROTOTYPE"

As the last step of our argument and, by way of final conclusion, we propose that, albeit at first they appear incompatible, prototypes in infant speech perception and the variability of BT speech can indeed be reconciled. The key to the resolution is that prototype be defined, not as a single *point* in phonetic space, but as a *function* that is established exclusively by experience and which will be tuned, during the course of acquisition, to express the lawful covariation between the aspect of the signal that undergoes modulation (in this study: vowel formant pattern) and the factors that induce that modulation (the several dimensions of vowel context: for example, loudness, F_0 variations, contextual modifications by adjacent consonants, stylistic transforms). Consequently, it seems possible to make some preliminary sense of phonetic BT variability. The main building blocks are "signal-driven phonetic memory" and "precompilation of context effects" and a redefinition of the notion of prototype.

ACKNOWLEDGMENTS

The research of the first author was supported by a research grant from the University Research Institute, The University of Texas at Austin. The research of the second author was supported by a grant from the Advanced

Research Program of the Texas Board of Coordination, grant No. BNS-9011894 from the National Science Foundation and by the HSFR (Humanistiska Samhällsvetenskapliga) of Sweden.

REFERENCES

Atal, B. S., & Schroeder, M. (1974). Recent advances in predictive coding applications to speech synthesis. In G. Fant, J. N. Holmes, & M. R. Schroeder (Eds.), *Speech communication, Vol. 1: Speech wave processing and transmission* (pp. 27–31). Stockholm : Almqvist & Wiksell.

Baran, J., Loffler, M., & Daniloff, R. (1977). Phonological contrastivity in conversation: A comparative study of voice onset time. *Journal of Phonetics, 5,* 339–350.

Bernstein-Ratner, N. (1982). *An acoustic study of mother's speech to language learning children: An analysis of vowel articulation characteristics.* Unpublished doctoral dissertation. Boston University.

Bernstein-Ratner, N. (1984). Phonological rule usage in mother-child speech. *Journal of Phonetics, 12,* 245–254.

Bernstein-Ratner, N. (1986). Durational cues which mark clause boundaries in mother-child speech. *Journal of Phonetics, 14,* 303–309.

Best, C., McRoberts, G., & Sithole, N. (1988). An investigation of young infants' perceptual representation of speech sounds. *Journal of Experimental Psychology: General, 117,* 21–33.

Brownlee, S. A. (1997). The role of sentence stress in vowel reduction and formant undershoot: A study of lab speech and informal, spontaneous speech. (Doctoral dissertation, University of Texas at Austin, 1996). *Dissertation Abstracts International, 58:1, 145–146,* DA9719308.

Carlson, R., Granström, B., & Fant, G. (1970). Some studies concerning perception of isolated vowels. *STL/QPSR 2/3* (pp. 19–35). Royal Institute of Technology, Stockholm, Sweden.

Estes, W. K. (1994). *Classification and cognition.* New York: Oxford University Press.

Fant, G. (1960). *Acoustic theory of speech production.* The Hague: Mouton.

Fant, G. (1968). Analysis and synthesis of speech processes. In B. Malmberg (Ed.), *Manual of phonetics* (pp. 173–277). Amsterdam: North-Holland.

Ferguson, C. A. (1977). Baby talk as a simplified register. In C. E. Snow & C. A. Ferguson (Eds.), *Talking to children: Language input and acquisition* (pp. 219–236). Cambridge, England: Cambridge University Press.

Fernald, A. (1984). The perceptual and affective salience of mothers' speech to infants. In L. Feagans, C. Garvey, & R. Golinkoff (Eds.), *The origins and growth of communication* (pp. 5–29). Norwood, NJ: Ablex.

Fernald, A. (1985). Four-month-old infants prefer to listen to motherese. *Infant Behavior and Development, 8,* 181–195.

Fernald, A. (1989). Intonation and communicative intent in mothers' speech to infants: Is the melody the message? *Child Development, 60,* 1497–1510.

Fernald, A. (1993). Human maternal vocalizations to infants as biologically relevant signals: An evolutionary perspective. In P. Bloom (Ed.), *Language acquisition: Core readings* (pp. 51–94). New York: Harvester Wheatsheaf: New York.

Fernald, A., & Simon, T. (1984). Expanded intonation contours in mother's speech to newborns. *Developmental Psychology, 20,* 104–113.

Fernald, A., Taeschner, T., Dunn, J., Papousek, M., Boysson-Bardies, B., & Fukui, I. (1989). A cross-language study of prosodic modifications in mothers' and fathers' speech to preverbal infants. *Journal of Child Language, 16,* 477–501.

Fónagy, I. (1983). *La vive voix.* Paris: Payot.

Fowler, C. A. (1986). An event approach to the study of speech perception from a direct-realist perspective. *Journal of Phonetics, 14*(1), 3–28.

Fowler, C. A. (1994). Speech perception: Direct realist theory. In R. E. Asher (Ed.), *Encyclopedia of language and linguistics* (pp. 4199–4203). New York: Pergamon.

Fujimura, O. (1962). Analysis of nasal consonants. *Journal of the Acoustical Society of America, 34*, 1865–1875.

Grieser, D., & Kuhl, P. K. (1989). Categorization of speech by infants: Support for speech sound prototypes. *Developmental Psychology, 24*(4), 577–588.

House, A. S., & Stevens, K. N. (1956). Analog studies of nasalization of vowels. *Journal of Speech and Hearing Disorders, 21*, 218–232.

Jakobson, R. (1960). Linguistics and poetics. In T. Sebeok (Ed.), *Style in language* (pp. 350–377). Cambridge, MA: MIT Press.

Jusczyk, P. W. (1994). Infant speech perception and the development of the mental lexicon. In J. C. Goodman & H. C. Nusbaum (Eds.), *The development of speech perception: The transition from speech sounds to spoken words* (pp. 227–270). Cambridge, MA: MIT Press.

Kent, R., & Read, C. (1992), *Acoustic analysis of speech*. San Diego: Singular press.

Klatt, D. H. (1979). Speech perception: A model of acoustic-phonetic analysis and lexical access. *Journal of Phonetics, 7*, 279–312.

Klatt, D. H. (1989). Review of selected models of speech perception. In W. Marslen-Wilson (Ed.), *Lexical representation and process* (pp. 169–226). Cambridge, MA: MIT Press.

Kluender, K. R., Diehl, R., & Killeen, P. (1987). Japanese quail can learn phonetic categories. *Science, 237*, 1195–1197.

Kuhl, P. K. (1991). Human adults and human infants show a perceptual magnet effect for the prototypes of speech categories, monkeys do not. *Perception and Psychophysics, 50*(2), 93–107.

Kuhl, P. K. (1993). Innate predispositions and the effects of experience in speech perception: The native language magnet theory. In B. de Boysson-Bardies, S. de Schonen, P. Jusczyk, P. MacNeilage, & J. Morton (Eds.), *Developmental neurocognition: Speech and face processing in the first year of life* (pp. 259–274). Dordrecht, Holland: Kluwer.

Kuhl, P. K. (1994). Learning and representation in speech and language. *Current Opinion in Neurobiology, 4*, 812–822.

Kuhl, P. K., Williams, K., Lacerda, F., Stevens, K. N., & Lindblom, B. (1992). Linguistic experience alters phonetic perception in infants by 6 months of age. *Science, 255*, 606–608.

Lacerda, F. (1995). The perceptual-magnet effect: An emergent consequence of exemplar-based phonetic memory. In K. Elenius & P. Branderud (Eds.), *Proceedings of the ICPhS 95* (Vol. 2, pp. 140–147). Stockholm.

Lacerda, F. (1999). *Distributed memory representations generate the perceptual-magnet effect.* Manuscript submitted for publication.

Lieberman, P. (1965). Some effects of semantic and grammatical context on production and perception of speech. *Language and Speech, 6*, 172–187.

Lindblom, B. (1963). Spectrographic study of vowel reduction. *Journal of the Acoustical Society of America, 35*, 1773–1781.

Lindblom, B. (1961/1991). Accuracy and limitations of sonagraph measurements. In *Proceedings of the IVth International Congress of Phonetic Sciences*. Mouton deGuyter. Also in R. J. Baken & R. Daniloff (Eds.), *Clinical spectrography of speech.* San Diego: Singular Publishing Group and Kay Elemetrics Corp.

Lindblom, B. (1990). Explaining phonetic variation: A sketch of the H&H theory. In W. J. Hardcastle & A. Marchal (Eds.), *Speech production and speech modeling* (pp. 403–439). Dordrecht, The Netherlands: Kluwer.

Lindblom, B., Brownlee, S. A., Davis, B., & Moon, S. -J. (1992). Speech transforms. *Speech Communication, 11*, 357–368.

Malsheen, B. (1980). Two hypotheses for phonetic clarification in the speech of mothers to children. In G. H. Yeni-Komshian, J. F. Kavanagh, & C. A. Ferguson (Eds.), *Child phonology, Vol. 2. Perception* (pp. 173–184). New York: Academic Press.

Mills, A. E. (1983). Acquisition of speech sounds in the visually handicapped child. In A. E. Mills (Ed.), *Language acquisition in the blind child: Normal and deficient* (pp. 46–56). London: Croom Helm.

Monsen, R. B., & Engebretson, A. M. (1983). The accuracy of formant frequency measurements: A comparison of spectrographic analysis and linear prediction. *Journal of Speech and Hearing Research, 26,* 89–97.

Moon, S. -J., & Lindblom, B. (1994). Interaction between duration, context and speaking style in English stressed vowels. *Journal of the Acoustical Society of America, 96*(1), 40–55.

Nelson, W. L. (1983). Physical principles for economies of skilled movements. *Biological Cybernetics, 46,* 135–147.

Nelson, W. L., Perkell, J. S., & Westbury, J. R. (1984). Mandible movements during increasingly rapid articulations of single syllables: Preliminary observations. *Journal of the Acoustical Society of America, 75*(3), 945–951.

Newport, E. L. (1975). *Motherese: The speech of mothers to children* (Tech. Rep. No. 52). San Diego: University of California, Center for Human Information Processing.

Öhman, S. (1966). Coarticulation in VCV utterances: Spectrographic measurements. *Journal of the Acoustical Society of America, 39*(1), 151–168.

Perkell, J. S., & Klatt, D. H. (Eds.). (1986). *Invariance and variability in speech processes.* Hillsdale, NJ: Lawrence Erlbaum Associates.

Peterson, G. E., & Barney, H. L. (1952). Control methods in a study of vowels. *Journal of the Acoustical Society of America, 24,* 175–184.

Pickett, J. M., & Pollack, I. (1963). Intelligibility of excerpts from fluent speech: Effects of rate of utterance and duration of excerpt. *Language and Speech, 6,* 151–164.

Pollack, I., & Pickett, J. M. (1964). Intelligibility of excerpts from fluent speech: Auditory vs. structural context. *Journal of Verbal Learning and Verbal Behavior, 3,* 79–84.

Potter, R. K., & Steinberg, J. C. (1950). Toward the specification of speech. *Journal of the Acoustical Society of America, 22,* 807–820.

Schulman, R. (1989). Articulatory dynamics of loud and normal speech. *Journal of the Acoustical Society of America, 85*(1), 295–312.

Shepard, R. N. (1984). Ecological constraints on internal representation: Resonant kinematics of perceiving, imagining, thinking and dreaming. *Psychological Review, 91*(4), 417–447.

Shockey, L., & Bond, Z. S. (1980). Phonological processes in speech addressed to children. *Phonetica, 37,* 267–274.

Snow, C. E. (1972). Mothers' speech to children learning language. *Child Development, 43,* 549–565.

Snow, C. E. (1977). The devlopment of conversation between mothers and babies. *Journal of Child Language, 4,* 1–22.

Stern, D. N., Spieker, S., Barnett, R. K., & MacKain, K. (1983). The prosody of maternal speech: Infant age and context related changes. *Journal of Child Language, 10,* 1–15.

Stevens, K. N. (1968). Acoustic correlates of place of articulation for stop and fricative consonants. *QPR, 89,* RLE, MIT, 199–205.

Stevens, K. N., & House, A. S. (1963). Perturbation of vowel articulations by consonantal context: An acoustical study. *Journal of Speech and Hearing Research, 6,* 111–128.

Stoel-Gammon, C. (1988). Prelinguistic vocalizations of hearing-impaired and normally hearing subjects: A comparison of consonantal inventories. *Journal of Speech and Hearing Disorders, 53,* 302–315.

Sundberg, J. (1987). *The science of the singing voice.* DeKalb, IL: Northern Illinois University Press.

Sundberg, U. (1993). Word accent 2 in child directed speech: A pilot study. *Perilus XVII Working Papers,* Stockholm University, Sweden. 65–74.

Sussman, H. M., Fructer, D., Hilbert, J., & Sirosh, J. (1999). Linear correlates in the speech signal: The orderly output constraint. *Brain and Behavioral Sciences, 21*, 241–299.

Sussman, H. M., McCaffrey, H., A. & Matthews, S. A. (1991). An investigation of locus equations as a source of relational invariance for stop place categorization. *Journal of the Acoustical Society of America, 90*, 1309–1325.

Traunmüller, H. (1981). Perceptual dimension of openness in vowels. *Journal of the Acoustical Society of America, 69*(5), 1465–1475.

Werker, J. F., & Polka, L. (1993), Developmental changes in speech perception: New challenges and new directions. *Journal of Phonetics, 21*, 83–101.

Werker, J. F., & Tees, R. C. (1984), Cross language speech perception: Evidence for perceptual reorganization during the first year of life. *Infant Behavior and Development, 7*, 49–63.

8

In the Beginning, Was the Word . . .

Peter W. Jusczyk
Johns Hopkins University

Students of language acquisition have traditionally attached a lot of importance to the first word. Indeed, long before studies of infant speech perception, it was assumed that the beginnings of language acquisition coincided with the production of the first words. However, we now know that there is considerable activity relevant to language acquisition that takes place long before the child utters her first word. Thus, there are indications in the child's own babbling, that these productions are being influenced by the sound structure of the native language (Boysson-Bardies, Hallé, Sagart, & Durand, 1989; Boysson-Bardies, Sagart, & Durand, 1984; Boysson-Bardies & Vihman, 1991; Levitt, 1993; Levitt & Wang, 1991; Whalen, Levitt, & Wang, 1991). Moreover, studies of perceptual capacities have revealed that young infants' exhibit some very adult-like behaviors in dealing with information in the speech signal. Not only do they give evidence of discriminating a wide range of phonetic contrasts (Aslin, Pisoni, Hennessy, & Perey, 1981; Eimas, 1974; Eimas, Siqueland, Jusczyk, & Vigorito, 1971; Levitt, Jusczyk, Murray, & Carden, 1988; Streeter, 1976; Trehub, 1976), but they seem to be able to recognize whether some utterance belongs to their native language or another language (Bahrick & Pickens, 1988; Mehler et al., 1988). In addition, they demonstrate some capacity to recognize different utterances of the same item despite the variability in the acoustic signal introduced by differences in talkers, speaking rate, or intonation patterns (Jusczyk, Pisoni, & Mullennix, 1992; Kuhl, 1980, 1983; Miller & Eimas, 1983).

There is growing evidence that the sound structure of the native language begins to impact on infants' perceptual capacities during the second trimester of the first year. Sensitivity to certain non-native speech contrasts begins to decline during this period (Best, 1995; Best, McRoberts, & Sithole, 1988; Werker & Tees, 1984, 1992). Some perceptual categories begin to get reorganized in ways that reflect those of adult speakers of the native language (Kuhl, 1993; Kuhl, Williams, Lacerda, Stevens, & Lindblom, 1992; Polka & Werker, 1994). Moreover, infants begin to display sensitivity to the frequency with which certain sound patterns, both prosodic and phonetic ones, occur in native language input (Jusczyk, Cutler, & Redanz, 1993; Jusczyk, Friederici, Wessels, Svenkerud, & Jusczyk, 1993; Jusczyk, Luce, & Charles Luce, 1994). All of these findings point to the fact that language acquisition is already in full swing by the time children begin to utter their first words.

The issue addressed in this chapter concerns the kind of preparatory activity that infants are engaged in that eventually leads to the acquisition and production of the first words. The traditional view of the prerequisites for learning words has tended to focus on the cognitive underpinnings needed to learn words. In other words, on the state of the child's conceptual structures and their abilities to pick up the relevant perceptual attributes of the objects to which the words refer.

There has been considerable discussion of the way in which the objects picked out by the child's use of the word do or do not correspond to the objects picked out by the adult's use of the word. So, a number of studies have focused on just which aspects of a word's meaning that children pick up, and how their meanings change until they come into line with adult meanings (Clark, 1983; 1991; Markman, 1991; Mervis, 1989; Waxman, 1991). The various investigations that documented overgeneralizations in the child's usage of words fall into this category (Anglin, 1977; Clark, 1973; Thompson & Chapman, 1977). There has also been a lot of interest in documenting the kinds of items that are likely to be named by the child, and the factors that govern how the child will extend the name to other objects. For example, whether the key factors have to do with the function or with the perceptual features of the objects (Clark, 1973; Nelson, 1973). There have also been discussions of the level of categorization that words become attached to (i.e., basic level categories as opposed to more general superordinates, or highly specific subordinates; Rosch & Mervis, 1975). Recently, there has been interest in how the naming of new objects relates to the lexical items that the child already knows. So, we have Markman's (1991) discussions of "mutual exclusivity" and Clark's (1991) "Principle of Contrasts" being applied to word learning. The point is that most of the work on early word learning has focused on the aspects which have to do with learning the meanings of words.

With the exception of the work of some child phonologists (Vihman, 1993), it is hard to find much mention of how the sound properties of a word impact on which words appear in a child's vocabulary. However, "knowing" a word requires that one attach a meaning consistently to a particular sound pattern. One has to be capable of identifying this sound pattern in the speech stream. It is this part of the sound–meaning equation that seems to get left out of most traditional accounts of how the child learns words. This is not some sinister plot on the part of developmental psycholinguists. Many can rightly claim that they are simply more interested in what happens on the conceptual side. However, I also think that the picture of the word learning process that most investigators have is that the child starts out with a concept in mind to name, and then looks around for the sound pattern that goes with it. Thus, the meaning side is primary and the sound side is secondary.

I now propose a different picture of the process of word learning—one that gives equal play to the role of sound properties in learning words. Please note that I do *not* make the claim that learning the sound patterns is primary and that finding meanings to go with these patterns is secondary. Rather, I think that in some cases the learner stores meanings away to attach a sound pattern to, and also stores away sound patterns in search of meanings. The view that I have been developing has been influenced by recent findings from three different projects that we have been working on. Although all of these projects are still ongoing, the data we have collected suggest that considerable groundwork for learning words is laid down during the second trimester of the first year. Broadly speaking, the three projects concern: the ability to recognize sound patterns of words in fluent speech; memory for sound patterns of words; learning names. In what follows, I discuss our work on each of these projects in turn.

DETECTION OF THE SOUND PATTERNS OF WORDS IN FLUENT SPEECH

Identification of the sound patterns of words would not be a very daunting task, if words were presented to the learner in isolation, one at a time. Then the sound patterns of individual words might be matched to information in fluent speech, thereby isolating nonfamiliar words from familiar ones, and adding the former to the lexicon as their meanings are learned (Suomi, 1993). However, most of the speech directed to infants consists of sentences or sentence fragments. Even in experiments in which mothers have been instructed to teach their children new words, the target words tend to be presented in isolation only about one fourth of the time (Woodward & Aslin, 1990). The problem with trying to pull words out of fluent speech contexts is that the acoustic shapes of words are often affected by the nature of surrounding words (Klatt, 1979, 1989). Boundaries between words are seldom well marked by distinct acoustic events. This fact has been a major stumbling block in producing machines that are effective at automatic speech recognition (Marcus, 1984; Reddy, 1976; Waibel, 1986). Yet adult users of a native language seem to have apparently little difficulty in recognizing words in fluent speech contexts. When do infants show any signs of being able to recognize words in fluent speech contexts?

There are reports in the language acquisition literature that children begin to show some limited comprehension of words at around 9 months (Benedict, 1979; Huttenlocher, 1974). However, other studies suggest that even at 11 months, comprehension skills are quite limited (Oviatt, 1980; Thomas, Campos, Shucard, Ramsay, & Shucard, 1981) and that it is not until 15 months that infants show signs of comprehending and recognizing novel words (McRoberts, 1991; Werker, 1994).

Typically, most of these investigations have used an approach that relies on attaching a label to some object, familiarizing the infant with the label in the presence of the object, and then later observing whether the infant will look at the object when the label appears in the context of fluent speech. There is no doubt that this is the kind of behavior that we expect from someone who is said to know a word. However, this task requires that the listener actually associate sound and meaning. As such, it may underestimate the ability of the listener to deal with only one half of the sound–meaning relationship. In other words, it could be the case that the listener really does have some capacity to recognize the familiar sound pattern when it occurs in fluent speech, but that this becomes obscured by the additional demands imposed by associating sounds and meanings.

When Dick Aslin and I began to think about this issue, we wondered whether a task that imposes few demands on infants might reveal earlier evidence of the ability to detect familiar sound patterns in fluent speech contexts (Jusczyk & Aslin, 1995). We created our task based on a couple of procedures that have been used to investigate the detection and recognition of words by adult listeners. One of these is word monitoring whereby listeners are presented with a word and, upon hearing a series of sentences, must indicate whenever they detect the occurrence of the word (Cutler & Norris, 1979; Foss & Swinney, 1973). Another paradigm is auditory priming in which a repeated auditory stimulus is followed by a recognition test using degraded versions of the familiar (primed) and unfamiliar (nonprimed) stimuli (Tulving & Schacter, 1990). We combined features of both of these paradigms with the Headturn Preference Procedure that has been used successfully to observe how infants respond to information in long passages of speech (Kemler Nelson et al., 1995). In the present case, we familiarized the infant with a particular word that was repeated several times in isolation. Then we tested infants' responses (i.e., their listening times) to passages containing the word versus those without the familiar word. We reasoned that if they listened longer to sentences containing the familiar word, then they must have detected some similarity between what they heard repeated in isolation and what occurred in the sentences.

As a starting point for our investigation, we decided to use the monosyllabic words, "feet," "dog," "cup," and "bike" as target items. These were chosen because they are content words containing stressed syllables and because each has a well-defined onset and offset. Moreover, the items contrast in their vowel qualities and can be used in sentences that one might speak to a child. We used words rather than nonwords so that they would not be unduly emphasized by the talker who recorded them. Each passage was composed of six short sentences, and the position of the target word was varied to occur twice near the beginning, middle, and end of the sentences. Here is an example of the passage for the word *dog*:

> The dog ran around the yard. The mailman called to the big dog. He patted his dog on the head. The happy red dog was very friendly. Her dog barked only at squirrels. The neighborhood kids played with your dog.

By familiarizing half of the infants with one set of two words, and the other half with the other set, we could determine the extent to which any prior familiarization with the words might affect performance. Because our prior research had suggested that infants tend to become more attuned to native language sound patterns between 6 and 9 months (Jusczyk, Cutler, et al., 1993; Jusczyk, Friederici, et al., 1993; Jusczyk et al., 1994), we decided to test 7½-month-olds. The results of our first experiment indicated that infants listened significantly longer to the familiar (8.29 sec) than to the unfamiliar (7.04 sec) passages. This difference in listening times is in line with the prediction that infants detected the familiar words in the fluent speech contexts.

In order to better understand the possible source of this effect, we used information obtained from a parental questionnaire to determine whether prior knowledge of the words could have been responsible for the pattern of results we observed. Infants' listening times did not correlate in any significant way with any of the data from the questionnaire, thus suggesting that prior familiarity with the words was not a critical factor. We also investigated whether the target words in the passages were more strongly emphasized relative to other words in the passages. Eight adult listeners judged the target word to be the most emphasized word in only 3 of the 24 sentences, and only by 3 to 5 judges even in these cases. Moreover, acoustic analyses indicated that the target words had substantially different pitch, duration, and formant structures in the isolated and sentential contexts. Thus, infants could not use a simple acoustic match as a basis for recognizing the similarity of the items across the two types of contexts.

Given that 7½-month-olds demonstrated they have some capacity for de-tecting the sound patterns of familiar words in fluent speech contexts, we wondered when this capacity might first appear. For this reason, we de-cided to test a group of younger infants. Because there are some recent re-ports of language-specific changes in sensitivity prior to 6 months (Kuhl et al., 1992; Polka & Werker, 1994), we chose a group of 6-month-olds. These in-fants had listening times of 8.45 sec for the passages with the familiar words and 7.97 sec for the ones with the unfamiliar words. This difference was not significant, so unlike the 7½-month-olds, the 6-month-olds did not show evi-dence of detecting the familiar targets in the fluent speech passages.

The next issue concerned the nature of the information that the 7½-month-olds were responding to when they listened longer to the fluent speech passages. For example, were these infants truly matching some representa-tion of a word-like sound pattern to comparable patterns in sentences or were they merely responding to some salient aspect of the words? For example, would infants be inclined to misperceive the words in the passages and re-spond to rather loose matches between the targets they heard in isolation and words that appeared in the passages? For instance, it is possible that an infant who stores information about a word like "feet" might encode only something about the vowel or syllable rime and thus false alarm to words like "bead" or "seat." To test this, Aslin and I replaced the familiarization words with the nonwords, "tup," "bawg," "zeet," and "gike." Note that these new nonword tar-gets differed minimally from the words in the passages; "zeet" differs from "feet" by two phonetic features, but all of the other changes involved a single phonetic feature difference. If infants only match salient properties from the acoustic signal, then they should have listened longer to the passages con-taining the words that sound most similar to the nonwords they heard in the familiarization phase. Our results indicated that this was not the case. The lis-tening times for the passages with the similar words (6.93 sec) versus those with the dissimilar words (6.57 sec) did not differ significantly. These results suggest that the infants in the earlier experiment were doing more than sim-ply matching vowels or syllable rimes to patterns in the fluent speech con-texts. Instead, it appears that the infants in the earlier study were operating with much more detailed representations of the words they heard during the familiarization phase.

More recently, we have extended the scope of these investigations to in-clude bisyllabic words such as "doctor," "candle," "hamlet," and "kingdom" (Jusczyk, Houston, & Newsome, 1999). The use of such items made it possi-ble for us to test not only whether infants are able to detect these longer items in fluent speech, but to investigate whether they might respond to partial matches involving only the strong syllables of these items. For exam-ple, after hearing "candle" and "doctor," would they respond to "can" and "dock"? The results of this investigation revealed several things. First, 7½-

month-olds can detect the occurrence of bisyllabic items in fluent speech contexts. However, infants at this age require more than a match of the strong syllables for these items (i.e., familiarization with "doctor" and "candle" does not lead to a tendency to listen longer to samples with "can" and "dock"). Second, 7½-month-olds do not detect bisyllabic words in fluent speech when these words begin with weak (i.e., unstressed) syllables, such as in the words "guitar" and "device". Instead, the infants appear to detect only the strong syllables (i.e., "tar" and "vice") of such words in fluent speech. It is not until 10½-months-of-age, that English-learners show some capacity to detect the occurrence of familiarized weak–strong words in fluent speech. Presumably, the older infants are able to detect these words because they are not relying solely on word stress cues to detect the onsets of new words in fluent speech. In particular, they may be able to use other types of word segmentation cues such as context-sensitive allophones (Church, 1987; Jusczyk, Hohne, & Bauman, 1999) and phonotactic cues (Cairns, Shillcock, Chater, & Levy, 1997; Mattys & Jusczyk, 1999; Mattys, Jusczyk, Luce, & Morgan, 1999).

Although it is impressive that 7½-month-olds have developed some capacity to match detailed representations of words heard in isolation to the same words in fluent speech contexts, one could argue that this ability is really only of limited utility to young infants in learning to identify words in fluent speech. As noted earlier, only a relatively small proportion of words used by mothers to their infants appear in isolation. Furthermore, because the offsets and onsets of words are not always clearly marked in fluent speech, it is likely that learning to recognize isolated words will be easier than learning to recognize them in fluent speech contexts. For these reasons, we have also conducted studies to determine whether infants who are exposed only to words in fluent speech contexts might show some subsequent recognition of these words. The approach that Dick Aslin and I took was to reverse the way we had been running our procedure. In other words, we exposed the infants to a couple of the passages for a brief familiarization period, then played them the isolated word samples during the test phase. Our results indicated that the infants listened to the isolated words that matched those heard in the passages (10.43 sec) than to the other isolated words (8.32 sec). These results suggest that the infants segmented, extracted, and remembered the repeated word from the passages. Moreover, recall that the acoustic analyses we carried out on these passages indicate that target words were seldom the most stressed words in the passages. Consequently, infants were extracting the words without the benefit of exaggerated stress, and in the presence of considerable acoustic variability among the tokens.

Repeated exposure to a lexical item apparently primes the infant to listen longer and/or more attentively to materials containing that item. This finding is interesting in light of studies of mother–infant dialogues (Bernstein Ratner, 1986) which show that mothers often do frequently repeat items with some variation when addressing their infant. The effect of this sort of communicative interaction may be to help infants form a representation of the sound patterns of frequently used words—one that can later be attached to an appropriate conceptual structure to add a new item to the infant's lexicon. But what evidence is there that the kinds of heightened sensitivity that infants show to sound patterns of repeated words is anything other than momentary? In other words, what reason do we have to believe that this might have a long-term impact on the development of the lexicon?

WHAT INFANTS REMEMBER ABOUT WORDS THEY HEAR

Earlier I alluded to the fact that there is a growing body of evidence to suggest that between 6 and 9 months, infants are becoming more attuned to the way in which sound patterns are distributed in the native language. Thus, they listen longer to items that embody frequently occurring sound patterns than they do to ones containing less frequently occurring patterns (Jusczyk, Cutler, et al., 1993; Jusczyk et al., 1994). Clearly, the infants are registering something about the structure of native language input, but it is still not clear just how specific the information is that they are encoding into long-term memory. For example, are they storing away information about individual lexical items? If so, what is the nature of this information? Is it a general abstract representation of a particular word or do they store away information about particular instances?

Around 1995, in proposing a model of the way in which speech perception capacities evolve to support word recognition, I suggested that infants might store away information about individual exemplars or tokens of a word, rather than an abstract prototype of the sound pattern of the word (Jusczyk, 1992, 1993, 1994). I suggested this possibility because data in the literature indicates that adult listeners appear to retain talker-specific information in their representations of spoken material (Craik & Kirsner, 1974; Martin, Mullennix, Pisoni, & Summers, 1989). Our interest in this general issue led us to wonder about the kind of information that infants store away about speech. In particular, we were interested in what kind of information infants remember about fluent speech they have heard. To be sure, the kind of situation in which infants might be expected to learn about the sound patterns of new words is one in which their attentional resources are heavily engaged, such as in a one-on-one interaction with a caregiver and in the presence of highly visible referents. However, there are a lot of uncontrolled variables in such a situation. So, we investigated the extent to which infants might even store away information under less engaging circumstances—such as when simply listening to a story (Jusczyk & Hohne, 1997; Jusczyk, Hohne, Jusczyk, & Redanz, 1993).

To explore this issue, we visited 7½-month-old infants in their homes 10 times over a 2-week period. During that time, we played them audio recordings of six children's stories. We avoided the most popular books and nursery rhymes to reduce the possibility that infants might have already been familiar with the stories. In our first experiment, two different female talkers recorded the stories, neither of whom was involved in the home visits. Half of the infants heard one of the talkers, the other half heard the other talker. During each visit, the stories were always played in the same order and the listening session lasted about 45 minutes.

Two weeks later, the infants were brought into the laboratory and assigned to one of two experimental groups. One group of 16 infants was assigned to what we called the Voice Recognition Condition, whereas the other group of 16 was assigned to the Word Recognition Condition. The stimulus materials for the Voice Recognition Condition consisted of 12 lists of words, all of which appeared in the stories the children had heard during the home visits. However, six of these lists were produced by the same storyteller who had read the versions of the stories that the infant had heard, whereas the other six lists were produced by the other storyteller. The words on the lists produced by one storyteller were the same as those produced by the other storyteller. The only difference in the two lists was in the identity of the talker. The stimulus materials for the Word Recognition Condition also consisted of 12 lists of words. Six of these contained words from the stories that the infant had heard and these were produced by the familiar storyteller. The other six lists, however, which were produced by the same story teller, were new words that were matched with respect to their overall frequency and phonetic characteristics (especially the vowels of their stressed syllables). We avoided words from the stories that were likely to be familiar to the child from other contexts (e.g., "cookie," "baby," and so forth). Within these constraints we tried to choose words that were repeated in the stories. An example of a typical pair of lists is shown in Table 8.1. The issue here was whether infants would show any tendency to listen longer to the lists containing the words that had actually appeared in the stories they had heard.

The infants were all tested using the Headturn Preference Paradigm. Let's look at the results first for the Voice Recognition Condition. As is evident in Fig. 8.1, there was a significant tendency for the infants to listen longer to the items produced by the familiar storyteller. These results suggest that the infants did retain information about the voice of the storyteller over a 2-week interval. This is impressive because they never actually had

TABLE 8.1
Examples of Lists in the Word Recognition Condition

Words From Stories	Foils
neighbor	sabre
prickers	slickers
feather	header
floated	bloated
robin	bobbin
gasped	rasped
mermaid	matron
snuffle	snuggle
sneezing	seedling
tiptoes	ticktocks
giggled	gargled
twirling	hurling

met or seen the storyteller, and because the items that they heard during the lab visit were isolated words produced in citation form. To check on whether the voice of one storyteller was simply more interesting to listen to than the other, we compared the data for Storyteller A to Storyteller B regardless of the familiarization during the home visit. There was no evidence of a preference for either voice. Thus, the preference that we observed is apparently attributable to the infant's responding to a familiar voice.

We now turn to the Word Recognition Condition. As is apparent from Fig. 8.2, the infants did not listen significantly longer to the lists of the words

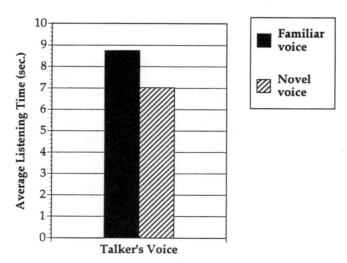

FIG. 8.1. Displays the average listening times in seconds for the Voice Recognition Condition to words spoken by the storyteller that the infant heard during the home visits (familiar voice) and by the other storyteller (novel voice).

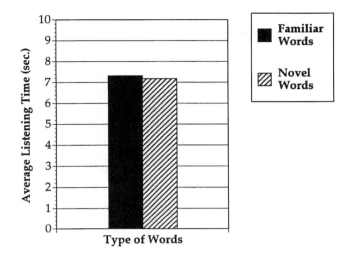

FIG. 8.2. Displays the average listening times in seconds for the Word Recognition Condition to words that occurred in the stories heard during the home visits (familiar words) and to the foils (novel words).

taken from the stories. Thus, there is no indication that infants stored representations of the sound properties of the words from the stories. On the one hand, the results of this first set of experiments suggest that infants store information that allows them to recognize a familiar talker. On the other hand, there was no indication that infants developed representations for the specific words that they heard in the stories. One possible explanation for the latter finding is that the kind of passive exposure condition used in this study was not sufficient for infants to store away an interesting sound pattern. Infants might need to be engaged more actively in pairing sounds and meanings in order to encode information about the sound patterns of words. However, another possibility also occurred to us. Perhaps the problem lay in the nature of the test materials. For example, our decision to avoid familiar words meant that we did not always choose the most frequent words that appeared in the stories. Moreover, because we used so many items from the stories, the frequency of some of these items was only once or twice per listening session. Similarly, we found that the 45-minute sessions tended to be too long to sustain the infants' attention, and that repeating the stories in the same order and always in the same voice also seemed to have diminishing returns on the infants' interest.

For this reason, we decided to modify our procedures and try again. We cut the number of stories to three, which reduced the home visit length to about 25 minutes. This increased the likelihood that infants would remain alert throughout the listening session. We also tried to increase infants' attention to the stories by having them recorded by five different talkers, and by using two different orders. This permitted us to use a unique story order–storyteller combination for each of the 10 days that we visited the infants in their homes. We reasoned that varying the materials in this way might put more emphasis on what was in the stories than on the voice characteristics of a particular storyteller. Moreover, to further engage the infants' attention, we created a picture book to go with each story, and the pages were turned as the stories progressed. Finally, we cut down the size of the word lists used in the test session to the 36 most frequently appearing content words in the stories. Each of these words appeared on two different lists in different combinations to create six lists of familiar story words. The foils list likewise consisted of 36 words that were matched in their frequency and likely familiarity to infants. An example of a list of each type is shown in Table 8.2.

This time we found evidence that infants did listen significantly longer to the lists containing the familiar story words (see Fig. 8.3). These results suggest that infants did seem to encode and remember information about the sound patterns of words that they heard in the stories. Furthermore, they were able to retain this information for at least as long as 2 weeks. Of course, it was possible that despite our best efforts to equate the lists in their prior familiarity for infants, that they may have known some of the words prior to the experiment and that this prior knowledge was responsible for the preference that they showed during the test session. To explore this possibility, we tested a new group of infants who had never been exposed to these stories. As is apparent from Fig. 8.3, this control group did not show any significant preference for the words from the familiar word lists. Thus, the preferences that we observed for infants who participated in the home visits appear to be related to their experiences in listening to the stories.

TABLE 8.2
Examples of Lists in the Second Home Visit Study

Words From Stories	Foils
ants	sloth
jungle	camel
grass	sand
mango	fennel
vine	ox
monkeys	ferrets
trees	plant
hornbill	heron
sneeze	aches
python	lanterns
fly	melt
birds	bugs

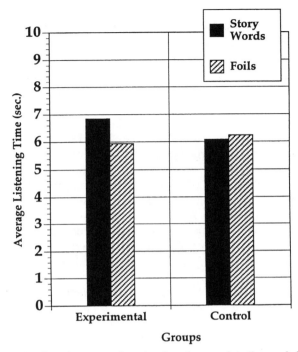

FIG. 8.3. Displays the average listening times in seconds to the words from the stories (story words) and to novel words (foils). The experimental group heard the stories on 10 occasions during home visits, whereas the control group was not exposed to the stories.

The picture that emerges from this set of studies is that infants retain information about the sound patterns of words and voices that they are frequently exposed to, even in the absence of any direct referents to attach these sound patterns to. More work is needed to establish whether or not infants are storing away talker-specific information along with their representations of lexical items. However, what is intriguing about our findings to date is that infants retain sufficient information about repeated items in fluent speech contexts to recognize them after a considerable delay. This pattern of results is consistent with the view that at least some lexical acquisition involves learning to attach meanings to stored representations of sound patterns of words.

LEARNING NAMES

The studies discussed thus far have focused on what infants pick up about the sound patterns of words during the early stages of the development of the lexicon. It is interesting that infants apparently remember sound patterns even when they may not have meanings to attach them to. However, at some point in the development of word learning, the infant will actually begin to make the links between sound and meaning. When might this process of linking sound patterns to specific meanings begin to take place?

As noted earlier, there are some reports of the beginnings of comprehension at around 9 months of age (Benedict, 1979; Huttenlocher, 1974; Oviatt, 1980; Thomas et al., 1981). Typically, these kinds of studies have focused on infants' responses to names of objects likely to be familiar to them. Recently, however, Denise Mandel, David Pisoni, and I wondered whether infants might not show earlier recognition of sound patterns related to items of greater personal significance to them. For example, one such item that infants are apt to hear repeated often in their presence, and when someone is making eye contact with them, is their own name. Thus, the child's own name could constitute one of the first cases in which a child might begin to associate a particular sound pattern with a particular meaning. To our surprise we were unable to find any information in the previous developmental literature on when infants begin to show any indications of recognizing their own names.

For this reason, we decided to explore when infants display signs of recognizing their own names (Mandel, Jusczyk, & Pisoni, 1995). One possible measure of infants' recognition of their own names is whether they orient more to their own name than to another name. For example, infants might actually listen longer to their own names than to other infants' names. To examine this possibility, we asked mothers with 2-month-olds who participated in some of our other experiments, whether they would participate in another experiment when their infant was $4\frac{1}{2}$ months old. Mothers who agreed, completed a short questionnaire. Among the questions listed was one that asked what name she and other family members used in addressing the infant. This allowed us to use the form of the name that the infant was most apt to be familiar with. At some point prior to each infant's next visit to the lab, an assistant recorded the form of the name most often used to address the infant. At the same time, she also recorded other names. Some of these were names of other infants who would be participating in the study, whereas others were recorded for use as foils in the experiment. The talker did not know which of the names actually belonged to the infants participating in the study. Each name was repeated 15 times to produce a sample for the infant to listen to. For each infant's name, there were three name-foils. One of the three had an identical stress pattern to the infant's name, whereas the other two had different stress patterns. An example of how the name "Corey" was presented with its foils is shown in Table 8.3. In many cases, the names for the foils were the names of other infants in the study. The use of an unfamiliar talker also helped to ensure that all the recorded names were more or less equated in emotional charge and in such

TABLE 8.3
Typical Trial Block

Trial 1:	Corey, Corey, Corey, Corey, . . . Corey
Trial 2:	Aaron, Aaron, Aaron, Aaron, . . . Aaron
Trial 3:	Denise, Denise, Denise, Denise, . . . Denise
Trial 4:	Michelle, Michelle, Michelle, Michelle, . . . Michelle

attention-getting features such as intonation and loudness. Twenty-four
4½-month-olds were tested using a version of the Headturn Preference Procedure. The infants were first acquainted with the operation of the procedure using musical passages. Then during the test phase, they heard test
trials arranged in four blocks of four (one trial for each of the four names).
On a given trial, the infants heard either their own name or one of the three
foil names for the entire duration of the trial. Each of the four names in a
given block of four trials occurred once in random order. The random or-
dering of the names varied from block to block. All infants were tested on
three blocks of trials.

As is apparent in Fig. 8.4, the infants' listened significantly longer to their
own names than to any of the foils, including, the one whose stress pattern

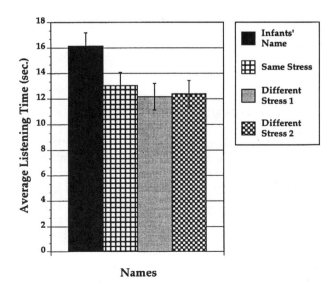

Names

FIG. 8.4. Displays the average listening times in seconds to the infant's own
name, another name with the same stress pattern as the infant's name, and
two other names with different stress patterns than the infant's name.

matched that of the infant's name. Hence, these results provide an indication that, by 4½ months, infants find their own names more interesting to listen to than someone else's name. Moreover, they prefer to listen to their own names even in the presence of prosaically similar foils. This suggests that by 4½ months, infants have a rather detailed representation of the sound patterns of their own names. They have learned to respond differentially to a particular sound pattern that will ultimately have special significance for them (Howarth & Ellis, 1961; Moray, 1959; Van Lancker, 1991; Wood & Cowan, 1995). In this sense, they have taken an important first step toward relating sounds to meanings.

We do not claim that this is necessarily the first or the only name the child has learned to respond to. It is certainly possible that they might show an equivalent interest in other frequently heard names. For example, infants might display similar recognition of other words that occur frequently in their language learning environments (e.g., other terms that relate to socially salient persons, objects, or events). What remains to be determined is whether infants at this early stage of language learning might show similar recognition to these other salient items. Regardless of whether there are other such items that are learned even earlier than the infant's own name, the present results demonstrate that infants as young as 4½ months of age are learning to recognize sound patterns that have special personal relevance for them. In this sense, infants display evidence of language comprehension well before previous estimates reported in the developmental literature (Bates et al., 1994; Benedict, 1979; Huttenlocher, 1974; Oviatt, 1980; Thomas et al., 1981). Moreover, they appear to have begun learning to attach some significance to the occurrence of certain salient sound patterns in speech.

SUMMARY AND CONCLUSIONS

In conclusion, I have provided a brief overview of the work we are doing to investigate factors related to acquiring words in the native language. The studies I have reviewed demonstrate that even 7½-month-olds attend to and encode rather detailed information about sound patterns that are frequently repeated in the input. Moreover, they display some capacity to recognize these patterns in fluent speech contexts. In addition, there are some indications from the home visit studies that infants' attention to recurring sound patterns leads to some long-term memory for information about such patterns. Finally, the process of associating sounds and meanings (at least for items with high personal relevance) might begin earlier in development than was previously thought. Infants, as young as 4½ months, orient significantly longer to their own names than to other names, even ones with the same stress patterns as their own names.

These sorts of findings demonstrate the plausibility of the view that some word learning may actually involve attaching meanings to previously stored sound patterns. Hence, although not denying the widely held view that word learning often involves learning the sound pattern that goes with some previously understood meaning, I think that new words also are sometimes acquired by learning the meaning that goes with some previously known sound pattern. If I am right about this, then I think we have to pay more careful attention to how phonological and semantic factors interact in the development and growth of the mental lexicon.

ACKNOWLEDGMENTS

The research described here was conducted while the author was supported by a Research Grant from NICHD (15795). I wish to thank Ann Marie Jusczyk for helpful comments she made on an earlier version of this manuscript.

REFERENCES

Anglin, J. M. (1977). *Word, object, and conceptual development.* New York: Norton.

Aslin, R. N., Pisoni, D. B., Hennessy, B. L., & Perey, A. J. (1981). Discrimination of voice onset time by human infants: New findings and implications for the effects of early experience. *Child Development, 52,* 1135–1145.

Bahrick, L. E., & Pickens, J. N. (1988). Classification of bimodal English and Spanish language passages by infants. *Infant Behavior and Development, 11,* 277–296.

Bates, E., Marchman, V., Thal, D., Fenson, L., Dale, P., Reznick, J. S., Reilly, J., & Hartung, J. (1994). Developmental and stylistic variation in the composition of early vocabulary. *Journal of Child Language, 21,* 85–124.

Benedict, H. (1979). Early lexical development: Comprehension and production. *Journal of Child Language, 6,* 183–201.

Bernstein Ratner, N. (1986). Durational cues which mark clause boundaries in mother-child speech. *Journal of Phonetics, 14,* 303–309.

Best, C. T. (1995). Learning to perceive the sound patterns of English. In C. Rovee-Collier & L. P. Lipsitt (Eds.), *Advances in infancy research* (Vol. 9, pp. 217–304). Norwood, NJ: Ablex.

Best, C. T., McRoberts, G. W., & Sithole, N. M. (1988). Examination of the perceptual re-organization for speech contrasts: Zulu click discrimination by English-speaking adults and infants. *Journal of Experimental Psychology: Human Perception and Performance, 14,* 345–360.

de Boysson-Bardies, B., & Vihman, M. M. (1991). Adaptation to language: Evidence from babbling, and first words in four languages. *Language, 67,* 297–319.

de Boysson-Bardies, B., Hallé, P., Sagart, L., & Durand, C. (1989). A cross-linguistic investigation of vowel formants in babbling. *Journal of Child Language, 16,* 1–17.

de Boysson-Bardies, B., Sagart, L., & Durand, C. (1984). Discernible differences in the babbling of infants according to target language. *Journal of Child Language, 11,* 1–15.

Cairns, P., Shillcock, R., Chater, N., & Levy, J. (1997). Bootstrapping word boundaries: A bottom-up corpus-based approach to speech segmentation. *Cognitive Psychology, 33,* 111–153.

Church, K. W. (1987). *Phonological parsing in speech recognition.* Dordrecht: Kluwer.

Clark, E. V. (1973). What's in a word? On the child's acquisition of semantics in his first language. In T. E. Moore (Ed.), *Cognitive development and the acquisition of language* (pp. 65–110). New York: Academic Press.

Clark, E. V. (1983). Meanings and concepts. In J. H. Flavell & E. M. Markman (Eds.), *Cognitive Development.* New York: Wiley.

Clark, E. V. (1991). Acquisitional principles in lexical development. In S. A. German & J. P. Byrnes (Eds.), *Perspectives on language and thought* (pp. 31–71). Cambridge, England: Cambridge University Press.

Craik, F. I. M., & Kirsner, K. (1974). The effect of speaker's voice on word recognition. *Quarterly Journal of Experimental Psychology, 26,* 274–284.

Cutler, A., & Norris, D. (1979). Monitoring sentence comprehension. In W. E. Cooper & E. C. T. Walker (Eds.), *Sentence processing: Psycholinguistic studios presented to Merrill Garrett* (pp. 113–134). Hillsdale, NJ: Lawrence Erlbaum Associates.

Eimas, P. D. (1974). Auditory and linguistic processing of cues for place of articulation by infants. *Perception & Psychophysics, 16,* 513–521.

Eimas, P. D., Siqueland, E. R., Jusczyk, P. W., & Vigorito, J. (1971). Speech perception in infants. *Science, 171,* 303–306.

Foss, D. J., & Swinney, D. A. (1973). On the psychological reality of the phoneme: Perception, identification and consciousness. *Journal of Verbal Learning and Verbal Behavior, 12,* 246–257.

Howarth, C. I., & Ellis, K. (1961). The relative intelligibility threshold for one's own name compared with other names. *Quarterly Journal of Experimental Psychology, 13,* 236–240.

Huttenlocher, J. (1974). The origins of language comprehension. In R. L. Solso (Ed.), *Theories in cognitive psychology* (pp. 331–368). New York: Wiley.

Jusczyk, P. W. (1992). Developing phonological categories from the speech signal. In C. A. Ferguson, L. Menn, & C. Stoel-Gammon (Eds.), *Phonological development: Models, research, implications* (pp. 17–64). Timonium, MD: York Press.

Jusczyk, P. W. (1993). From general to language specific capacities: The WRAPSA Model of how speech perception develops. *Journal of Phonetics, 21,* 3–28.

Jusczyk, P. W. (1994). Infant speech perception and the development of the mental lexicon. In J. C. Goodman & H. C. Nusbaum (Eds.), *The development of speech perception: The transition from speech sounds to spoken words* (pp. 227–270). Cambridge, MA: MIT Press.

Jusczyk, P. W., & Aslin, R. N. (1995). Infants' detection of the sound patterns of words in fluent speech. *Cognitive Psychology, 29,* 1–23.

Jusczyk, P. W., Cutler, A., & Redanz, N. (1993). Preference for the predominant stress patterns of English words. *Child Development, 64,* 675–687.

Jusczyk, P. W., Friederici, A. D., Wessels, J., Svenkerud, V. Y., & Jusczyk, A. M. (1993). Infants' sensitivity to the sound patterns of native language words. *Journal of Memory and Language, 32,* 402–420.

Jusczyk, P. W., & Hohne, E. A. (1997). Infants' memory for spoken words. *Science, 277,* 1984–1986.

Jusczyk, P. W., Hohne, E. A., & Bauman, A. (1999). Infants' sensitivity to allophonic cues for word segmentation. *Perception & Psychophysics, 61,* 1465–1476.

Jusczyk, P. W., Hohne, E. A., Jusczyk, A. M., & Redanz, N. J. (1993). Do infants remember voices? *Journal of the Acoustical Society of America, 93,* 2373.

Jusczyk, P. W., Houston, D. M, & Newsome, M. (1999). The beginnings of word segmentation in English-learning infants. *Cognitive Psychology, 38,* 159–207.

Jusczyk, P. W., Luce, P. A., & Charles Luce, J. (1994). Infants' sensitivity to phonotactic patterns in the native language. *Journal of Memory and Language, 33,* 630–645.

Jusczyk, P. W., Pisoni, D. B., & Mullennix, J. (1992). Some consequences of stimulus variability on speech processing by 2-month old infants. *Cognition, 43,* 253–291.

Kemler Nelson, D. G., Jusczyk, P. W., Mandel, D. R., Myers, J., Turk, A., & Gerken, L. A. (1995). The headturn preference procedure for testing auditory perception. *Infant Behavior & Development, 18,* 111–116.

Klatt, D. H. (1979). Speech perception: A model of acoustic-phonetic analysis and lexical access. *Journal of Phonetics, 7,* 279–312.

Klatt, D. H. (1989). Review of selected models of speech perception. In W. Marslen-Wilson (Eds.), *Lexical representation and process* (pp. 169–226). Cambridge, MA: MIT Press.

Kuhl, P. K. (1980). Perceptual constancy for speech-sound categories in early infancy. In G. H. Yeni-Komshian, J. F. Kavanagh, & C. A. Ferguson (Eds.), *Child phonology: Perception* (pp. 41–66). New York: Academic Press.

Kuhl, P. K. (1983). Perception of auditory equivalence classes for speech in early infancy. *Infant Behavior and Development, 6,* 263–285.

Kuhl, P. K. (1993). Innate predispositions and the effects of experience in speech perception: The native language magnet theory. In B. de Boysson-Bardies, S. de Schonen, P. Jusczyk, P. McNeilage, & J. Morton (Eds.), *Developmental neurocognition: Speech and face processing in the first year of life* (pp. 259–274). Dordrecht, The Netherlands: Kluwer.

Kuhl, P. K., Williams, K. A., Lacerda, F., Stevens, K. N., & Lindblom, B. (1992). Linguistic experiences alter phonetic perception in infants by 6 months of age. *Science, 255,* 606–608.

Levitt, A. G. (1993). The acquisition of prosody: Evidence from French- and English-learning infants. In B. de Boysson-Bardies, S. de Schonen, P. Jusczyk, P. McNeilage, & J. Morton (Eds.), *Developmental neurocognition: Speech and face processing in the first year of life* (pp. 385–398). Dordrecht, The Netherlands: Kluwer.

Levitt, A. G., Jusczyk, P. W., Murray, J., & Carden, G. (1988). The perception of place of articulation contrasts in voiced and voiceless fricatives by two-month-old infants. *Journal of Experimental Psychology: Human Perception and Performance, 14,* 361–368.

Levitt, A. G., & Wang, Q. (1991). Evidence for language-specific rhythmic influences in the reduplicative babbling of French- and English-learning infants. *Language and Speech, 34,* 235–249.

Mandel, D. R., Jusczyk, P. W., & Pisoni, D. B. (1995). Infants' recognition of the sound patterns of their own names. *Psychological Science, 6,* 315–318.

Marcus, S. M. (1984). Recognizing speech: On the mapping from sound to word. In H. Bouma & D. G. Bouwhuis (Eds.), *Attention and performance: Control of language processes* (pp. 151–163). Hillsdale, NJ: Lawrence Erlbaum Associates.

Markman, E. M. (1991). The whole-object, taxonomic, and mutual exclusivity assumptions as initial constraints on word meanings. In S. A. Gelman & J. P. Byrnes (Eds.), *Perspectives on language and thought* (pp. 72–106). Cambridge, England: Cambridge University Press.

Martin, C. S., Mullennix, J. W., Pisoni, D. B., & Summers, W. V. (1989). Effects of talker variability on recall of spoken word lists. *Journal of Experimental Psychology: Learning, Memory, and Cognition, 15,* 676–684.

Mattys, S. L., & Jusczyk, P. W. (1999). *Phonotactic cues for segmentation of fluent speech by infants.* Manuscript submitted for publication.

Mattys, S. L., Jusczyk, P. W., Luce, P. A., & Morgan, J. L. (1999). Phonotactic and prosodic effects on word segmentation in infants. *Cognitive Psychology, 38,* 465–494.

McRoberts, G. (1991, April). An experimental study of lexical comprehension at 12, 15, and 18 months. Paper presented at the *Biennial meeting of the Society for Research in Child Development,* Seattle, WA.

Mehler, J., Jusczyk, P. W., Lambertz, C., Halsted, N., Bertoncini, J., & Amiel-Tison, C. (1988). A precursor of language acquisition in young, infants. *Cognition, 29,* 144–178.

Mervis, C. B. (1989). Child-basic object categories and lexical development. In U. Neisser (Ed.), *Concepts and conceptual development: Ecological and intellectual factors in categorization* (pp. 201–233). Cambridge, England: Cambridge University Press.

Miller, J. L., & Eimas, P. D. (1983). Studies on the categorization of speech by infants. *Cognition, 13*, 135–165.

Moray, N. (1959). Attention in dichotic listening: Affective cues and the influence of instructions. *Quarterly Journal of Experimental Psychology, 11*, 56–60.

Nelson, K. (1973). Structure and strategy in learning to talk. *Monographs of the Society for Research in Child Development, 38*(149).

Oviatt, S. L. (1980). The emerging ability to comprehend language: An experimental approach. *Child Development, 51*, 97–106.

Polka, L., & Werker, J. F. (1994). Developmental changes in perception of non-native vowel contrast. *Journal of Experimental Psychology: Human Perception and Performance, 20*, 421–435.

Reddy, R. (1976). Speech recognition by machine: A review. *Proceedings of the IEEE, 64*, 501–531.

Rosch, E., & Mervis, C. B. (1975). Family resemblances: Studies in the internal structure of categories. *Cognitive Psychology, 7*, 573–605.

Streeter, L. A. (1976). Language perception of 2-month old infant shows effects of both innate mechanisms and experience. *Nature, 259*, 39–41.

Suomi, K. (1993). An outline of a developmental model of adult phonological organization and behavior. *Journal of Phonetics, 21*, 29–60.

Thomas, D. G., Campos, J. J., Shucard, D. W., Ramsay, D. S., & Shucard, J. (1981). Semantic comprehension in infancy: A signal detection analysis. *Child Development, 52*, 798–803.

Thompson, J. R., & Chapman, R. S. (1977). Who is "Daddy" revisited: The status of two-year-olds' overextended words in use and comprehension. *Journal of Child Language, 4*, 359–375.

Trehub, S. E. (1976). The discrimination of foreign speech contrasts by infants and adults. *Child Development, 47*, 466–472.

Tulving, E., & Schacter, D. L. (1990). Priming and human memory systems. *Science, 247*, 301–306.

Van Lancker, D. (1991). Personal relevance and the human right hemisphere. *Brain and Cognition, 17*, 64–92.

Vihman, M. M. (1993). Variable paths to early word production. *Journal of Phonetics, 21*, 61–82.

Waibel, A. (1986). Suprasegmentals in very large vocabulary word recognition speech perceptions. In E. C. Schwab & H. C. Nusbaum (Eds.), *Pattern recognition by humans and machines* (pp. 159–186). New York: Academic Press.

Waxman, S. R. (1991). Convergence between semantic and conceptual organization in preschool years. In S. A. Gelman & J. P. Byrnes (Eds.), *Perspectives on language and thought* (pp. 107–145). Cambridge, England: Cambridge University Press.

Werker, J. F. (1994, June). *Changing input, changing perceptual abilities, and changing cognitive skills: Toward a more comprehensive account of age-related changes in cross-language speech perception.* Paper presented at 9th International Conference on Infant Studies, Paris.

Werker, J. F., & Tees, R. C. (1984). Cross-language speech perception: Evidence for perceptual reorganization during the first year of life. *Infant Behavior and Development, 7*, 49–63.

Werker, J. F., & Tees, R. C. (1992). The organization and reorganization of human speech perception. *Annual Review of Neuroscience, 15*, 377–402.

Whalen, D. H., Levitt, A., & Wang, Q. (1991). Intonational differences between the reduplicative babbling of French- and English-learning infants. *Journal of Child Language, 18*, 501–506.

Wood, N., & Cowan, N. (1995). The cocktail party phenomenon revisited: How frequent are attention shifts to one's own name in an irrelevant auditory channel? *Journal of Experimental Psychology: Learning, Memory, and Cognition, 21*, 255–260.

Woodward, J. Z., & Aslin, R. N. (1990, April). *Segmentation cues in maternal speech to infants.* Paper presented at 7th biennial meeting of the International Conference on Infant Studies, Montreal, Quebec, Canada.

9

Domain Specificity and the Epistemic Triangle: The Development of the Concept of Animacy in Infancy

Maria Legerstee
York University

This chapter reviews research on the origin of the concept of animacy, and, in particular, on the development of the ability to distinguish between people and graspable objects during the first year of life. The background to this work is the traditional Piagetian assumption that an understanding of the social and physical world needs to be constructed through acting on it during the infancy period. Through these actions mental structures develop that permit infants to separate self from the environment and to understand that there are social and nonsocial objects in the world. Theories that put forth such assumptions view the infant as born into a world of chaotic stimuli that are perceived through unintegrated sensory modalities. These theories view the baby as lacking an awareness of space, time, and causality, and consequently of self and the physical and social environment. However, current infancy research suggests that Piaget's view should be questioned. There is evidence of cross-modal integration in 4-month-old infants because they will vocalize when hearing the voices of invisible people, but make reaching movements when hearing the sounds of invisible toys. Thus, the sound had come to indicate the identity of a *specific* object, a realization that is likely to come with the understanding that objects continue to exist when out of sight. These same infants also respond differentially to people and objects in a game of hide and seek. They will reach toward the occluder behind which objects have disappeared, but call for people in order to bring them back to view (Legerstee, 1994a). Because the infants were making inferences about the properties of people and objects that they could not perceive, this example suggests in addition to cross-modal integration, some type of conceptual understanding of how to interact with people and things long before the infancy period has ended.

The ability to differentiate between animate and inanimate objects is not only foundational for normal human development, but the two classes require distinctive methods of scientific inquiry. This problem was understood by Henri Bergson (1907/1945), whose treatises on the contrast between living and nonliving things related closely to the natural scientific debates of the 1890s. He argued that living things, in contrast to nonliving things are always in the process of becoming, and should therefore not be analyzed with the same ideas we use for the study of the inanimate world. Unlike objects, humans act upon the world, and are constantly creating themselves in their actions with the environment.

The idea that people and objects are different and that their complexity can only be described using rules and regulations that are specific to each domain has generated much controversy that extends to its foundations. For instance, in contrast to Bergson (1907/1945), Piaget (1954) believed that information about social and nonsocial domains, is processed by the same mechanism or "structures of the whole." The findings of recent empirical investigations on the animate–inanimate distinction in general and person–object differentiation in particular cast doubt on this interpretation, because these data show that babies act in ways that domain-general theorists would have difficulty explaining (Karmiloff-Smith, 1992; Legerstee, 1997a; Spelke, 1991).

In this chapter I propose to do the following. First, I provide empirical support for the suggestion that infants come equipped with repertoires of response pattern that are different for social and nonsocial objects. These response pattern are not simply reflexive actions to particular stimuli. Rather, evidence of recall and interpretation in young infants suggests that conceptual knowledge guides their actions. This knowledge appears driven by domain specific predispositions that are present at birth. Second, I consider the implications of these results for theories of the original nature of infant cognition, by using the development of the concept of animacy as a case in point. The chapter concludes by considering transitions in structures and action and in the infants' resulting understanding of people and things during the infancy years. It is argued that although the infants' interactions with the social and nonsocial worlds reveal that they come prepared to act appropriately with people and inanimate objects from the start, many of the attributes that define these classes still need to be constructed. The construction of this knowledge, although constrained by innate specifications, takes place through interactions with objects in the environment under active guidance of a co-subject (Chapman, 1992). More specifically, the developmental process is seen as one in which infants'

structural determinants give rise to complex interactions with the properties of the social and nonsocial world. As a result, new mental structures
can emerge as components of the individual and environment self-organize.
New structures representing more elaborate concepts and action pattern
may arise as the individual and environment mutually constrain each
other's actions (Fogel, 1993). This cognitive flexibility not only allows for
the individual's creativity, but it reveals that human cognition is the consequence and the cause of its development.

THE CONCEPT OF ANIMACY

A concept of Animacy is defined as the ability to differentiate between living and nonliving things. It entails knowing that both classes have physical
properties such as size and shape, but that only animate objects have biological functions (Chi, 1988). When does a concept of Animacy develop in
people? Concepts are mentally represented structures. The structures underlying concepts can be poor, providing only minimal information to the
subject about the concept, in which case, one would have a global understanding of the category under study. Researchers would call such concepts primitive (Mandler, 1992); skeletal (Gelman, 1990; Karmiloff-Smith,
1992) or core concepts (Spelke, 1991). A concept can also be detailed, providing more elaborate information about a particular category. It appears
that infants come endowed with both, global and more detailed concepts.
For instance, an understanding of object permanence (Baillargeon, 1987;
Spelke, 1991); causality (Leslie & Keeble, 1987; Spelke, 1991), numerical and
linguistic relevant data (Gelman, 1990; Karmiloff-Smith, 1991) appears to be
more detailed or complete from the outset.

Recent work has begun to investigate the onset of the infants' understanding of the psychological world as contrasted to their understanding of
the physical world (Gelman & Spelke, 1981; Legerstee, 1992; Spelke, Phillips
& Woodward, 1995) in order to shed light on the onset of the animate-inanimate distinction. Many authors interested in the concept of Animacy
have focused on conceptual changes in animism during childhood (Carey,
1985; Chi, 1988; Gelman, 1990). In contrast to Piaget's (1930/1950) contention
that misconceptions in attributing life to inanimate objects (animism) continues until late childhood, these authors found that preschoolers can distinguish between living and nonliving things if different tasks (other than
explanations) are used (Gelman, Spelke, & Meck, 1983; Keil, 1979). For example, when Piaget asked children in the concrete operational stage (8 years
old) whether a cloud was alive, children would answer "Yes, because it
moves sometimes." However, if tasks are used during which perceptual or
affective responses are required children show an earlier appreciation of

animacy. For instance, Golinkoff and Harding (1980; cited in Golinkoff, Harding, Carlson, & Sexton, 1984) found that infants as young as 12 months looked longer (interpreted as surprise) when inanimate objects, such as chairs appeared to move by themselves, and Carlson (1980; cited in Golinkoff et al., 1984) who trained 10-month-old infants to push a knob toward or away in order to have either a picture appear in a window, a mechanical dog bark, or a female experimenter smile and wave, found that infants pushed the knob significantly more toward rather than away from the inanimate event, but that there was no difference in type of pushing (away or toward) when the animate event was presented. It was as if the infants were aware that physical contact was necessary with inanimate but not with animate objects. This suggestion is supported by a recent study by Poulin-Dubois, Lepage, and Ferland (1996, Exp. 3), in which 9-month-olds expected a novel inanimate object to be constrained by the principle of contact. They were exposed to a self-propelled small robot and a female stranger, both moving according to the verbal commands of the infant who was present in the room. Infants from both age groups stared longer at the robot acting at a distance than at the person doing the same. Thus infants expected people to move independently, but not objects. Other aspects of the stimuli such as familiarity and sociality also seem to be important in facilitating discrimination in infants. Berzonsky (1971) revealed that young children provided more competent explanations about animate and inanimate objects if the objects were familiar. In addition, Carey (1985) suggested that children perform better if the living things were people, since animistic thinking is related to how their biological knowledge is organized, which tends to center on humans as the prototype of living things.

EVIDENCE FOR A GLOBAL CONCEPT OF ANIMACY IN INFANTS

As suggested earlier, it would appear that a *precursor* to a concept of animism in infants is the ability to distinguish between people and graspable objects. My own work, and that of others, on very young infants' ability to differentiate people from inanimate objects suggests, based on the appropriateness of infant behavioral responses, that infants have organized knowledge that they use correctly to classify the stimuli. From very early on, babies treat people in a special way and different from the way they treat objects. In a recent review of a range of evidence, it was concluded that by 2 months of age babies treat people as social objects, smiling, vocalizing, and imitating their actions, but objects as toys to be looked at and to be manipulated (Legerstee, 1992; 1997a; Spelke et al., 1995). For instance, as early as 5 weeks, infants become upset when caregivers refrain from communicating with them. They do not show this type of behavior in front of objects that remain immobile (Legerstee, Pomerleau, Malcuit, & Feider, 1987). By age 2 to 3 months infants smile and coo more to their mother and a female stranger than to interactive novel and familiar objects (Ellsworth, Muir, & Hains, 1993; Legerstee, 1991a; Legerstee, Corter, & Kienapple, 1990; Legerstee et al., 1987). It has been suggested that infants expect people to communicate reciprocally with them, each partner working actively to sustain and regulate the interaction (Stern, 1985; Trevarthen, 1979; Tronick, Ricks, & Cohn, 1982). Infants will also imitate actions of people, but not of objects simulating human gestures (Legerstee, 1991b). This suggests that infants are aware that *only* people can act in kind, and seems to support the suggestion, also proposed by Marler (1991) that each species accommodates most readily with those aspects of experience that are compatible with its nature. Even newborns react differently to people and objects, because they produce different manual actions to the two classes (Rönnqvist & von Hofsten, 1994). Moreover, there is an interesting convergence here with data on infants with Down syndrome. These babies also show person–object differentiation in their responsiveness, albeit at a later chronological age (4 to 6 months) than normal infants but when the subjects have approximately the same mental age (Legerstee & Bowman, 1989; Legerstee, Bowman, & Fels, 1992).

It could be argued, that this differential responsiveness of infants to people and objects is related to the different *perceptual* stimulation emanating from the two classes rather than a product of general knowledge about the roles that people and objects occupy. It would seem that in order for infants to be said to have a *conceptual* understanding of people and things evidence is needed that would indicate that infants are able to draw on this knowledge when perceptual stimulation is not available. We showed that when 4-month-old precrawling infants were allowed to search for people and objects hidden behind a screen in a game of hide and seek they reacted with different responses to the two classes. Most infants reached for the occluder behind which the object had disappeared, but they vocalized toward the occluder behind which people had disappeared (Legerstee, 1994a). These results suggest that infants in this situation appreciated that an object has been hidden, the object was either animate or inanimate and that different procedures were necessary to retrieve these objects.

Although the foregoing data appear to indicate that infants are endowed with a system of knowledge, containing principles that identify living and nonliving things, it could be argued that infants simply have a category of "person" and have associated with it various attributes such as a person communicates, and moves independently. In order for infants to have a concept of animacy, infants should include in this concept other examples of social objects (e.g., infants as well as adults) and also other examples of living things (e.g., nonhuman as well as human animals). A concept of Animacy cannot be applicable to only a single exemplar for the reason that in this case it would not longer constitute a concept.

To find out whether infants categorize images of self and other babies as social objects, we presented 5- and 8-month-old infants with video images of self, a same-aged peer, and dolls matched on skin and hair color and dressed in yellow bibs (see Fig. 9.1; Legerstee, Anderson, & Schaffer, 1998). All infants received two visits. During the first visit, the infants were filmed in interaction with their mothers in order to obtain visual and auditory material of a smiling and cooing baby. Of this 5-minute interaction tape, we cut a 60-second demonstration tape for the second visit. These demonstration tapes showed babies that moved their faces, and vocalized in a burst and pause pattern (three successive bursts of vocalizations of a total of approximately 6 sec and a 2-sec pause during which the babies did not vocalize, repeated for a total of 60 sec). We used a burst and pause pattern in order to

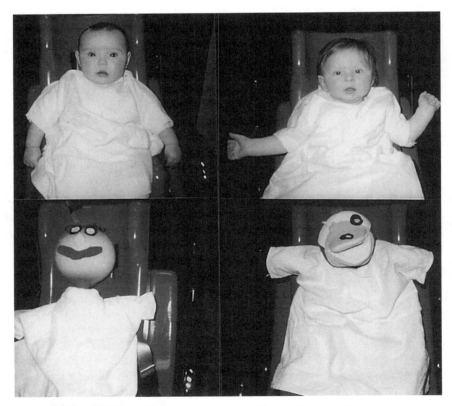

FIG. 9.1. Examples of faces of self (top), peer (top right), external moving object (bottom left), and internal moving object (bottom right).

simulate human interaction patterns. We hoped that this pattern would mo-
tivate infants to action rather than to mere visual fixation. During the second visit, the infants were placed in front of a large television screen and
were presented with the demonstration tapes of self, peers, and dolls. To
examine the role of movement in the recognition of the faces, the images
were presented in moving and static conditions. In the moving conditions,
the doll would move externally (the body swayed sideways and up and
down) or internally (an experimenter would move the internal abstract facial features of a hand puppet), and the infants moved as they naturally do
when interacting with adults. In the static condition the infants saw a frozen
image of self, peer, or doll. The moving and static visual conditions were
presented *without sound*. The results showed, that when 5- and 8-month-olds
were presented with silent moving video images of self, peer, or dolls, they
not only looked longer at the peer (novelty preference) and least long at
self (familiarity) at both ages, but they smiled and vocalized more to the social images than to the nonsocial images. In the static condition infants
looked longer at their own facial image, but the infants again produced
more social responses to the social images than to the nonsocial images.
Thus infants recognized their distinctive features as familiar and socioaf-
fective stimuli.

Aside from visual recognition of the face, infants also attend preferentially to human auditory input and recognize their own vocalizations as familiar sounds. In the auditory conditions, infants of both ages were presented with the social demonstration tapes, but now the visual image was
obscured, so that only the vocalizations were heard. The nonsocial sounds
were made either by bells or by a synthesizer and matched to the rhythm
and frequency (burst–pause pattern) of the infant vocalizations. Infants
looked longer (novelty) when hearing the peer's vocalizations than when
hearing their own (familiarity), and least long when hearing inanimate
sounds. Smiles and vocalizations occurred most frequently when infants
heard human voices, with most of the vocalizations occurring when they
listened to their own voices. Thus, the infants not only discriminated between their vocalizations and nonsocial sounds, but they recognized these
vocalizations as familiar, and similar to sounds they produce themselves.
The findings that 5-month-old babies recognize their faces and voices as familiar and social stimuli indicates that their responses are species, peer,
and self-specific.

Infants not only categorize babies and adults as social objects, different
from inanimate objects, but they also differentiate between inanimate objects and animals. Mandler and McDonough (1994) found that when they
presented 7-, 9-, and 11-month-olds, with 3-dimensional replicas of real objects in each of the vehicle and animal category, the infants showed *different*
exploratory behaviors toward animate and inanimate objects that looked

similar, such as birds and airplanes, but *similar* exploratory behaviors to objects that belonged to the animate category, but where the perceptual differences were low, such as dogs and fish. In another study, Ricard and Allard (1993) compared the responses of 9- to 10-month-old infants to a live rabbit and a stranger. Infants seem to know that animals are not inanimate (they can move themselves) and neither human (one cannot communicate with them). These findings on the infant's abilities to differentiate between living and nonliving things would support the suggestion that during their first year of life infants have developed a rudimentary or global concept of animacy.

DOMAIN SPECIFIC MECHANISM GUIDE ANIMACY

On what basis do infants differentiate between animate and inanimate objects? One of the most obvious differences between man and things is contained in the word "animate." Human beings are seen as the origin of motion, as internally motivated, sometimes as a center of consciousness (Legerstee, 1998). That is, they are seen as having an internal locus of causality (De Charmes, 1968). Piaget (1954) acknowledged this distinction in his writings when he discussed horizontal decalage in favor of person over object permanence toward the end of the sensori-motor period. He proposed that infants noticed people to be independent sources of causality and not objects, consequently people are more cognitively motivating to infants than objects and should therefore produce more rapid accommodations than objects (see Legerstee, 1994b).

The suggestion, that infants use various aspects of biological motion to differentiate animate from inanimate objects has also been proposed by more recent theorists (Gergely, Nadasdy, Csibza, & Biro, 1995; Watson, 1985). For instance, Watson (1985) suggested that it is the perception of contingent movement that enables infants to distinguish between social and nonsocial objects. He argued that people not only react to smiles, vocalizations, and motor movements of infants with similar actions of their own, but their variable interactions are more arousing to babies than the immediate and perfect responses of inanimate objects. Mandler (1992) argued that infants are born with a perceptual analysis device that enables them to perceive whether an object begins to move *on its own*, moves *irregularly* and *contingently*, in which case the infant assigns that object to the animate category. This perceptual category accrues other knowledge such that animate objects communicate, have feelings and intentions and other things do not. Thus conceptions develop from internal abstractions that are made specific by the perceptual system (Mandler, 1992).

To investigate the effects of contingent, independent, and irregular movement of people and inanimate objects on the infants' ability to dis-

criminate between people and things, we conducted the following two experiments, in which (a) onset and offset of the actions of people and things
were made contingent upon the infant response, (b) onset and offset of the
actions of people and things were non-contingent, but were yoked instead
to the responses of infants in the previous contingent performance, and (c)
the contingent and yoked interactions were followed by a transfer task during which the effect of the previous interactions were evaluated on the infants' subsequent interest in a cognitive task (a visual and auditory stimulus; Legerstee, 1997b). In the first experiment, sounding inanimate objects,
moved in a smooth, irregular way by an invisible experimenter, and people
saying "hello baby, how are you," alternately provided contingent or yoked
reinforcement to the vocalizations of the infants. The effects of these interactions were evaluated in the subsequent transfer tasks. The results
showed that infants found the contingent person most stimulating and the
non-contingent person most distressing. In addition, infants that had experienced contingent interactions with a person remained positively engaged
on the subsequent transfer task, those that had experienced noncontingent
interactions with a person lowered their interest to the stimulus on the
transfer task. No such regulation of emotion was noted toward the contingent or yoked inanimate objects, nor to the subsequent transfer tasks.
Thus, the infants' social interactive experiences affected their emotions.
This effect was then carried forward onto their next task. Because people
and objects acted in a continuous way to the infant vocalizations, their differential responsiveness could not be due to different schedules of contingencies. However, it could be argued, that infants attend selectively to people because they have a general preference to attend to human faces and
voices. They may have learned that interesting events occur where faces
and voices are and thus the stimuli may have acted as an "attention magnet" (Watson, 1972). In order to address this issue, in Experiment 2, the
same scenario was presented except that this time the inanimate object
had facial rather than abstract features and the stimuli moved in a silent
way to the infants' gazes. Despite changes in facial and auditory aspects of
the stimuli, the results of Experiment 2 closely paralleled those of Experiment 1. The finding that the infants differentiated between contingent relationships of people and objects, but that only the response contingent stimulation of persons affected their subsequent performance on a cognitive
task, suggests that the transfer effects that were obtained were dependent
upon the quality of the *social* stimulation infants received and less on their
overall ability to perceive a contingency or to process information. Presumably, the contingent and sensitive interactions of people create a positive
mood which then increases infant motivation to learn, whereas insensitive
interactions of people disturbs infants and interferes with subsequent
learning. Thus, by 3 months, infants do not seem to mistake a nonsocial ob-

ject for a social object on the basis of contingency, independent movement or irregular path of movement.

It has been suggested that infants respond differentially to people and objects because the history of contingency learning (variable social reinforcement vs. immediate nonsocial reinforcement) from birth to 3 months has created a difference in such young infant reactions to nonsocial objects (Watson, 1985). However, it is difficult to see how infants learn to differentiate between people and objects through a process of differential conditioning. Although by 3 months of age infants may have had ample practice playing contingency games with people, it is likely that in the natural world infants would have little experiences with objects to perceive and analyze "perfect and clear contingencies" given their limited abilities to act on objects. Watson (1972, pp. 323–324) himself states that "during the first three months, the combination of slow response recovery and short contingency memory prohibits [the infant of] becoming aware of contingencies between his behavior and its stimulus effects in the physical environment." Our results suggest, that rather than having an innate ability to perceive contingencies or independent movement, infants may be born with predispositions that allow them to appreciate in some primitive way that conspecifics not only act contingently and independently (Mandler, 1992; Watson, 1972, 1985) but are similar to themselves (Legerstee, 1997a). For instance, Gelman, Durgin, and Kaufman (1995) argued that infants are born with domain specific structures that draw infant attention to the various details that distinguish animate from inanimates. The animate structures specify that people (and other animates) are capable of self-generated movements and the inanimate structures specify that objects need agents to move them. However, Gelman does not believe that the distinction between people and objects is made on a perceptual (spatio-temporal) level, because perceptual information is usually ambiguous or incomplete. Rather, the structures allow infants to *interpret* movement of objects differently depending on whether the movement is made by an animate or inanimate stimulus. To give an example, Gelman wrote (Gelman et al., 1995): "If we encounter a round object in the desert with needles we may think it is a cactus until it begins to move, then we realize that it is an echidna and would not maintain that it was a cactus on what it looked like initially" (p. 183). Thus according to Gelman, infants interpret perceptual information from both movement and external features when drawing conclusions about animacy. However, even if infants are aware that animates can move by themselves and should look a certain way, it would seem that in order to classify animates as social objects, they need to appreciate that humans act according to social rules. Various authors view the ability to perceive intentions in others as a prerequisite to a conceptual understanding of people. They argue that it allows for a clear differentiation between the social and the physical (Fry, 1981; Tomasello, 1995; Wellman, 1993).

It appears that by 9 months, infants' interactions with people undergo major transformations. Infants for the first time begin to direct people's attention to objects and events outside the dyad. They start to engage in joint attention (Tomasello, 1995; Legerstee & Weintraub, 1997) and produce communicative gestures, such as protodeclaratives (e.g., Bates Benigni, Bretherton, Camaioni, & Volterra, 1979; Legerstee, Verbeek, & Varghese, 1998). It has been suggested that this behavior implies an understanding of the other participants as people who share intentional relations to them (Hobson, 1989; Tomasello, 1995). How do infants progress from interactions with either people or objects, to triadic interactions that include attention to objects? It would seem that before infants understand, that they can affect people's attention or mental state through instrumental behaviors in which they show that they have goals "in mind" ahead of time and use various means for attaining them, infants need to be sensitive to a functional link between people and other things. Thus infants need to be aware that people relate to things in the environment and that these relationships are different for social and nonsocial objects. They need to know that people communicate and interact at a distance with other people, but manipulate inanimate objects.

Before infants understand people as intentional, they show surprise when people's hands do unexpected things (Leslie, 1994; Woodward, 1998). Woodward (1998) found that between 5 and 9 months, infants connect a hand with the object it grasps, but do not make such relationships between an inanimate rod and an object it touches. These results revealed that infants construe the movements of people and objects differently, even when the trajectory on which the animate and inanimate objects moved were identical.

In addition to associating human actions with objects, they need to know that when people reach or speak, their actions are *related* to something. In order to find out whether infants expect people to speak to persons, but to act on inanimate objects, we examined whether they attend selectively to the consequences of these actions (Legerstee, Barna, & DiAdamo, in press; see also Molina, Spelke, & King, 1996). We randomly assigned infants to two experimental and one control condition. In the experimental conditions, the infants were habituated to two videotaped events in which they saw an actor either talk to or manipulate something behind an occluder. After the infants were habituated, one screen was moved to cover the actor and the other was moved to reveal that the stimulus was either a person or an object. The inanimate objects were a black broom with a blue handle, or a black shovel with a wooden handle. To match the size and form of the objects to the social stimulus, a Styrofoam ball was attached to the top of the broom handles. The social stimuli were women, that were of the same height as the inanimate stimuli. They wore either blue or beige slacks, with white or black blouses and black shoes (see Fig. 9.2). Infant looking time was coded in each condition. We hypothesized that if infants expected people to communicate with persons, but not with inanimate objects, then they should look longer at events that appear to violate these expectations following habituation (e.g. people speaking to objects or acting on people). Thus in these experiments, the person and object test events

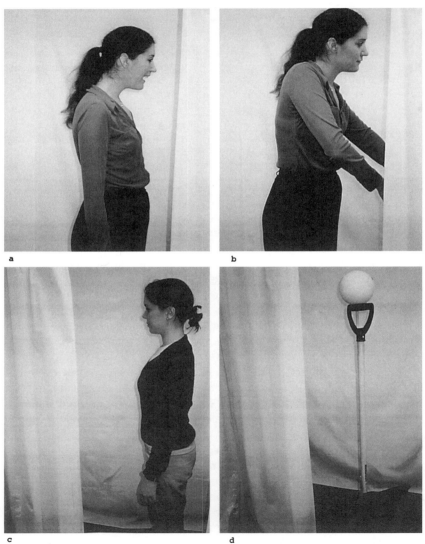

FIG. 9.2. Actor talking (a) or reaching and swiping (b) during habituation. Test displays (c) person, (d) inanimate object.

were the same, and if the analysis shows a main effect, then this must be due to a preference for one stimulus over another. However, if the analysis shows a Stimulus × Action interaction for the experimental conditions only, then the difference in responding to the person or the object conditions indicates that the infants had developed expectations about the different actions (speaking versus manipulating) that they had observed during habituation.

The results showed, that when 6-month-olds see people talk, they expect these actions to be directed at persons, and not at inanimate objects. Infants who were familiarized with the profile of an actor who appeared to talk to something hidden behind an occluder looked longer when the recipient of the actions was revealed to be an inanimate object, rather than a person. In contrast, infants who had been habituated to an actor who reached for and appeared to swipe with something hidden behind an occluder, looked longer when the hidden object turned out to be animate. These responses could not have been the result of the visual difference between the two stimuli, because infants did not show such differential looking during the control conditions. Instead, the infants' differential looking pattern varied as a result of the different types of actions to which they had been habituated. These findings indicate that infants are sensitive to the target of adults' communications. We would like to propose that the infants' differential responsiveness to people and objects during the test events suggest that they construe intentional actions such as talking and reaching in terms of actions directed toward objects.

One could argue that infants by 6 months of age may have developed associations between human actions and the types of objects toward which the actions tend to be directed. People usually tend to talk to distal objects that are human rather than inanimate, and they tend to proximally manipulate inanimate objects rather than persons. These behavioral sequences become familiar events, and if they are changed then they become novel or unfamiliar. We suggest however, that rather than associations, these behaviors are internal experiences about something. The infants not only have to infer that the adults' actions are indeed directed toward something they can't see, but they have to remember this experience when they eventually see the person and objects alone.

Such precocious awareness of how people behave appears to indicate that these conceptions do not originate from perception and action (cf. Piaget, 1954; Merleau-Ponty, 1942/1963). Rather the evidence suggests that it develops from its own roots and that the earliest conceptions of animacy in infants, albeit primitive, form the core of later mature conceptions. Spelke suggested about these early concepts that, "they are enriched and refined as knowledge grows, but they are rarely overturned" (Spelke, Breinlinger, Macomber, & Jacobson, 1992, p. 606).

ORGANIZATION OF EARLY KNOWLEDGE

If infants have domain specific predispositions by which to categorize animate and inanimate objects how is this initial knowledge organized? It appears that this early knowledge is not only primitive but it is organized in a procedural form. What this means is that the available predispositions allow infants to respond appropriately to the social and nonsocial environment but it prevents infants from using knowledge of one domain in the service of the other. Through domain specific constraints, infants remain centered on either the social or nonsocial aspects of the environment. With development, and because of plasticity of early brain development (Johnson, 1990), domain specific structures not only become more specified, but decentration occurs which allows for knowledge to become explicit.

Developmental change in human cognition is a function of dynamic processes of self-organization and interactions with people and objects. However, the general constraints provided by the environment favor particular interactions, such that "resonance between autonomous cognitive structures and the social environment is inevitable" (Lewis, 1994, p. 159). In this model, transitions in development, stability and order, do not arise as a consequence of domain specific predispositions or of environmental influences alone, rather, they emerge dynamically through the interaction of their cooperative elements (Fogel, & Thelen, 1987). The infant's information-seeking principles select feedback from the environment, and this feedback specifies subsequent information seeking. Thus the conceptual structures infants have and those they will acquire are constrained by the individual's epistemic history, yet they are propelled by the general maturational and environmental constraints toward specification and integration (Chapman, 1992).

Piaget (1954) also emphasized that new cognitive structures could only arise if the infant was put into a sufficiently challenging environment. Because he was interested in the infants' understanding of the physical environment, Piaget did not describe in any detail how different social contexts would be responsible for different intellectual performances. Indeed, Piaget neglected to describe the ways in which social factors were implicated in the generativity of human cognition (Chapman, 1992). This is surprising, because it would seem essential that in order for infants to acquire a detailed concept of Animacy, they would have to interact with animate as well as inanimate objects. Properties of people and objects are produced in interaction. They do not reside in the object, nor are they arbitrary and subjective (Oyama, 1985). Infants may find out about the physical properties of objects during solitary play (e.g., the objects' multimodal qualities, permanence, and so forth), but in order for infants to construct functional concepts of objects, interaction with people appears essential. Similarly, in order for infants to find out about people they will have to communicate with them. Thus cognitive development involves not only equilibration between subject and object, but also equilibration between subjects (Chapman, 1992, p. 50). Bruner (1983) argued that we do not construct a reality solely on the basis of private encounters with exemplars of natural states, but that most of our approaches to the world are mediated through negotiation with others. Hence, rather than viewing the infant as a lone scientist coping with the social and nonsocial world of the unknown, in the present model of developmental theorizing, the infant, in constructing concepts of people and things, is regarded as a scientist in a shared social context. The development of human cognition has an irreducibly triadic structure involving the infant, the thing to be known and the co-subject (Chapman, 1992). The particular interactions infants have with people over objects result in progressive specification of social and nonsocial domain knowledge, and promotes the subsequent coupling of the two domains. As a consequence, both domain specific predispositions and the environment determine the course of cognitive development, and changes and variability in development are viewed as a function of the infants' cognitive structures and the milieu in which they play.

People are not only things to be apprehended, but also social agents that bring about hierarchical changes in infant cognition. Through interacting with people, infants notice that people reciprocate, elaborate on their actions, and negotiate with them. From such interactions, where the participants share their individual knowledge, it is possible that new knowledge is constructed that neither partner possessed before (Chapman, 1992).

CROSS-CONNECTING OF DOMAINS

Throughout the first 4 to 5 months, the infant's domain specific structures are placed into the organizing dynamics of social interaction, where they select feedback from ever changing contexts. The result of this development is not only progressive domain specification, but increased refinement that allows for the formation of new systems that then take on lives of their own and whose structures were not initially specified. The development of new structures becomes evident by the end of the first 6 months of life when the two ways of interacting become coordinated. Rather than focusing uniquely on people or objects, infants begin to shift their gazes between the partner's face and the toy in which the infant is interested (Legerstee & Weintraub, 1997), and they are sensitive to the target of adult communication to a third party (Legerstee, et al., in press). This capacity does not indicate that infants understand the mentalistic aspects of people's focus of attention, but it reveals the infants' own intentionality and may lead them to perceive aspects of the event that are important to the understanding of intentional behavior. By the end of the first year, when playing with caretakers, the coordination of attention between people and things becomes routine. Infants now readily communicate non-verbally about things in the environment and use their gazes to signal to social partners their desire for an object of interest (Legerstee, et al., 1998). Mature social partners seem essential in the initial production of these behaviors because infants will coordinate their attention more when interacting with adults than when playing with same-aged peers. The development of coordinated attention is regarded as the beginning of referential communication and as the foundation for language development (Bruner, 1983, Butterworth, 1991; Legerstee & Weintraub, 1997; Tomasello & Farrar, 1986; Vygotsky, 1978).

The proposition that infants begin life with domain specific structures that become more sophisticated and may cross-connect as a result of dynamic social interactions finds support from developmental neuropsychology. If infants have domain specific structures that predispose them to respond differently to social and nonsocial stimuli, then deficits in one domain could produce impairments in the developmental phase where the two interact. Sequential analyses have shown that object, rather than person involvement is a significant precursor to the display of coordinated attention in normal infants (Bakeman & Adamson, 1984; Legerstee & Weintraub, 1997). Infants with Down syndrome do not show much interest in objects during the first year of life, which makes it difficult for parents to encourage infants to coordinate their attention between them and their toys. The factors must contribute to the significant delay in the development of coordinated attention and subsequent language development of infants with Down syndrome (Legerstee & Weintraub, 1997). The findings provide support for domain specificity of the cognitive systems and points to the importance of social factors in structuring interaction between the domains. Whether infants with Down syndrome involve nonsocial domain specific deficits which then affect later linguistic functioning, or linguistic deficits or both remains an empirical question. It would appear that domain general theorists have difficulty explaining such within and across domain deficits.

CONCLUSION

In summary, it appears that rather than acquiring the concept of Animacy through a process of conditioning, where the items to be learned, such as people and objects, their attributes and their functions, are repeatedly associated, infants understanding of animacy is guided by domain specific principles. It is this ability that allows infants to recognize at birth that they are similar to other people, and to differentiate them from objects and consequently living from nonliving things. However, the existence of early structures does not imply that infants do not develop new structures, containing more elaborate knowledge. The evidence shows that not everything is known at birth and that many of the attributes that differentiate people from things still need to be constructed with age. The role of the predispositions is to give the epigenetic process a head start in each domain and to guide the infants' subsequent involvement with social and nonsocial objects in an orderly, albeit varied and flexible way. The duality of initial structures and of subsequent rich development should not be seen as contradictory. "The only way we can understand the dynamics of change is in terms of what might be viewed as the constants of the system" (Pylyshyn, 1985, p. 403). It would seem that in order for developmental theories to have predictive and explanatory value, not everything can be seen to vary. Rather, they have to outline the universal mechanism of the infants' cognitive systems and to study their development in order to reveal their forms of variation over time, as well as the construction of new forms.

Although increasingly more complex interactions with objects and people result in a more sophisticated knowledge of the two, it is through interactions with people that new structures are created. The infants' understanding that they are similar to members of their own species leads the two partners not only to share the knowledge that each alone possesses, but they may construct knowledge that neither one of them possessed alone (Chapman, 1992; Fogel, 1993; Oyama, 1985).

ACKNOWLEDGMENTS

This work was supported by a grant from the Social Sciences and Humanities Research Council of Canada (410-96-1693).

REFERENCES

Baillargeon, R. (1987). Young infants' reasoning about the physical and spatial properties of a hidden object. *Cognitive Development, 2*, 179–220.

Bakeman, R., & Adamson, L. (1984). Coordinating attention to people and objects in mother-infant and peer-infant interaction. *Child Development, 55*, 1278–1289.

Bates, E., Benigni, L., Bretherton, L., Camaioni, L., & Volterra, V. (1979). *The emergency of symbols: Cognition and communication in infancy.* New York: Academic Press.

Bergson, H. (1907/1945). *L'evolution creatrive.* Geneve: Editions Albert Skira.

Berzonsky, M. D. (1971). The role of familiarity in children's explanations of physical causality. *Child Development, 43*, 705–715.

Bruner, J. (1983). *Child's talk: Learning to use language.* New York: Norton.

Butterworth, G. (1991). The ontogeny and phylogeny of joint visual attention. In A. Whiten, *Natural theories of mind: Evolution, development and simulation of everyday mindreading* (pp. 223–232). London, England: Basil Blackwell.

Carey, S. (1985). *Conceptual change in childhood.* Cambridge, MA: MIT Press.

Chapman, M. (1992). Equilibration and the dialectics of organization. In H. Beilin & P. Putfall (Eds.), *Piaget's theory: Prospects and possibilities* (pp. 39–59). Hillsdale, NJ: Lawrence Erlbaum Associates.

Chi, M. T. H. (1988). Children's lack of access and knowledge reorganization: An example from the concept of animacy. In F. E. Weinert & M. Perlmutter (Eds.), *Memory development: Universal changes and individual differences* (pp. 169–194). Hillsdale, NJ: Lawrence Erlbaum Associates.

De Charmes, R. (1968). *Personal causation,* New York: Academic Press.

Ellsworth, C. P., Muir, D. W., & Hains, S. M. J. (1993). Social competence and person-object differentiation: An analysis of the still-face effect. *Developmental Psychology, 29,* 63–73.

Fogel, A. (1993). *Developing through relationships: Origins of communication, self and culture.* Illinois: The University of Chicago Press.

Fogel, A., & Thelen, E. (1987). Development of early expressive and communicative action: Reinterpreting the evidence from a dynamic system perspective, *Developmental Psychology, 23,* 747–761.

Fry, D. (1981). Developmental changes in strategies of social interaction. In M. Lamb and L. Sherrod (Eds.). *Infant Social Cognition* (pp. 315–331). Hillsdale, NJ: Lawrence Erlbaum Associates.

Gelman, R. (1990). First principles organize attention to and learning about relevant data: Number and the animate-inanimate distinction as examples. *Cognitive science, 14,* 79–106.

Gelman, R., Durgin, F., & Kaufman, L. (1995). Distinguishing between animates and inanimates: Not by motion alone. In D. Sperber, D. Premack, & A. J. Premack, (Eds.), *Causal cognition: A multidisciplinary debate* (pp. 150–184). Oxford: Clarendon Press.

Gelman, R., & Spelke, E. (1981). The development of thoughts about animate and inanimate objects: Implications for research on social cognition. In J. H. Flavell & L. Ross (Eds.), *Social cognition development: Frontiers and possible futures.* New York: Cambridge University Press.

Gelman, R., Spelke, E. S., & Meck, E. (1983). What preschoolers know about animate and inanimate objects. In D. Rogers & J. A. Sloboda (Eds.), *The acquisition of symbolic skills* (pp. 297–326). New York: Plenum.

Gergely, G., Nadasdy, Z., Csibza, G., & Biro, S. (1995). Taking the intentional stance at 12 months of age. *Cognition, 56,* 165–193.

Golinkoff, R. M., Harding, C., Carlson, V., & Sexton, M. E. (1984). The infant's perception of causal events: The distinction between animate and inanimate objects. In L. P. Lipsitt & C. Rovee-Collier (Eds.), *Advances in infancy research* (Vol 3., pp. 145–151). Norwood, NJ: Ablex.

Hobson, P. (1989). On sharing experiences. *Development and Psychopathology, 1,* 197–203.

Johnson, M. H. (1990). Cortical maturation and the development of visual attention in early infancy. *Journal of cognitive neuroscience, 2,* 81–95.

Karmiloff-Smith, A. (1991). Beyond modularity: Innate constraints and developmental change. In S. Carey & R. Gelman (Eds.), *The epigenesis of mind* (pp. 171–197). Hillsdale, NJ: Lawrence Erlbaum Associates.

Karmiloff-Smith, A. (1992). *Beyond modularity: A developmental perspective on cognitive science.* Cambridge, MA: MIT Press.

Keil, F. (1979). *Semantic and conceptual development: An ontological perspective.* Cambridge, MA: Harvard University Press.

Legerstee, M., Barna J., & DiAdamo, C. (in press). Precursors to intentional behavior: Understanding people and their actions. *Developmental psychology.*

Legerstee, M. (1991a). Changes in the quality of infant sounds as a function of social and nonsocial stimulation, *First language, 11,* 327–343.

Legerstee, M. (1991b). The role of person and object in eliciting early imitation, *Journal of Experimental Child Psychology, 51, 3,* 423–433.

Legerstee, M. (1992). A review of the animate-inanimate distinction in infancy: Implications for models of social and cognitive knowing. *Early Development and Parenting, 1,* 57–67.

Legerstee, M. (1994a). Patterns of 4-month-old infant responses to hidden silent and sounding people and objects. *Early Development and Parenting, 3,* 71–80.

Legerstee, M. (1994b). The role of familiarity and sound in the development of person and object permanence. *British Journal of Developmental Psychology, 12,* 455–468.

Legerstee, M. (1997a). Changes in social conceptual development: Domain specific structures, self-organization and indeterminism. In A. Fogel, M. C. D. P. Lyra, & J. Valsiner (Eds.), *Dynamics and indeterminism in developmental and social processes* (pp. 245–260). Mahwah, NJ: Lawrence Erlbaum Associates.

Legerstee, M. (1997b). Contingency effects of people and objects on subsequent cognitive functioning in three-month-old infants. *Social Development, 6,* 307–321.

Legerstee, M. (1998). Mental and bodily awareness in infancy: Consciousness of self-existence in 6-month-old infants. *Journal of Consciousness, 5,* 627–644.

Legerstee, M., Anderson, D., & Schaffer, M. (1998). Five and eight month-old infants recognize their face and voice as familiar and social stimuli. *Child Development, 69,* 37–50.

Legerstee, M., & Bowman, T. (1989). The development of responses to people and a toy in infants with Down syndrome. *Infant Behavior and Development, 12*(4), 462–473.

Legerstee, M., Bowman, T. G., & Fels, S. (1992). People and objects affect the quality of vocalizations in infants with Down syndrome. *Early Development and Parenting, 1, 3,* 149–156.

Legerstee, M., Corter, C., & Kienapple, K. (1990). Hand, arm and facial action to social and nonsocial stimuli, *Child Development, 61,* 774–784.

Legerstee, M., Pomerleau, A., Malcuit, G., & Feider, H. (1987). The development of infants' responses to people and a doll: Implications for research in communication. *Infant Behavior and Development, 10,* 81–95.

Legerstee, M., Verbeek, Y., & Varghese, J. (1998, April). *Effects of didactic strategies on symbolic behavior in infants with and without Down syndrome.* Paper presented at the 11th Biennial International Conference on Infant Studies, Atlanta, Georgia.

Legerstee, M., & Weintraub, J. (1997). The integration of person and object attention in infants with and without Down syndrome. *Infant Behavior and Development, 20,* 71–82.

Leslie, A., & Keeble, S. (1987). Do six-month-old infants perceive causality? *Cognition, 25,* 265–288.

Leslie, A. M. (1994). Infant perception of a manual pick up event. *British Journal of Developmental Psychology, 2,* 19–32.

Lewis, M. (1994). Reconciling stage and specificity in Neo-Piagetian Theory: Self-organizing conceptual structures. *Human Development, 37,* 143–169.

Mandler, J. (1992). How to build a baby: II. Conceptual primitives. *Psychological Review, 99,* 587–604.

Mandler, J., & McDonough, L. (1994). Concept formation in infancy. *Cognitive Development, 8,* 291–318.

Marler, P. (1991). The instinct to learn. In S. Carey & R. Gelman, (Eds.), *The epigenesis of mind: Essays on biology and cognition* (pp. 37–66). Hillsdale, NJ: Lawrence Erlbaum Associates.

Merleau-Ponty, M. (1942/1963). *The structure of behavior* (A. L. Fisher, Trans.). Boston, MA: Beacon Press.

Molina, M., Spelke, E. S., & King, D. (1996). The animate-inanimate distinction in infancy: Sensitivity to distinctions between social interactions and object manipulations. *Infant Behavior and Development, 19,* 625.

Oyama, S. (1985). *The ontogeny of information: Developmental systems and evolution.* Cambridge, England: Cambridge University Press.

Piaget, J. (1930/1950). *The child's conception of physical causality* (M. Gabian, Trans.). London: Routledge & Kegan Paul.

Piaget, J. (1954). *The construction of reality in the child* (M. Cook, Trans.). New York: Basic Books.

Poulin-Dubois, D., Lepage, A., & Ferland, D. (1996). Infants' concept of animacy. *Cognitive Development, 11,* 19–36.

Pylyshyn, Z. (1985). Plasticity and invariance in cognitive development. In: J. Mehler & R. Fox (Eds.), *Beyond the blooming, buzzing confusion* (pp. 403–415). Hillsdale, NJ: Lawrence Erlbaum Associates.

Ricard, M., & Allard, L. (1993). The reaction of 9- to 10-month-old infants to an unfamiliar animal. *Journal of Genetic Psychology, 154,* 15–16.

Rönnqvist, L., & von Hofsten, C. (1994). Neonatal finger and arm movements as determined by a social and an object context. *Early development and parenting, 3,* 81–93.

Spelke, E. (1991). Physical knowledge in infancy: Reflections on Piaget's theory. In S. Carey & R. Gelman (Eds.), *The epigenesis of mind* (pp. 133–169). Hillsdale, NJ: Lawrence Erlbaum Associates.

Spelke, E. S., Breinlinger, K., Macomber, J., & Jacobson, K. (1992). Origins of knowledge. *Psychological Review, 99,* 605–632.

Spelke, E. S., Phillips, A. T., & Woodward, A. L. (1995). Infants knowledge of object motion and human action. In D. Sperber, D. Premack, & A. J. Premack (Eds.), *Causal cognition: A multidisciplinary debate* (pp. 44–78). Oxford, England: Clarendon Press.

Stern, D. N. (1985). *The interpersonal world of the infant.* New York: Basic Books.

Tomasello, M., & Farrar, M. J. (1986). Joint attention and early language. *Child Development, 57,* 1454–1463.

Tomasello, M. (1995). Joint attention as social cognition. In C. Moore & P. Dunham (Eds.), *Joint attention: Its origin and role in development* (pp. 103–130). Hillsdale, NJ: Lawrence Erlbaum Associates.

Trevarthen, C. (1979). Communication and cooperation in early infancy: A description of primary intersubjectivity. In M. Bullowa (Ed.), *Before speech: The beginning of interpersonal communication* (pp. 321–347). Cambridge, England: Cambridge University Press.

Tronick, E. Z., Ricks, M., & Cohn, J. F. (1982). Maternal and infant affective exchange: Patterns of adaptation. In T. Field & A. Fogel (Eds.), *Emotion and early interaction* (pp. 93–100). Hillsdale, NJ: Lawrence Erlbaum Associates.

Vygotsky, L. (1978). *Mind in society.* Cambridge, MA: Harvard University Press.

Watson, J. S. (1972). Smiling, cooing and "the game." *Merrill-Palmer Quarterly, 18,* 323–339.

Watson, J. S. (1985). Contingency perception in early social development. In T. M. Field & N. A. Fox (Eds.), *Social perception in infants* (pp. 157–176). Norwood, NJ: Ablex.

Wellman, H. M. (1993). Early understanding of mind: The normal case. In S. Baron-Cohen, H. Tager-Flusberg, & D. J. Cohen (Eds.), *Understanding other minds: Perspectives from autism* (pp. 10–39). Oxford, England: Oxford University Press.

Woodward, A. (1998). Infants selectively encode the goal of an actor's reach. *Cognition, 69,* 1–34.

10

"Discovery Procedures" for People and Things—The Role of Representation and Identity

Andrew N. Meltzoff
M. Keith Moore
University of Washington, Seattle

Infancy research has captured the attention of a broad array of cognitive scientists, neuroscientists, and philosophers. In a relatively short time researchers have discovered many nonobvious facts about infant behavior. The field is now in search of a theoretical framework that encompasses these new discoveries.

One influential view is that the concepts used by young infants are essentially adult-like in nature. The concepts may later be enriched somewhat around the edges, but what is available to newborns is essentially unchanged over the course of development. The justification for this view is that infant experience in the world is both too chaotic and too impoverished to extract the mature concepts. Thus, mature concepts are needed to organize experience and do not derive from it. This view has been called the "core-knowledge" thesis (Spelke, 1994). *The slogan is that infants have adult concepts.*

A second view is that adults have concepts, but preverbal infants do not. On this view, behavior is complex because infants are sophisticated processors of the regularities in the perceived world. This allows them to extract the pattern and time-course of events, adapting their behavior to events without recourse to conceptual analysis. This view has been articulated in "dynamic-systems" theories (e.g., Thelen & Smith, 1994). *The slogan is that infants have no concepts—to explain infant behavior at a cognitive level is misguided.*

This chapter presents a third alternative. Central to this approach is identifying the minimum initial structure that infants could use to develop the conceptual structures of the adult and to describe the mechanism of this transformative process. The notion is that evolution has bequeathed human infants not with adult concepts, but with initial mental structures that serve as "discovery procedures" for developing more comprehensive and flexible concepts. Development is thus an open-ended process. *The slogan is that infants have concepts that are different from, but the developmental foundation for, adult concepts—there are conceptual revolutions in infancy.*

The aim of this chapter is to flesh out the notion of infant "discovery procedures." We draw on two lines of empirical research: (a) infants' representation and imitation of actions that are no longer visible, *deferred imitation*, and (b) their representation of the existence, location, and movement of objects that are no longer visible, *object permanence*. We deduce three theoretical premises from the evidence: (a) infant representations persist, (b) spatiotemporal parameters of objects are the primary criteria for numerical identity, and (c) object features and functions serve as secondary identity criteria. Starting with these premises, we propose a model of the early representational system. Our proposal is developmental without denying innate structure and elevates the power of perception and representation while being cautious about attributing mature concepts to young infants. We show how the model helps to resolve one of the crucial paradoxes in infancy research—the dissociation between young infants' reactions to object disappearance as measured by visual attention versus manual search.

MARSHALLING THE EVIDENCE

Young Infants Are Representational Beings

One phenomenon bearing on infant representation is deferred imitation. Infants can observe an act at Time *t1* without imitating, and at a subsequent *t2* can re-enact the behavior in the absence of the model. This demonstrates a capacity for acting on the basis of a stored representation of a perceptually absent event. Deferred imitation provides a close parallel to the problem of searching for hidden objects. For both, observation alone, prior to action, provides the critical target information. For both, the problem is posed by invisibility that cuts off perceptual contact with the target. One difference is in the content of the representation—in the deferred case an absent *act* and in the permanence case an absent *object*. This difference has implications for assessing representation. In object-disappearance tasks, representation of the object serves as a goal that can be obtained by organizing a separate action (manual search) or indexed by another reaction (increased looking), neither of which is specified by the original representation. In deferred imitation the original representation intrinsically specifies the act to perform and to measure. Consequently, deferred imitation has long been thought to measure representation.

In classical developmental theory, infants first became capable of deferred imitation at about 18 months of age (Piaget, 1962). Modern research has discovered evidence for deferred imitation at substantially younger ages. The most extensive work on deferred imitation of object-related acts has been done with infants about 1 year of age, but as we will see, work has also been done with even younger infants.

This pre-18-month-old deferred imitation could have been fragile and highly constrained. However, the research showed it is not. A recent study demonstrated that 14-month-olds can imitate with fidelity after delays as long as 4 months (Meltzoff, 1995b). Research has also documented deferred imitation of completely novel acts (Meltzoff, 1988). Further, early deferred imitation is powerful enough to generalize across a change of context. Infants who witnessed an action-on-an-object at home or in a day-care center imitated several days later when presented with the object by a different person in a different setting (Barnat, Klein, & Meltzoff, 1996; Hanna & Meltzoff, 1993; Klein & Meltzoff, 1999).

Moreover, the capacity to imitate perceptually absent acts seems to be part of the initial state, not a product of development, at least when simple body actions such as facial gestures are used. One study intervened between the stimulus and response by having infants suck on a pacifier while the adult demonstrated mouth opening and tongue protrusion (Meltzoff & Moore, 1977). The adult terminated the demonstration, assumed a neutral face, and only then removed the pacifier. The results showed that 3-week-old infants imitated the gestures in the subsequent response period. Other studies have also reported imitative effects when the gesture is no longer visible (Fontaine, 1984; Heimann, Nelson, Schaller, 1989; Heimann & Schaller, 1985; Legerstee, 1991; Meltzoff & Moore, 1989). Further, infants have been shown to imitate across longer delays. In one study, 6-week-olds saw different gestures on Day 1 and returned on Day 2 to see the adult with a neutral pose. The results showed that 6-week-old infants imitated the gestures they saw 24-hours earlier (Meltzoff & Moore, 1994).

Taken as a whole, the new results suggest that the ability to act on the basis of a stored representation of perceptually absent stimuli is the starting point for infant development, not its culmination. The findings support three inferences about the nature and scope of early representations: (a) Representations can be formed from observation alone, prior to action. Infants create representations at *t1* without having to perform the act themselves, and moreover do so for nonhabitual, novel acts. Perception without synchronous motor action is sufficient to form representations. (b) Representations persist. Even after relatively brief observation periods, infant representations are long lived, persisting mental entities. (c) Representations are a sufficient basis on which to organize action. Perceptually derived representations from *t1* are sufficient to generate motor production at *t2*.

Theoretical Premise #1: Representations Persist. The foregoing data warrant a strong inference, which we label theoretical premise #1. The data suggest that young infants do not live solely in a here-and-now world with finely attuned, stimulus-driven reactions and nothing more than that. That representations persist over lengthy delays means that infants live in contact with the past as well as the present. We call this aspect of early cognitive capacity *representational persistence*. One of the larger implications of representational persistence is that infants can use their experience with past events to interpret the present and even predict the future.

Young Infants Are Concerned About the Identity of People and Things

Representational persistence immediately raises a question of identity: Is this object (*O*) now present to perception the same as *O'* previously encountered and now represented? If each object encountered required a new representation to be set up, representations would proliferate endlessly. The evidence from two lines of research shows that young infants operate more economically—one investigating features and categorization, the other investigating the numerical identity of objects.

One of the first topics addressed in infancy research concerned the recognition of "sameness" at a featural level, whether a currently perceived display looks like one seen (or heard) before. For example, studies explored whether infants treat a pattern or object as familiar or novel (e.g., Cohen, 1979; Fagan, 1990; Fantz, 1964: Kuhl, 1983, 1994). The notion of identity or sameness underlying this research concerns appearances—the features of this display are "the same as" or identical to the features of that display. When representational persistence operates with this meaning of sameness, it groups people and things into categories. Economy is achieved by forming equivalence classes (bull's-eyes, dogs, /a/ sounds) which treat new exemplars as "another of those."

However, newer research has explored another meaning of identity that concerns whether the currently perceived object is the same *individual* again. This is the idea William James so colorfully described as "Hollo! thingumbob again!" Philosophers have dubbed this meaning of sameness, "numerical identity" (e.g., Strawson, 1959). Adults are engaged with determining the numerical identity of objects (e.g., Kahneman, Treisman, & Gibbs, 1992; Treisman, 1992). Infants also analyze events in terms of numerical identity (Bower, 1982; Meltzoff & Moore, 1998; Moore, Borton, & Darby,

1978; Moore & Meltzoff, 1999; Spelke, Kestenbaum, Simons, & Wein, 1995; Xu & Carey, 1996). Numerical identity does not ask whether this looks the *same as* that, but rather whether this is the *same one* again. The concept of numerical identity allows us to understand that two encounters with featurally identical objects need not be contacts with the same object. Conversely, it allows us to understand that one and the same thing may have different appearances. When representational persistence operates with numerical identity, it organizes multiple encounters as re-encounters with the same individual. Here the economy comes from treating different appearances as manifestations of a single entity. Over multiple disappearances and reappearances, my "Rover," is not just another exemplar of dog. Instead, he is the same individual seen repeatedly. In determining numerical identity, representation mediates between two encounters with an object such that these are taken as two instantiations of one underlying entity in the external world.

Numerical identity is chiefly determined by spatiotemporal criteria, not by featural analysis. To know which can of Coke is one's own requires tracing its location and movements over time. There is evidence that young infants use spatiotemporal criteria in determining numerical identity. For example, in one study, 5-month-olds were shown an object moving at a constant speed and direction before it disappeared behind a screen. A featurally identical object then emerged on the other side of the screen, but too soon, given the original object's trajectory (see Fig. 10.1, "Violation"). Infants did not accept the featurally identical object as "the same one" they were following, because they looked back for the one on the original trajectory. This was a particularly compelling example because infants had to look away and disengage from an interesting, moving object to search an empty portion of the display. Evidently, the violation of trajectory overrides a featurally identical appearance in determining an object's numerical identity at 5 months of age (Moore et al., 1978).

This concern with numerical identity was also found in younger infants viewing people instead of inanimate objects. In one study, 6-week-olds were shown two people who alternately disappeared and reappeared in their field of view (Meltzoff & Moore, 1992). To maximize featural differences, one person was the infant's mother, and the other a male stranger. The measure of whether the infant individuated them as two different people was differential imitation. Under one condition, one person moved on one trajectory and the other on a different trajectory as they disappeared and reappeared, thus differentiating them by the spatiotemporal criterion of trajectory. In this condition, infants imitated each person in turn. In the second condition, the same two adults were used, but infants did not have the differential trajectory information. In this case, infants imitated the person they saw before, rather than the one currently perceived. The compelling

TRAJECTORY EVENTS

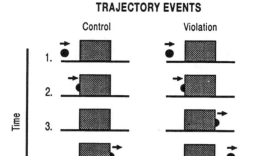

FIG. 10.1. The trajectory event used to diagnose whether 5-month-olds were sensitive to violations of spatiotemporal criteria for identity (adapted from Moore et al., 1978).

aspect of this reaction was that infant imitation overrode what they saw being done in front of them. Our interpretation was that, without spatiotemporal information to differentiate the people, infants were unsure whether one or two individuals were involved. Their "deferred imitation" resulted from the identity confusion (for fuller details, see Meltzoff & Moore, 1992). Evidently, for very young infants spatiotemporal criteria are fundamental for determining numerical identity, and without them identity confusions can arise even for people as familiar as one's own mother. Of course, this is not to say that infants cannot featurally discriminate mother from stranger. The point is that neither featural difference nor featural similarity indexes numerical identity.

Taken as a whole, these results suggest that infants in the first half year of life rely on spatiotemporal criteria for determining numerical identity. Based on this and other research (Meltzoff & Moore, 1998), our summary of infants' initial spatiotemporal identity rules are: A moving object is the "same one again" if it is encountered on the same *trajectory of motion*, and a stationary object is the same one again if it is encountered in the same *place or location*. Conversely, if the trajectory or place of the second encounter is different from the original, these encounters are interpreted as involving different objects.

Theoretical Premise #2: Spatiotemporal Parameters Are the Primary Criteria for Object Identity. Persisting representations carry more than just the form and features of an object—what an object looks like. The persisting representations of a last encounter also carry spatiotemporal parameters. Representational persistence paired with spatiotemporal identity criteria form a representational system. Operating with such spatiotemporal parameters allows the system to function prospectively, to anticipate future locations of perceived objects, and retrospectively, to reidentify objects seen earlier.[1]

With Development, Featural and Functional Criteria Come to Bear on Numerical Identify

Infants strive to keep track of individuals in the perceptual field, economically "conserving" them rather than repeatedly setting up representations of new entities. They do so primarily using spatiotemporal criteria for identity. However, if infants operated solely with spatiotemporal criteria for object identity, they would err in a fundamental way. Whenever a second object appears in a location predicted from the movements (or location) of a first object, it will be interpreted as the same individual regardless of featural or functional differences, the "substitution error."

This error has been reported in the literature and seems to be characteristic of infants younger than 3- to 5-months-of-age (Bower, 1982; Piaget, 1954; and for older infants see Xu & Carey, 1996). This phase of infancy is not the final state, which suggests development beyond the initial, spatiotemporally based system. In commonsense adult psychology, people and things are often identified as "the same one again" by nonspatiotemporal means. One knows one's spouse by face, voice, distinctive behavior patterns, and other such "qualitative identifiers," even when unexpectedly encountered.

A few studies have investigated the development of infants' use of qualitative identifiers. They suggest that infants begin to take qualitative identifiers into account within the first half year of life, thus beginning to overcome the substitution error. The spatiotemporal criteria remain primary, but qualitative identifiers come to play a secondary role, at least calling into question the maintenance of numerical identity when there are radical changes in features and functions.

In one such study using inanimate objects, 5-month-olds were shown a moving object that disappeared behind a screen. At the time and place specified by the initial trajectory, a featurally different object emerged on the other side of the screen. Infants did not accept the object as "the same one" even though it appeared when and where it should have. Infants searched the display for the original (Moore et al., 1978). Evidently, by 5

---

[1]The spatiotemporal criteria of place and trajectory are not the same as Spelke et al.'s (1995) "principle of continuity." Place and trajectory identity criteria are used to keep track of which object is the same one again; Spelke's continuity principle treats objects as continuously existing, even when out of sight. As used here place and trajectory are *identity* criteria; Spelke's principle of continuity confers *permanence*. For a further discussion about the difference between object identity and object permanence, see Meltzoff and Moore (1998).

months of age a change in the object's features is sufficient to raise questions as to its identity, even when spatiotemporal criteria are maintained (see also, von Hofsten & Lindhagen, 1982; Wilcox & Baillargeon, 1998).

The use of featural appearance in determining numerical identity seems particularly relevant for people. Our adult intuition is that the facial features of people, like their fingerprints, uniquely identify them. The foregoing mother–stranger experiment (Meltzoff & Moore, 1992) suggests that facial features are not *decisive* determinants for very young infants. Despite the salient featural differences in the adults (mother vs. male stranger), infants who did not trace the separate trajectories of the people did not differentially imitate them. However, other research using people showed that the features are not wholly irrelevant to infants' concerns. In a study showing 6-week-old imitation after a 24-hour delay, the person who demonstrated the gesture on Day 1 returned with a neutral face on Day 2 (Meltzoff & Moore, 1994). The results showed that the features of the person were sufficient for infants to recall the particular gestures he presented the previous day, even though there were no spatiotemporal means for re-identifying the person as the same one again.

Taking these findings from people and things together, we infer that features and behavioral characteristics can at least *raise questions* about which individual is present, even though spatiotemporal parameters (place and trajectory) would be needed for making a conclusive determination.[2]

Theoretical Premise #3: Features and Functions Serve as Secondary Criteria for Object Identity. These findings suggest that by the end of the first half year of life infants use three criteria for understanding the identity of objects—spatiotemporal, featural, and functional. Spatiotemporal refers to location in space and time; featural refers to perceptual properties; and functional refers to how an object acts or how one can act with it.

Synthesis of the Evidence. Four characteristics of the early representational system that relate to numerical identity are:

1. Even for young infants, representations persist over breaks in sensory contact.
2. The numerical identity of objects is initially specified by spatiotemporal criteria (place and trajectory).

---

[2]Elsewhere we have shown how development may work to allow infants to use an object's functions as secondary identity criteria (Meltzoff & Moore, 1995, 1998). Human actions—in particular the distinctive acts we call "gestural signatures"—are used to differentiate individuals. These are the precursors to our everyday adult notion that individual people have distinctive mannerisms, styles, and modes of behavior that can be expected from them.

3. Featural and functional identity criteria develop.

4. Representation operates both prospectively, anticipating future contacts with an object, and retrospectively, reidentifying an object as the same one again.

A MODEL OF HOW YOUNG INFANTS MAINTAIN OBJECT IDENTITY

This section provides a model of how young infants determine the identity of physical objects, both people and things. We think that a central function of the early representational system is to trace the numerical identity of objects, allowing infants to treat a second object encounter as the same one again. If this is a second contact with an old object, all that needs to be entered into representation is the object's new position, an "update," rather than an entirely new individual.

Assumptions of the Model

The model assumes that infants are evolutionarily prepared for interacting with and representing objects in a "steady-state world" (Moore, 1975; Moore & Meltzoff, 1978). The idea that young infants are set for a steady-state world is suggested by several considerations: (a) Human perceptual systems are adapted to "middle-sized objects" lying somewhere between planets and atoms. (b) Such middle-sized objects obey Newton's laws of motion that assume a steady-state in which objects at rest remain at rest, and objects in motion continue in motion. (c) Cognitive and neurophysiological studies show that the perceptual system registers an object's trajectory of motion as well as its location in space (e.g., Kahneman et al., 1992; Watamaniuk, McKee, & Grzywacz, 1995). We think (a)–(c) are captured by Premise #2—infants' initial identity criteria are *trajectory* (object in motion) and *place* (object at rest).

The early representational system has evolved to take into account the dynamic nature of objects. Young infants not only represent what an object looks like but also parameters such as its location in space and direction and speed of motion. We call these parameters *spatiotemporal descriptors*. When infants encounter an object, they compare the perceived object to ones already represented. If the spatiotemporal descriptors (place, trajectory) are equivalent, this is a re-encounter. If not, a representation of the new individual may be required. For the cases that are equivalent, the representation links the two separate encounters as being contacts with the self–same entity in the world.

Because represented objects have spatiotemporal descriptors, the changes produced by an object continuing to move in space or by a stationary object remaining in place as an observer moves are not occasions for

setting up a representation of a new individual. Such changes are perceived, but economically represented as movements of a unitary object or
as movements of the observer relative to that object. Such a dynamic representational system is prospective, allowing predictions about events that
are as yet unseen, for example, a future object position as a function of its
trajectory. This is adaptive, because it enables young infants to intersect
the world as it will be rather than as it was when an act was initiated.

The infant's representational system also takes into account what an object looks like and how it acts or can be used. We call these *featural and functional descriptors*. A represented object can be called to mind by any one of its
three descriptors. We hypothesize that infants strive to achieve congruence
between the multiple descriptors of a previously encountered but now represented object, and a currently perceived object, which confers a primitive understanding of the external object and its identity.

How the Model Works

Figure 10.2 provides a model of how the representational system maintains
object identity at approximately 5 months of age. It shows how infants maintain a steady-state representation of the perceptual field using multiple object descriptors as coordinated criteria for identity. The model is a snapshot
of the infant's state when all three criteria are first incorporated.

The chief components of the model are depicted by the five bold boxes.
The box labeled perceived object field (POF) is not further analyzed and
presupposes the findings on infants' perception showing that they process
inputs from the physical world to yield a layout of distal objects in 3-D
space (e.g., Bower, 1982; Kellman, 1993; Spelke, 1990). The box labeled
steady-state representation of objects (SSR) functions as a directory or index, keeping track of individual objects (Os) over steady-state changes in
the perceptual field by mapping multiple appearances of Os onto the same
underlying representation. The Os in the POF are compared to those in representation by operations displayed in the comparator box. The other two
boxes labeled functional equilibrator and spatiotemporal equilibrator serve
to restore consonance between perception and representation as described next.

The process of determining object identity begins with a global comparison of the Os in the POF and those in SSR (depicted by the bold arrows). Os
are compared in terms of their spatiotemporal descriptors and features.
There are four possible outcomes of the initial comparison, indicated by
the lines numbered [1]–[4] in the figure.

The typical outcome is maintenance of numerical identity (outcome line
[1]). This case occurs when the spatiotemporal descriptor of an O in the POF
corresponds to one in representation and the O's features match. This perceived O is treated as the numerically identical individual despite changes in

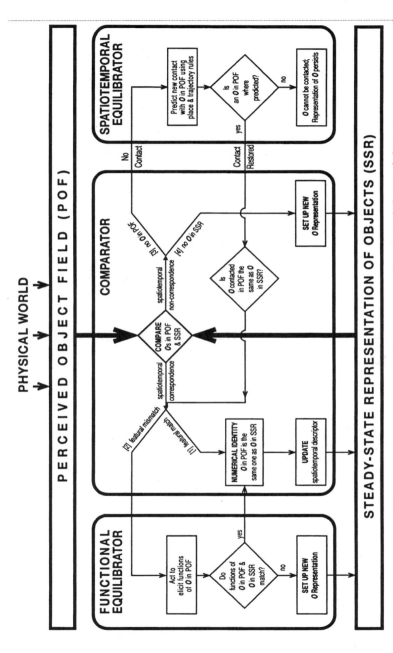

FIG. 10.2. A model showing how young infants determine the numerical identity of objects in the perceptual field. The five major components are shown in bold boxes. O indicates object; POF indicates perceived object field; SSR indicates steady-state representation of objects (from Meltzoff & Moore, 1998).

the field (e.g., an *O* seen moving on the same trajectory and with the same features remains the same individual). The spatiotemporal descriptor of the *O* in representation is updated with its currently perceived location.

A second outcome (line [2]) occurs when an *O* in the POF and a represented one correspond on spatiotemporal grounds, but their features do not match. Thus the two identity criteria conflict. In this case, the functional equilibrator collects information about the third identity criterion by observing and eliciting the functions of the perceived *O*. For physical things, it may involve manual manipulation to elicit the *O*'s functions; for people it may involve performing the person's act as a way of eliciting the behavior. There are two possible results of this functional probing. (a) *Yes* branch—If the functions of the perceived *O* match the functional descriptors of the represented *O*, it is recognized as the same individual but with a change in appearance. (b) *No* branch—If the functions of the perceived *O* do not match the functional descriptors of the represented one, the perceived *O* is a different individual, and a new representation is set up.

A third outcome (line [3]) arises when perceptual contact ceases with an *O* already in representation. In this case, there is no *O* in POF corresponding to the one in SSR, which is input to the box labeled spatiotemporal equilibrator. For example, an *O* leaves the field of view or moves behind an occluder. This dissonance between perception and representation is processed in the spatiotemporal equilibrator. When there is a loss of contact with a desired *O*, future contact points are predicted from the spatial descriptors of the *O* in representation by applying the place/trajectory rules. There are two possible results. (a) *Yes* branch—If an *O* is contacted where predicted, the pathway re-enters the comparator to determine whether it is the same one with which contact was lost (the line returns to the fork between [1] vs. [2]). (b) *No* branch—If no *O* is contacted in the predicted location, then the same one is not in the field. The representation persists but it no longer refers to an entity in the perceptual world.

A fourth outcome (line [4]) is that a new *O* representation needs to be set up. This case occurs when there is no existing representation corresponding to an *O* currently in the perceptual field, for example a new *O* unexpectedly enters the field.

RESOLVING THE PARADOX OF EARLY PERMANENCE: DOES INCREASED LOOKING-TIME REFLECT OBJECT IDENTITY OR OBJECT PERMANENCE?

One problem for theories of early cognition is the "paradox of early permanence." The paradox is posed by studies of young infants' reactions to objects that have disappeared from the perceptual field. Infants in the first half year of life are reported to understand that objects are permanent when assessed by preferential-looking-to-novelty methods (e.g., Baillargeon, 1993; Spelke, Breinlinger, Macomber, & Jacobson, 1992). However, another indicator of permanence, manual search for hidden objects, is at odds with this interpretation (e.g., Moore & Meltzoff, 1999). The youngest age at which infants can recover hidden objects is about 8 months. The explanation for this discrepancy is hotly debated. The foregoing model might shed light on the paradox.

We suggest that the operation of the early representational system underlies the preferential-looking effects to disappearance events. Our argument is premised on the idea that young infants trace the *identity* of objects before they know or reason about *permanent* objects (Meltzoff & Moore, 1998; Moore, 1975; Moore et al., 1978; Moore & Meltzoff, 1978).

When an infant watches an object disappear behind a screen, the permanence interpretation is that the object continues to exist behind the screen—the screen merely blocks the view of it. A failure to emerge constrains its location to a definite part of space (behind the screen). On this account, what unifies the components of the occlusion event (object disappearance→no movement→object reappearance) is the physical entity that continues to exist in the world—the enduring object. Anticipatory looking to the other side of the screen is based on the permanence of the object behind the screen. We think this is too "rich" an interpretation of what infants are doing in the first half year of life.

There is a more conservative interpretation based on object identity instead of permanence. The identity interpretation is that the infant extrapolates the initial trajectory (defined by the *O*'s already-seen speed and direction, the spatiotemporal descriptors of the foregoing model) beyond the screen to anticipate where and when the same object will next be visible (in this case, the trailing edge of the screen). The two encounters on either side of the screen are interpreted as being manifestations of the same object because they lie on two visible portions of the same trajectory. The crucial point, which is at once logical and developmental, is that *recognizing this sameness does not force young infants to infer existence between* encounters. Young infants need not understand that the object resides behind the screen in order to succeed. What allows infants to treat the disparate components as a unitary event is the maintenance of object identity—the two encounters are interpreted as manifestations of one and the same object by the trajectory rule for object identity. On this account, prospective looking to the other side of the screen is based on extrapolating the *visible*, preocclusion trajectory of the object.

This identity interpretation is embodied in the foregoing model. The movement of an object behind an occluder corresponds to the loss of contact with an object that was in the field, as shown in Fig. 10.2, line [3]. The model shows that infants predict future contact points with a moving object using the object's spatiotemporal descriptors. This would allow infants to anticipate the appearance of the object on the far side of an occluder. Permanence of the object while out of sight behind the occluder is not required.

The import of the model is that infants' systematic reaction to disappearance can be explained without recourse to permanence. It is generated by a perceptual-cognitive system in which representations persist and which operates with rules for numerical identity. Thus, in our view, there is no discrepancy between the visual measures and the search measures. There is no real paradox. The apparent anomaly posed by the looking-time studies is resolved by differentiating infants' reactions based on object identity from those based on object permanence. The visual measures typically reported do not show that infants understand object permanence. Infants do not act to recover objects in the classic object permanence tests because they do not know where the objects are. Successful manual search requires that infants understand that the invisible object resides in a particular location behind the occluder. The motivation for search is to recover the object by revealing the place. This is why spatially directed measures (such as manual or visual search) are such strong assessments of object permanence.

Of course, the validity of this argument is best tested by examining whether it can be used to reinterpret existing findings and predict new ones. The former is no mean feat given the large and ever-growing corpus of studies based on preferential-looking methods. Elsewhere (Meltzoff & Moore, 1998), we have offered a detailed reinterpretation of some of the classic findings using the current framework (Baillargeon's drawbridge and rabbit studies, Spelke's discontinuity test, and Xu & Carey's tests of numerical identity in 10- to 12-month-olds). We also used this framework to create new tests of object permanence and investigate how it develops (Moore & Meltzoff, 1999).

AN EMERGING VIEW OF COGNITION
IN EARLY INFANCY

At the outset of this chapter we noted that the new discoveries in infancy research have outpaced classical theories. Much recent energy in the field has been devoted to finding a theoretical framework that is consistent with the recent discoveries. Several candidates have been offered. The "core-knowledge" thesis is that infants already possess adult-like concepts. The "dynamical-systems" view is that there are no infant concepts, behavior reflects perceptuomotor adaptations. We advocate a third alternative. We think conceptual development occurs within infancy, although infants do not begin with mature adult concepts. The challenge is to specify an initial psychological structure that is sufficiently rich to lead to the adult mind without assuming it as part of the initial state. If the initial structure is too impoverished, it would not lead to the adult mind; if it's too rich, it would solve the problem, but do so unparsimoniously.

We tried to characterize such an initial structure in the Fig. 10.2 model of the steady-state representational system. In this view, the spatiotemporal rules for determining object identity (place, trajectory) can be seen as "discovery procedures" for interpreting the behavior of objects. Similarly, the imitation of human acts can be seen as discovery procedures for interpreting the behavior of people, as we have shown elsewhere (Meltzoff, 1995a; Meltzoff & Moore, 1995, 1997).

Although the initial discovery procedures exhibit cognitive processing, they do not embody the mature adult notions of people and things. For example, Xu and Carey (1996) showed that under certain circumstances infants as old as 10 months are unsure, based on features alone, whether a blue elephant and a red truck are actually two different objects. Infants require spatiotemporal information to make this distinction. This is obviously quite different from the everyday adult concept of object identity—for adults blue elephants cannot turn into red trucks. Some development in the notion of identity must be occurring. Another example of development can be drawn from work with people. Adults regard faces as akin to fingerprints, unique unto the individual. However, Meltzoff and Moore (1992) showed that facial features alone are insufficient for 6-week-olds to conclusively individuate two people in the absence of spatiotemporal information. Once again, development must occur in infants' notion of identity as applied to people. It seems clear that initial knowledge is not adult knowledge, at least regarding the identity of people and things.

Developmental claims have also been made for a radical restructuring in infants' understanding of the existence and location of occluded objects, that is, for object permanence. For example, there is evidence that failures of young infants to search for absent objects indicate a deficit in understanding permanence rather than problems with motor skill or means-ends coordination (e.g., Moore & Meltzoff, 1999; Munakata, McClelland, Johnson, & Siegler, 1997). Of course, the hypothesis that a notion of permanence develops from experience with object disappearance-reappearance has met with objections. One counterclaim to this view is that such experience is too impoverished for learning an abstract notion like permanence—it has to be built-in to begin with. A second counterclaim is that experience is sufficiently orderly that a notion of permanence is superfluous—one can learn to make re-appearance predictions based on regularities in the world without positing abstract concepts about invisible entities.

Both cannot be true. The argument of this chapter is that there is a way out of this dilemma. The initial identity rules serve as something like discovery procedures for developing a concept of permanence. If permanence is not fully specified innately but develops through experience with objects disappearing and reappearing in the world, numerical identity must be a necessary precursor. Without numerical identity, the (re)appearance of an object that has disappeared is merely another object. Unless appearance is understood as a *re*-appearance of the same one, there is no question of where it was when out of sight and no data on which to infer permanence. Without a prior notion of object identity, object permanence development cannot get off the ground (Moore & Meltzoff, 1999). Thus, the characterization of the infant's initial structure presented here affords a basic foundation from which the more mature notions of permanence may develop.

This argument for the development of object permanence can be seen as an exemplar of a more general view of infancy and childhood that has come to be called the "theory theory" (Gopnik & Meltzoff, 1997; Gopnik, Meltzoff, & Kuhl, 1999). This view does not portray infants' similarity to adults in terms of unchanging core knowledge, but rather in the striving for a coherent interpretation of the world, and, in particular, a coherent understanding of the behavior of people and things. Infants are not born with adult concepts, but rather with discovery procedures that lead to the development of adult concepts.

ACKNOWLEDGMENTS

The order of authorship is alphabetical; this article is a co-equal creation. Work on this chapter was supported by a grant from the National Institutes of Health (HD-22514).

REFERENCES

Baillargeon, R. (1993). The object concept revisited: New directions in the investigation of infants' physical knowledge. In C. Granrud (Ed.), *Visual perception and cognition in infancy* (pp. 265–315). Hillsdale, NJ: Lawrence Erlbaum Associates.

Barnat, S. B., Klein, P. J., & Meltzoff, A. N. (1996). Deferred imitation across changes in context and object: Memory and generalization in 14-month-old infants. *Infant Behavior and Development, 19*, 241–251.

Bower, T. G. R. (1982). *Development in infancy* (2nd ed.). San Francisco: W. H. Freeman.

Cohen, L. B. (1979). Our developing knowledge of infant perception and cognition. *American Psychologist, 34*, 894–899.

Fagan, J. F., III. (1990). The paired-comparison paradigm and infant intelligence. In A. Diamond (Ed.), *The development and neural bases of higher cognitive functions.* New York: Annals of the New York Academy of Sciences, *608*, 337–364.

Fantz, R. L. (1964). Visual experience in infants: Decreased attention to familiar patterns relative to novel ones. *Science, 146*, 668–670.

Fontaine, R. (1984). Imitative skills between birth and six months. *Infant Behavior and Development, 7*, 323–333.

Gopnik, A., & Meltzoff, A. N. (1997). *Words, thoughts, and theories.* Cambridge, MA: MIT Press.

Gopnik, A., Meltzoff, A. N., & Kuhl, P. K. (1999). *The scientist in the crib: Minds, brains, and how children learn.* New York: Morrow Press.

Hanna, E., & Meltzoff, A. N. (1993). Peer imitation by toddlers in laboratory, home, and daycare contexts: Implications for social learning and memory. *Developmental Psychology, 29*, 701–710.

Heimann, M., Nelson, K. E., & Schaller, J. (1989). Neonatal imitation of tongue protrusion and mouth opening: Methodological aspects and evidence of early individual differences. *Scandinavian Journal of Psychology, 30*, 90–101.

Heimann, M., & Schaller, J. (1985). Imitative reactions among 14-21 day old infants. *Infant Mental Health Journal, 6*, 31–39.

Hofsten, C. von, & Lindhagen, K. (1982). Perception of visual occlusion in 4½-month-old infants. *Infant Behavior and Development, 5*, 215–226.

Kahneman, D., Treisman, A., & Gibbs, B. J. (1992). The reviewing of object files: Object-specific integration of information. *Cognitive Psychology, 24*, 175–219.

Kellman, P. J. (1993). Kinematic foundations of infant visual perception. In C. Granrud (Ed.), *Visual perception and cognition in infancy* (pp. 121–173). Hillsdale, NJ: Lawrence Erlbaum Associates.

Klein, P. J., & Meltzoff, A. N. (1999). Long-term memory, forgetting, and deferred imitation in 12-month-old infants. *Developmental Science, 2*, 102–113.

Kuhl, P. K. (1983). Perception of auditory equivalence classes for speech in early infancy. *Infant Behavior and Development, 6*, 263–285.

Kuhl, P. K. (1994). Learning and representation in speech and language. *Current Opinion in Neurobiolgy, 4*, 812–822.

Legerstee, M. (1991). The role of person and object in eliciting early imitation. *Journal of Experimental Child Psychology, 51*, 423–433.

Meltzoff, A. N. (1988). Infant imitation after a 1-week delay: Long-term memory for novel acts and multiple stimuli. *Developmental Psychology, 24*, 470–476.

Meltzoff, A. N. (1995a). Understanding the intentions of others: Re-enactment of intended acts by 18-month-old children. *Developmental Psychology, 31*, 838–850.

Meltzoff, A. N. (1995b). What infant memory tells us about infantile amnesia: Long-term recall and deferred imitation. *Journal of Experimental Child Psychology, 59*, 497–515.

Meltzoff, A. N., & Moore, M. K. (1977). Imitation of facial and manual gestures by human neonates. *Science, 198*, 75–78.

Meltzoff, A. N., & Moore, M. K. (1989). Imitation in newborn infants: Exploring the range of gestures imitated and the underlying mechanisms. *Developmental Psycholgy, 25*, 954–962.

Meltzoff, A. N., & Moore, M. K. (1992). Early imitation within a functional framework: The importance of person identity, movement, and development. *Infant Behavior and development, 15*, 479–505.

Meltzoff, A. N., & Moore, M. K. (1994). Imitation, memory, and the representation of persons. *Infant Behavior and Development, 17*, 83–99.

Meltzoff, A. N., & Moore, M. K. (1995). Infants' understanding of people and things: From body imitation to folk psychology. In J. Bermúdez, A. J. Marcel, & N. Eilan (Eds.), *The body and the self* (pp. 43–69). Cambridge, MA: MIT Press.

Meltzoff, A. N., & Moore, M. K. (1997). Explaining facial imitation: A theoretical model. *Early Development and Parenting, 6*, 179–192.

Meltzoff, A. N., & Moore, M. K. (1998). Object representation, identity, and the paradox of early permanence: Steps toward a new framework. *Infant Behavior and Development, 21*, 201–235.

Moore, M. K. (1975, April). Object permanence and object identity: A stage-developmental model. In M. K. Moore (Chair), *Object identity: The missing link between Piaget's stages of object permanence.* Symposium at the meeting of the Society for Research in Child Development, Denver, CO.

Moore, M. K., Borton, R., & Darby, B. L. (1978). Visual tracking in young infants: Evidence for object identity or object permanence? *Journal of Experimental Child Psychology, 25,* 183–198.

Moore, M. K., & Meltzoff, A. N. (1978). Object permanence, imitation, and language development in infancy: Toward a neo-Piagetian perspective on communicative and cognitive development. In F. D. Minifie & L. L. Lloyd (Eds.), *Communicative and cognitive abilities—Early behavioral assessment* (pp. 151–184). Baltimore: University Park Press.

Moore, M. K., & Meltzoff, A. N. (1999). New findings on object permanance: A developmental difference between two types of occlusion. *British Journal of Developmental Psychology, 17,* 563–584.

Munakata, Y., McClelland, J. L., Johnson, M. H., & Siegler, R. S. (1997). Rethinking infant knowledge: Toward an adaptive process account of successes and failures in object permanence tasks. *Psychological Review, 104,* 686–713.

Piaget, J. (1954). *The construction of reality in the child.* New York: Basic Books.

Piaget, J. (1962). *Play, dreams, and imitation in childhood.* New York: Norton.

Spelke, E. S. (1990). Principles of object perception. *Cognitive Science, 14,* 29–56.

Spelke, E. S. (1994). Initial knowledge: Six suggestions. *Cognition, 50,* 431–445.

Spelke, E. S., Breinlinger, K., Macomber, J., & Jacobson, K. (1992). Origins of knowledge. *Psychological Review, 99,* 605–632.

Spelke, E. S., Kestenbaum, R., Simons, D. J., & Wein, D. (1995). Spatiotemporal continuity, smoothness of motion and object identity in infancy. *British Journal of Developmental Psychology, 13,* 113–142.

Strawson, P. E. (1959). *Individuals: An essay in descriptive metaphysics.* London: Methuen.

Thelen, E., & Smith, L. B. (1994). *A dynamic systems approach to the development of cognition and action.* Cambridge, MA: MIT Press.

Treisman, A. (1992). Perceiving and re-perceiving objects. *American Psychologist, 47,* 862–875.

Watamaniuk, S. N. J., McKee, S. P., & Grzywacz, N. M. (1995). Detecting a trajectory embedded in random-direction motion noise. *Vision Research, 35,* 65–77.

Wilcox, T., & Baillargeon, R. (1998). Object individuation in infancy: The use of featural information in reasoning about occlusion events. *Cognitive Psychology, 37,* 97–155.

Xu, F., & Carey, S. (1996). Infants' metaphysics: The case of numerical identity. *Cognitive Psychology, 30,* 111–153.

Neonatal Imitation— A "Fuzzy" Phenomenon?

Mikael Heimann
Göteborg University, Sweden

Although our knowledge about young infants' ability to imitate has been largely expanded during the last 2 decades, there are still controversies concerning the nature of this early imitative capacity. One such area of concern relates to the large variability in infants' responses that has been noted in several studies. This variance has been interpreted in many different ways: as pure error variance, as a result of the various methods used in different studies, and as an indication of individual differences among infants. It has also been suggested that the variation in imitation observed among newborn children might be related to their emerging personality traits.

This chapter takes a new look at early variation in imitation and discusses how it might be interpreted. Observations made in three Swedish studies are presented, and the combined data make it difficult to dismiss the observed variation in imitation as only error variance. The chapter is organized into three main parts: The first part provides a brief description of some basic assumptions; the second part presents empirical observations of variation in the imitative responses of neonates and young infants; the last part is a discussion of how we might envision the role of the nervous system in the occurrence of neonatal imitation.

SOME BASIC ASSUMPTIONS

As pointed out by Heimann (1998), the basic procedure in almost all studies investigating neonatal imitation (NI) has been to compare the frequency of the modeled behavior (e.g., tongue protrusion) with the observed frequency in some control situation (an alternate modeling: mouth opening or a baseline). These observed frequencies, or some type of imitation indexes based on them, are then used for computing the appropriate statistics. Some researchers have used other measures (e.g., duration, the longest act), but overall these approaches are rare in the literature. Thus, when we speak or write about NI, we almost always base our interpretations and our assumptions on purely behavioral and statistical observations: An increase in one specific behavior (e.g., mouth opening) after modeling of that behavior as compared with the observed frequency of mouth opening after presentation of an alternative gesture.

Using this behavioral definition of NI I have little doubt concerning the robustness of the phenomenon. Findings indicating imitation among newborns (and among newborns with Down syndrome, see Heimann, Ullstadius, & Swerlander, 1998) have been reported by many independent research groups worldwide (see Heimann, 1998; Meltzoff & Moore, 1994; Ullstadius, 1998, for a comprehensive list of studies). But skeptics still exist: Even today, more than 20 years after the publication of Meltzoff and Moore's first report in 1977, and more than 25 years after Maratos' observations of NI in the early 1970s, the phenomenon is still being questioned (Anisfeld, 1996). Thus, it is not surprising that several researchers have spent considerable time conducting studies toward proving or disproving NI. In my view, the field must move beyond this rather primitive fight about whether or not NI actually exists. Instead, more viable research agenda should focus on the implications of the phenomenon both theoretically and in the real world, using observed interactions between infants and their parents. Recently, this has been the approach taken by a number of researchers (e.g., Heimann, 1999; Kugiumutzakis, 1993; Meltzoff & Moore, 1998, chap. 10, this volume; Trevarthen, Kokkinaki, & Fiamenghi, 1998; Ullstadius, 1998). Most theorists think that NI plays an important role during early development, and some evidence for that claim does exist (e.g., Fiamenghi, 1996; Heimann, 1989, 1999; Meltzoff & Moore, 1994). However, the verdict is out on this point, and we still risk finding out that NI exists but plays no major role in early infant development. Although the support for this position has become weaker, it is theoretically possible that neonatal imitation is primarily an antecedent of a later emerging behavior (e.g., fully intentional imitation as seen around 8 to 9 months of age), with no particular function of its own during the neonatal period (but see Heimann, 1998, for a different view).

However, this chapter does not dwell on issues relating to the robustness of NI. Instead, we rest on the assumption that NI is a real phenomenon (using the earlier operational definition), but that detailed information regarding the specific processes involved is still missing. More specifically, the following areas are addressed:

Problem 1: The Large Variation Observed. Substantial variation among infants' responses has been noted by many researchers over the years (e.g., Dunkeld, 1978; Hayes & Watson, 1981; Heimann, Nelson, & Schaller, 1989; Meltzoff & Moore, 1977). Although this variation has mostly been regarded as error variance, some studies have suggested that individual differences might already be apparent in early infancy. In addition, the differences in methodology employed across studies may surround these discrepancies. These issues are discussed in some detail shortly.

Problem 2: What Mechanism? How can we ever know what is actually going on inside the child's mind? If imitation does occur, then there must be a part of the nervous system, something in the child's biological make-up, that allows the infant to perceive the modeled act, map this perception onto some sort of body schema (or the equivalent thereof) and then transform this mapping into a motor output (a matching or imitative response). This process is discussed in the section on "fuzzy" mapping processes, where I argue that "fuzzy" processes must be involved because: We know that the child's response is inexact and crude at first; the nervous system is very immature at birth (especially true for the neocortex); and the exact use of imitation—the exact meaning of an imitative act—for any individual develops transactionally over time within the emerging first relationship.

Problem 3: The Use of NI. I argue that NI should not only be viewed as a capacity of the child's brain or as a skill that the child can use or as an act the individual performs. Instead, I see NI as having its function within the ongoing interactive flow between the child and his or her parents. The child's imitation will serve a purpose within the relationship and will have an impact upon the caregivers. This effect will lead the parents to change or modulate their responses (a modulation they might be completely unaware of) toward their child, and NI could thus play a role in establishing an early dialogue between the infant and the parents (cf. Bråten, 1988, 1994; Fogel, 1993; Trevarthen et al., 1998).

Three Swedish studies (Heimann, 1989, 1991, 1997, 1998; Heimann, Nelson, & Schaller, 1989; Heimann & Schaller, 1985) form the database for this chapter. Overall, slightly different strategies for investigating neonatal imitation have been used in these studies, although all infants fulfilled similar inclusion criteria (see Table 11.1).

TABLE 11.1
A Brief Description of the Three Swedish Studies Forming the Empirical Database for This Chapter

	Study 1	Study 2	Study 3
Participants			
N	11	32	33
Sex (M/F)	5/6	18/14	17/16
Gestational age	38–42	38–42	38–42
Apgar (5 min)	>7	>7	>7
Age at Observation 1 (days)	14–21	3	2
Age at Observation 2–4 (weeks)	--	3, 12, 52	12, 26,60[a]
Procedure			
Gesture presented by	Mother	Experimenter	Experimenter
Facial gestures	TP, MO	TP, MO, LP	TP, MO
Setting Observation 1	Home	Hospital	Hospital

[a]Only data from Observation 1 are presented here.

OBSERVED VARIATION IN YOUNG CHILDREN'S IMITATION

Methodology

Although a clear majority of the studies on NI report evidence in favor of an early imitative capability, differences still exist. A few studies published in the early 1980s did fail to find evidence of NI and in a relatively recent review (Anisfeld, 1991), it was claimed that solid evidence only exists for matching of one gesture (= tongue protrusion). However, Anisfeld's (1991) review is in my view flawed in that not all studies are included (e.g., Dunkeld, 1978; Kugiumutzakis, 1985); he misinterprets already published observations, he fails to inform the reader when his interpretations are at odds with those reported in the original publication (i.e., Heimann et al., 1989), and he misrepresents the procedure used is some studies (i.e., Heimann & Schaller, 1985).

   One obvious reason for the occurrence of divergent results is that no general agreement exists as to how neonatal imitation ought to be defined and studied. In a previous review, Heimann (1991) noted that differences among the studies could be observed in sample size, modeled behavior, mode of presentation, length of response period, definition and coding of responses, and setting. Thus, there is no agreement regarding how many times a certain gesture should be presented or how fast this presentation should be. Nor is there any agreement about the length of the response periods. Should we only count responses emitted directly after the presentation as imitative or should we also include gestures observed 20, 40, or 120 seconds later? And to make matters even worse: When we have observed the child, how do we code the responses? When is a tongue protrusion a tongue protrusion and when is it not?

Gestures Used. Of the studies included in Heimann's (1991) review, a clear majority focused on imitation of tongue protrusion (21 studies) and mouth opening (12 studies). All other types of behavior (e.g., facial expressions, hand opening, lip protrusion, and others) were used in less than five studies each. Furthermore, it was noted that widely varying rules for presenting the gestures and also different lengths of the response period were used in the studies. For example, Meltzoff and Moore (1977), McKenzie and Over (1983), and Koepke, Hamm, Legerstee, and Russell (1983) used a 15-seconds long presentation period and a 20-seconds long response period, whereas Hayes and Watson (1981) presented their stimulus until the infant had been attentive for 15 seconds, and followed this with a 150-seconds long response period. Moreover, Jacobson (1979) modeled the behavior four times within a 20-second period, after which there was an interval of 10 seconds. Those 30 seconds were repeated three times for each gesture to be presented. Similar methods—shorter presentation and response periods that are repeated—have been used by several investigators. To mention a few, Neuberger, Merz, and Selg (1983) used four presentations during 10 seconds plus a 15 seconds long response period repeated twice; Maratos (1973, 1982) presented the gesture four times with a 30-seconds long response period and repeated this three times, and Meltzoff and Moore (1983) used a 20-seconds long presentation period plus a 20-seconds long response period and repeated the sequence over a total length of 4 minutes.

Definitions. As for the length of presentation and of the response period, Heimann (1991) also noted large differences in the rules used for judging whether or not the infant has imitated. The following list exemplifies how tongue protrusion (TP) has been defined by various research groups to date:

1. The tongue has to pass "clearly beyond lip" (Neuberger, Merz, & Selg, 1983; McKenzie & Over, 1983).
2. TP = "distinct tongue protrusions" (Maratos, 1973, 1982).
3. The tongue has to "pass the lower lip" (Dunkeld, 1978).
4. The tongue must be seen to have "clearly left the mouth" (Fontaine, 1984).

5. "Tongue must be seen to leave the mouth" (Kugiumutzakis, 1985).
6. The tongue must be "visible on screen for more than .5 seconds" (Jacobson, 1979).
7. The tongue has "crossed the back edge of the lip" (Meltzoff & Moore, 1983).
8. Some studies have attempted to divide responses into two (e.g., Abravanel & Sigafoos, 1984; Lewis & Sullivan, 1985; Vinter, 1986; Wolff, 1987), three (Heimann et al., 1989), or four categories (Meltzoff & Moore, 1994).

Taken together, it is not difficult to accept the possibility that sample and procedural variations explain, to some extent, the contradictory findings reported in the literature. However, no simple relation seems to exist between the methods that have been implemented and the probability of positive reports of imitation, except the fact that negative reports are rare among studies using larger samples ($n > 15$), which supports the conclusion that methodological factors at least account for part of the variance observed. In addition, we must also be prepared to consider other aspects such as the possibility of real individual differences among infants very early in life. This is also the focus of the next section:

Individual Differences

Observation 1: Do Mothers Notice Imitative Responses Among Newborns? Heimann and Schaller (1985) found that, overall, only one comparison reached significance: The number of tongue protrusions after modeling of tongue protrusion was significantly higher than during baseline. However, a different pattern emerged when the mother's opinion was added as an additional factor. Nearly half of the infants were perceived by their mothers as imitating and this was also confirmed by the blind scoring of the tapes. The result was significant for both mouth opening and tongue protrusion. In short, these observations suggest that individual differences in imitation might be evident very early, and also, that mothers are sensitive to the kinds of responses made by their infants.

Observation 2: Short-Term Stability During the First Month of Life. Our second study (Heimann, 1991; Heimann et al., 1989) specifically focused on the occurrence of individual differences in imitation very early in life. Several imitation indexes were constructed in order to judge whether a particular child imitated a gesture or not, and this classification was used to investigate possible relationships between children's tendency to imitate at one age and observed imitation at a later age. In short, strong and significant correlations were obtained for imitation of both mouth opening ($r =$

.68; $p < .01$) and tongue protrusion ($r = .49$; $p < .05$) between observations when the children were 3 days and 3 weeks old. Thus, some stability in imitation exists already during the neonate's first weeks of life. For example, 72% of the children that were observed for mouth opening at both occasions received the same classification (imitating or nonimitating) at both ages.

Observation 3: High Imitators at Birth and at 3 Months. Additional observations made in our second study did indicate a possible link between children judged as high imitators at Day 3 and facial imitation at 3 months (see Heimann, 1998). This was investigated by comparing the number of gestures imitated at each age, in order to determine which children tended to imitate several of the gestures (= high imitators) and which tended to imitate few of them (= low imitators). A significant relationship was found between imitation observed at the 3-day and the 3-month observation (see Table 11.2; Fisher exact test, $p = .026$). Thus, children displaying very low imitation levels (imitation of only one or none of the gestures) shortly after birth tended to be judged as low imitators at 3 months as well. Similarly, children who were high imitators (imitation of two or three gestures) during the first days of life were also more likely to be high imitators 3 months later. These results indicate that long-term stability within groups of high and low imitators *might* exist as early in life as from birth to 3 months of age.

Furthermore, our current knowledge of early brain development suggests that stability in response patterns over the first 3 months of life ought to be rare (Bronson, 1982; Dawson & Fischer, 1994). Major changes take place during this early phase of life. This is exemplified by the marked increase in the development of connections between neocortex and subcortical areas (e.g., visual pathways) as well as between different cortical areas during these first months (Johnson, 1998; Trevarthen & Aitken, 1994). These changes in neural organization should make it difficult to observe stability when comparing behavior observed during the first week of life and later behavior at 3 months of age. Thus, our finding indicating a relationship between high– low imitation levels at birth and at 3 months must be regarded as one of those rare findings of early long-term stability, if indeed it is not an artifact.

TABLE 11.2
The Relationship Between High and Low Imitators at 3 Days of Age and at 3 Months in Study 2

| | *Imitation at 3 Months* | | |
Imitation at 3 days	Low	High	*Fisher Exact Test*
Low	7	2	
High	3	9	$p < .05$

Observation 4: Imitation and Temperament. The observed variation among infants in their tendency to imitate motivated Field (1982) to suggest that these differences might be an early sign of different personality traits (e.g., internalizers and externalizers). In a subsequent study, Field, Woodson, Greenberg, and Cohen (1986) reported that 40% of their subjects were consistently good imitators, indicating a stability over time for imitation of facial expressions (that is, happy, sad, and surprised faces). Stability in expressiveness per se has also been reported (Field, 1985), further supporting the existence of important early individual differences. However, there exists to date no published report linking observed imitation of facial gestures in young infants with temperament as assessed through a standard questionnaire. Presented here are findings from two of our Swedish studies on possible relationships between imitation and temperament in children not older than 3 months.

As part of our two last studies we asked the parents to complete a temperament questionnaire (the Baby Behavior Questionnaire (BBQ); Hagekull, 1985; Hagekull, Lindhagen, & Bohlin, 1980) when the child was 3 months old. The BBQ is composed of six subscales and is developed and standardized within Sweden (see Table 11.3 for brief description of the subscales).

TABLE 11.3
The Baby Behavior Questionnaire: A Brief Description of the Subscales

Subscale	Number of Items	Description
1. Approach–Withdrawal	3	Tendency to show inhibition in social situations
Example		*One item asks whether the child "adjusts after a short while in new situation" or "does not adjust after half an hour in new places or situation." For this item a score of 5 means that the child adjusts quickly, and a score of 1 means that the child does not adjust even after half an hour or more.*
2. Intensity/Activity	10	Output of energy
3. Regularity	6	Rhythmicity (e.g., as expressed in sleeping and eating)
4. Sensory Sensitivity	3	Reaction to strong stimulation (e.g., light flash, loud noise)
5. Attentiveness	7	Reactivity to small environmental details and changes
6. Manageability	5	Mood and persistence in various activities/situations, reflecting level of negative emotionality/irritability

Note. Adapted from Hagekull (1985) and Hagekull et al. (1980).

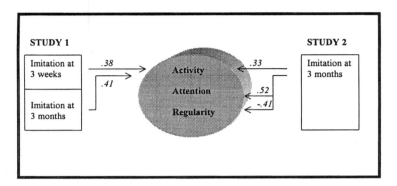

FIG. 11.1. Significant correlations between imitation (at 3 weeks and 3 months) and temperament (at 3 months) as observed in two studies.

The results from our second study, depicted in Fig. 11.1, show a significant relationship between the subscale Intensity/Activity and imitation at both 3 weeks and 3 months ($r = .38$; $p < .05$ and $r = .41$; $p < .05$). None of the remaining comparisons between the BBQ at 3 months and imitation at 2 days, 3 weeks, or 3 months were significant. This relationship between the Intensity/Activity subscale and imitation was almost replicated ($r = .33$; $p < .10$) in our third study (Heimann, 1994, 1998). However, this time we also detected other interesting relationships. A significant positive correlation was noted between imitation overall and the subscale Attentiveness ($r = .52$; $p < .01$), whereas a negative relationship was observed for the relationship between regularity and imitation of mouth opening ($r = -.41$; $p < .05$).

Taken together, these observations lend support to the hypothesis that temperamental or personality factors might explain part of the variability found in young infants' tendency to imitate (e.g., between 9% and 16% of the variance is explained by the subscale Attentiveness). The observed positive relationships between imitation and the Intensity/Activity scale seem to fit Field's (1982) notion that more expressive infants are to be found among infants that imitate.

Observation 5: Imitation and Gaze Aaversion. An exploratory analysis of the relationship between observed imitation and interactive behaviors observed during a mother–infant interaction was carried out as part of Study 2 (Heimann, 1989). A brief face-to-face observation was included at the 3-month observation, and the most striking result was a negative relationship between the infants' brief gaze aversion while interacting with the mother and experimentally elicited imitation of tongue protrusion and mouth opening at 3 days, 3 weeks, and 3 months (range of $r = -.49$ to $-.61$). These observations suggest that mother–infant interactive styles and the infants' early tendencies to imitate might be related. Imitation may exert a positive influence on the early mother–infant relationship. Perhaps imitation facilitates each participant's sensitivity to the subtle social cues embedded in the rich interactive flow between the two partners (the mother and her infant).

Observation 6: Imitation at 3 Months and at 12 Months. The children who participated in Study 2 were also followed up at 12 months, and this revealed only two significant findings (see Heimann, 1998, for a fuller description). One correlation between tongue protrusion at 3 months and vocal imitation at 12 months ($r = .42$, $p < .05$), and one between mouth opening at 3 months and imitation of action on objects at 12 months ($r = .38$, $p < .05$). Thus, imitation observed around the third month of life was partly linked to imitative responses observed 9 months later. It is, however, important to note that no significant correlations were observed between imitation during the neonatal period and imitation at 12 months.

Observation 7: Deferred Imitation at 9 and 14 Months. Recently, we also found indications of individual differences in a longitudinal study on deferred imitation (action on objects) among sixty-two 9- to 14-month-old children (Heimann & Meltzoff, 1996). Besides replicating Meltzoff's (1988) earlier findings on deferred imitation, the findings from this Swedish sample suggest that children displaying very low levels of deferred imitation at 9 months tend to stay low also at 14 months.

The infants were classified into dichotomous categories of either being *low* or *high* imitators. Low imitation at 9 months was defined as scoring 0, that is producing no target actions, while a high imitative tendency was defined as a score of 1, 2, or 3 (each correct target action equaling 1 point). This isolated five subjects who were at the bottom end of the scoring range. The division at 14 months was slightly different, because only two subjects in the experimental group failed to display any target actions. Thus, for the 14-month-old infants, a score of 0 or 1 indicates low imitation and a score of 2 or 3 a high level of imitation. This division revealed that about two thirds of the children (17 out of 26) could be classified as high imitators at both ages, whereas 15% (4 out of 26) remained low at both ages. Thus, overall, more than 80% of the infants (21 of 26) were stable in their imitative tendency.

Taken together, the observations presented so far indicate a relatively strong support for the notion of individual differences in imitation already during the first year of life. This evidence suggests that short-term stability exists during the first months of life, that temperament might explain a small but significant part of the variance at around 3 months, and that some stability in imitative behavior can be observed between 3 and 12 months for immediate imitation as well as between 9 and 14 months for deferred imitation. However, it is still unclear whether any stability can be found across the first 2 or 3 months of life, although some observations pointing in that direction have been presented.

Transition Periods

Observed variation in imitation might also be linked to periods of rapid change during the first year of life. Recent findings indicate the existence of several periods of rapid change (Trevarthen, Aitken, & Plooij, 1999) linked to developmental transitions within the infancy period (0 to 15 months), but no consensus exists as to exactly how many periods are to be expected. The most common assumption, that three periods centered around the ages of 2, 7, and 12 months exist (see Fischer, 1987), contrasts with recent observations. Findings that indicate as many as nine transition periods between birth and 15 months of age (at 4–5, 7–9, 11–12, 14–19, 22–26, 32–37, 40–46, 49–52, and 61–64 weeks of age; Plooij & van der Rijt-Plooij, 1989; van der Rijt-Ploiij & Plooij, 1992). Observations that have been partly replicated by research groups in Sweden, Spain, and England (e.g., Lindahl, Heimann, & Ullstadius, 1997; Sadurni & Rostan, 1997).

If as many as nine normal regression periods exist during the first 15 months of a child's life, it will have a profound influence on our understanding of early infancy. A regression period refers to periods in which infants' temporarily loose stability due to intrinsic reorganization. They become difficult to handle for the parents, they cry more and sleep less. Thus, we might expect observed imitation also to be affected. A child observed while in the middle of a transition "crisis" will not be as easily motivated to partake in an imitation game as a child observed at a different time point.

THE "FUZZY" PROCESSES BEHIND NEONATAL IMITATION

For neonatal imitation (NI) to occur some matching between sensory input and motor output must take place. Thus, the nervous system has to carry out *some* sort of analysis at *some* particular level within the central nervous system. This process must be able to transfer incoming sensory information from one modality (vision) to a different output modality (motor) as pointed out by Meltzoff and Moore in their 1977 article. Exactly where in the brain such a system might operate very early in life is an open question. However, it has been my belief (e.g., Heimann, 1991, 1999) that we should look for a system that uses mainly subcortical parts of the infants' brain during the first weeks of life, a hypothesis also previously proposed by others (Goldman-Rakic, 1985; Stein & Meredith, 1993; Stein, Meredith, & Wallace, 1994; Vinter, 1986). The problem with this model is that we have to assume

some sort of preprogrammed analysis in the brain without knowing anything about the parameters of the program, how the program is controlled,
or what triggers it to run. These questions remain unanswered today.

I propose (as several have done before me) that the child's early imitation is the result of a perception of an event that is transformed—via some
unknown motivational process (see Trevarthen et al., 1998)—into an action,
and that this action is an attempt to match what the child just has perceived. This system allows perception to be carried over to a motor response already at a subcortical level (maybe in the superior colliculus via
multimodal sensory mapping as suggested by Stein and Meredith, 1993).
This process is based on the primacy of faces (Johnson, 1998; Johnson &
Morton, 1991), but it also requires that the child is both attentive, motivated, and alert, a state that is relatively rare during the first hours and
days of life. Thus, we should not expect a fast and exact reproduction, and
we should not even expect imitation to occur every time imitation, in theory, could be observed.

It is also my view that the capacity to imitate belongs to our biological
set-up, and that this capacity is encoded in the brain in a *partly* preprogrammed as opposed to hardwired (reflex-like) fashion. Instead, I suggest a
softwired system, a system that develops through maturation and constant
transactional interactions with the environment. Neonatal imitation is not
fixed in the brain (Bjorklund, 1987) or governed by an innate releasing
mechanism (Anisfeld, 1996). To me,

the concept 'fuzzy dynamical processes' (FDP) is a good way to conceptualize
both the ability of the nervous system to process and respond to complex social situations already at birth and the problem the young infant has in responding to complex social situations. Thus, the system is not specific to imitation but, rather, an effect of the initial settings (the initial weights and
existing connections before any clear visual input has acted upon the child's
brain) and constraints governing the immature nervous system. (Heimann,
1999, p. 15).

If we take into account obvious facts such as the immaturity of the nervous
system in a newborn child, the fact that the sensory systems are far from
fully developed at birth, and that the visual processing probably takes
place primarily within subcortical parts of the brain (Bronson, 1982; but see
Johnson, 1998, for early involvement of deeper layers in primary visual cortex), then we cannot expect the child to give a perfect response, if any response at all! This is also what has been observed: The newborn child
works him- or herself up to an imitative response, as has been noted in several studies (Heimann et al., 1989; Holmlund, 1995; Kugiumutzakis, 1985;
Meltzoff & Moore, 1977, 1983, 1994). Heimann et al. also noted that evidence

of imitation could only be observed for responses emitted after presentation, but not for responses seen while the model still presented the gesture. In other words, the child needed 30 to 60 seconds in order for a clear differentiating response to emerge. Meltzoff and Moore (1994) demonstrated that infants imitated "large tongue protrusions to the side," but only after several presentations over three different days. Finally, Holmlund (1995), who studied imitation and mother–infant interaction longitudinally, also observed a similar phenomenon. She explicitly suggests that a child less than 1 month old needs 60 to 90 seconds in order to process a complex social event and to make a clear response. According to Holmlund, the immature nervous system is capable of responding to an interaction, but only at a very slow rate. Thus, it is common for parents to miss their baby's responses because they do not always wait long enough for a response.

In sum, the proposed model suggests that the baby has a fuzzy "knowledge" of the modeled act (compare AIM and Meltzoff & Moore's discussion in their 1994 paper and Meltzoff & Moore, chap. 10, this volume). This act is perceived and mapped through fuzzy processes within a neural net. This network combines sensory and motor information in an amodal fashion. The end result *might* be an imitative response, provided that the situation also has motivated the infant to absorb what is going on and to focus on the relevant aspects of the visual information provided at the moment. Later in development, when attentional networks in both the parietal and the frontal lobe have developed, the child will display more intentional and controlled responses. This also means that cortical processes play a larger role (maybe via mirror neurons in the frontal cortex as suggested by Rizzolatti & Arbib, 1998) for later imitation.

In addition, other factors might also affect imitation early in life: The child's state, the infant's overt attention, the child's capacity for sustained attention, the salience of the model, the temporal organization of the modeled behavior, the distance between the model and the baby, the way the baby is being held, the light in the observation room, the noise from the camera, and so forth. It might also be the case that children differ in terms of how much they attend to information coming from different sensory systems. Some might be more prone to react to visual information, others to tactile stimulation (Fogel, personal communication, April 1995). Thus, the capacity of the brain and the CNS is only one aspect of the intricate transaction between the child's mind and the adult's mind—a transaction that provides the setting for neonatal imitation. The difficulty of the task (i.e., how the gesture is presented or the type of behavior used), the physical aspects of the environment (i.e., lightning in the room), and the ability of the presenter to tune into the child's window of attention (emotional regulation) are all additional examples of factors that affect the outcome. All these factors or parameters interact with each other and, simultaneously, function both as facilitators and constraints. It is no wonder that neonatal imitation is hard to capture!

ACKNOWLEDGMENTS

The research presented in this chapter has been supported by grants from the Bank of Sweden Tercentenary Foundation (# 89/313), Stockholm, the Swedish Council for Research in the Humanities and the Social Sciences (HSFR F709/94), and the Swedish First of May Flower Foundation, Göteborg, Sweden, to Mikael Heimann. Special thanks are also due to all participating children and their families.

REFERENCES

Abravanel, E., & Sigafoos, A. D. (1984). Exploring the presence of imitation during early infancy. *Child Development, 55,* 381–392.

Anisfeld, M. (1991). Neonatal imitation: Review. *Developmental Review, 11,* 60–97.

Anisfeld, M. (1996). Only tongue protrusion modeling is matched by neonates. *Developmental Review, 16,* 149–161.

Bjorklund, D. (1987). A note on neonatal imitation. *Developmental Review, 7,* 86–92.

Bråten, S. (1988). Dialogic mind: The infant and the adult in protoconversation. In M. E. Carvallo (Ed.), *Nature, cognition, and system I* (pp. 187–205). Dordrecht, The Netherlands: Kluwer.

Bråten, S. (1994, August). *Self-other connections in the imitating infant and in the dyad. The companion space theorem.* Paper presented at the Symposium on Intersubjective Communication and Emotion in Ontogeny: Between Nature, Nurture and Culture, The Norwegian Academy of Science and Letters, Oslo.

Bronson, G. W. (1982). Structure, status, and characteristics of the nervous system at birth. In P. Stratton (Ed.), *Psychobiology of the human newborn* (pp. 99–118). New York: Wiley.

Dawson, G., & Fischer, K. W. (Eds.). (1994). *Human behavior and the developing brain.* New York: Guilford Press.

Dunkeld, J. (1978). *The function of imitation in infancy.* Unpublished doctoral dissertation, University of Edinburgh, UK.

Fiamenghi, G. A., Jr. (1996). Intersubjectivity and infant-infant interaction: Imitation as a way of making contact. Research and Clinical Center for Child Development, Hokkaido University, Japan: *Annual Report No. 19* (pp. 15–21).

Field, T. M. (1982). Individual differences in the expressivity of neonates and young infants. In R. S. Feldman (Ed.), *Development of nonverbal behavior in children.* New York: Springer-Verlag.

Field, T. M. (1985). Neonatal perception of people: Motivation and individual differences. In T. M. Field & N. A. Fox (Eds.), *Social perception in infants.* Norwood, NJ: Ablex.

Field, T. M., Woodson, R., Greenberg, R., & Cohen, D. (1982). Discrimination and imitation of facial expressions by neonates. *Science, 218,* 179–181.

Fischer, K. W. (1987). Relation between brain and cognitive development. *Child Development, 58,* 623–632.

Fogel, A. (1993). *Developing through relationships.* Chicago: University of Chicago Press.

Fontaine, R. (1984). Imitative skills between birth and six months. *Infant Behavior and Development, 7,* 323–333.

Goldman-Rakic, P. S. (1985). Toward a neurobiology of cognitive development. In J. Mehler & R. Fox (Eds.), *Neonate cognition: Beyond the blooming buzzing confusion* (pp. 285–306). Hillsdale, NJ: Lawrence Erlbaum Associates.

Hagekull, B. (1985). Individual stability in dimensions of infant behavior. *Infant Behavior and Development, 4,* 97–108.

Hagekull, B., Lindhagen, K., & Bohlin, G. (1980). Behavioral dimensions in one-year-olds and dimensional stability in infancy. *International Journal of Behavioral Development, 3,* 351–364.

Hayes, L. A., & Watson, J. S. (1981). Neonatal imitation: Fact or artifact? *Developmental Psychology, 17,* 655–660.

Heimann, M. (1989). Neonatal imitation, gaze aversion, and mother-infant interaction. *Infant Behavior and Development, 12,* 495–505.

Heimann, M. (1991). Neonatal imitation: A social and biological phenomenon. In T. Archer & S. Hansen (Eds.), *Behavioral biology: The neuroendocrine axis* (pp. 173–186). Hillsdale, NJ: Lawrence Erlbaum Associates.

Heimann, M. (1994, July). *Do temperamental factors influence young infants' tendency to imitate?* Poster presented at the 13th Biennial Meeting of the International Society for the Study of Behavioral development, Amsterdam, The Netherlands.

Heimann, M. (1997, September). *The never ending story of neonatal imitation.* Poster presented at the 8th European Conference on Developmental Psychology, Rennes, France.

Heimann, M. (1998). Imitation in neonates, in older infants and in children with autism: Feedback to theory. In S. Bråten (Ed.), *Intersubjective communication and emotion in early ontogeny* (pp. 89–104). Cambridge, England: Cambridge University Press.

Heimann, M. (1999). Imitation in early infancy: A fuzzy picture or a clear vision? *Proceedings of the AISB'99 symposium on imitation in animals and artifacts* (pp. 12–16). The Society for the Study of Artificial Intelligence and Simulation of Behaviour: Edinburgh, Scotland.

Heimann, M., Nelson, K. E., & Schaller, J. (1989). Neonatal imitation of tongue protrusion and mouth opening: Methodological aspects and evidence of early individual differences. *Scandinavian Journal of Psychology, 90,* 90–101.

Heimann, M., & Meltzoff, A. N. (1996). Deferred imitation in 9- and 14- months old infants: A longitudinal study of a Swedish sample. *British Journal of Developmental Psychology, 14,* 55–64.

Heimann, M., & Schaller, J. (1985). Imitative reactions among 14-21 day old infants. *Infant Mental Health Journal, 6,* 31–39.

Heimann, M., Ullstadius, E., & Swerlander, A. (1998). Imitation in eight young infants with Down's syndrome. *Pediatric Research, 44*(5), 780–784.

Holmlund, C. (1995). Development of turntakings as a sensorimotor process in the first 3 months: A sequential analysis. In K. E. Nelson & Z. Réger (Eds.), *Children's language. Vol. 8* (pp. 41–64). Hillsdale, NJ: Lawrence Erlbaum Associates.

Jacobson, S. W. (1979). Matching behavior in the young infant. *Child Development, 50,* 425–430.

Johnson, M. H. (1998). Developing an attentive brain. In R. Parasuraman (Ed.), *The attentive brain* (pp. 427–443). Cambridge, MA: MIT Press.

Johnson, M. H., & Morton, J. (1991). Biology and cognitive development: The case of face recognition. Oxford, England: Basil Blackwell.

Koepke, J. E., Hamm, M., Legerste, M., & Russell, M. (1983). Neonatal imitation: Two failures to replicate. *Infant Behavior and Development, 6,* 97–102.

Kugiumutzakis, J. (1985). *Development of imitation during the first six months of life* (Uppsala Psychological Reports, No. 377). University of Uppsala, Sweden.

Kugiumutzakis, J. (1993). Intersubjective vocal imitation in early mother-infant interaction. In J. Nadel & L. Camioni (Eds.), *New perspectives in early communication development* (pp. 23–47). London: Routledge.

Lewis, M., & Sullivan, M. W. (1985). Imitation in the first six months of life. *Merrill-Palmer Quarterly, 31*, 315–333.

Lindahl, B. L., Heimann, M., & Ullstadius, E. (1997, October). *Occurrence of regressive periods in the normal development of Swedish infants*. Paper presented at the Research Conference on Regression Periods in Early Infancy (M. Heimann, Chair). Department of Psychology, Gothenburg University, Sweden.

Maratos, O. (1973). *The origin and development of imitation in the first six months of life*. Paper presented at the Annual Meeting of the British Psychological Society, Liverpool, UK.

Maratos, O. (1982). Trends in the development of imitation in early infancy. In T. G. Beaver (Ed.), *Regressions in mental development: Basic phenomena and theories* (pp. 81–101). Hillsdale, NJ: Lawrence Erlbaum Associates.

McKenzie, B., & Over, R. (1983). Young infants fail to imitate manual and facial gestures. *Infant Behavior and Development, 6*, 85–95.

Meltzoff, A. N. (1988). Infant imitation and memory: Imitation by nine-month-olds in immediate and deferred tests. *Child Development, 59*, 217–225.

Meltzoff, A. N., & Moore, M. K. (1977). Imitation of facial and manual gestures. *Science, 198*, 75–80.

Meltzoff, A. N., & Moore, M. K. (1983). Newborn infants imitate adult facial gestures. *Child Development, 54*, 702–709.

Meltzoff, A. N., & Moore, M. K. (1994). Imitation, memory, and the representation of persons. *Infant Behavior and Development, 17*, 83–99.

Meltzoff, A. N., & Moore, M. K. (1998). Object representation, identity, and the paradox of early permanence: Steps toward a new framework. *Infant Behavior and Development, 21*(2), 201–235.

Neuberger, H., Merz, J., & Selg, H. (1983). Imitation bei Neugeboren—eine kontroverse Befundlage. *Zeitschrift für Entwicklungspsychologoie und Pädagogische Psychologie, XV*, 267–276.

Plooij, F. X., & Rijt-Plooij, H. H. C. van der (1989). Vulnerable periods during infancy: Hierarchically reorganized systems control, stress and disease. *Ethology and Sociobiology, 10*, 279–296.

Rizzolatti, G., & Arbib, M. A. (1998). Language within our grasp. *Trends in Neuroscience, 21*(5), 188–194.

Rijt-Plooij, H. H. C. van der, & Plooij, F. X. (1992). Infantile regressions: Disorganization and the onset of transition periods. *Journal of Reproductive and Infant Psychology, 10*, 129–149.

Sadurni, M., & Rostan, C. (1997, October). *Regression periods in infancy: A case study from Catalonia*. Paper presented at the Research conference on Regression periods in early infancy (M. Heimann, Chair). Department of Psychology, Gothenburg University, Sweden.

Stein, B. E., & Meredith, M. A. (1993) *The merging of the senses*. Cambridge, MA: MIT Press.

Stein, B. E., Meredith, M., & Wallace, M. T. (1994). Development and neural basis of multisensory integration. In D. J. Lewkowicz & R. Lickliter (Eds.), *The development of intersensory perception: Comparative perspectives* (pp. 81–105). Hillsdale, NJ: Lawrence Erlbaum Associates.

Trevarthen, C., & Aitken, K. J. (1994). Brain development, infant communication, and empathy disorders: Intrinsic factors in child mental health. *Development and Psychopathology, 6*, 597–633.

Trevarthen, C., Aitken, K., & Plooij, F. X. (1999). *Can age-related brain developments explain behavioural 'regressions' in infancy*. Manuscript submitted for publication.

Trevarthen, C, Kokkinaki, T., & Fiamenghi, G. A., Jr. (1998). What infants' imitations communicate: With mothers, with fathers and with peers. In J. Nadel & G. Butterworth (Eds.), *Imitation in infancy: Progress and prospects of current research* (pp. 127–185). Cambridge, England: Cambridge University Press.

Ullstadius, E. (1998). *Exploring early imitation*. Doctoral dissertation, Göteborg University, Sweden.

Vinter, A. (1986). The role of movement in eliciting early imitations. *Child Development, 57*, 66–71.

Wolff, P. H. (1987). *Behavioral states and expression of emotions in early infancy*. Chicago: University of Chicago Press.

Author Index

Subject Index